I0806229

The Ethics of Earth Art

AMANDA BOETZKES

# The Ethics of Earth Art

UNIVERSITY OF MINNESOTA PRESS | Minneapolis • London

Published by the University of Minnesota Press
111 Third Avenue South, Suite 290
Minneapolis, MN 55401-2520
http://www.upress.umn.edu

Printed in the United States of America on acid-free paper

Library of Congress Cataloging-in-Publication Data

Boetzkes, Amanda.
The ethics of earth art / Amanda Boetzkes.
p. cm.
Includes bibliographical references and index.
ISBN 978-0-8166-6588-4 (hc : alk. paper)
ISBN 978-0-8166-6589-1 (pb : alk. paper)
1. Earthworks (Art)—Moral and ethical aspects.
2. Art and morals. I. Title.
N6494.E27B65 2010
709.04'076—dc22

2010027202



18 17 16 15 14 13 12 11 10 10 9 8 7 6 5 4 3 2 1

# Contents

# Illustrations

# Acknowledgments

This book is dedicated to Aron Vinegar, with heartfelt thanks. I am grateful for your insights, and for our many spirited conversations, which have enriched these pages. Special thanks go to Christine Ross, for her perceptive recommendations and advice. You have inspired me more than words can say. I am indebted to those individuals who provided me with invaluable feedback at different stages of this project: Jennifer Roberts, Erika Suderberg, David Woods, Dana Arnold, Jackie Brookner, Alex Potts, Johanne Sloan, Bronwen Wilson, Angela Vanhaelen, Hajime Nakatani, Andrew Shelton, Vibha Arora, Alexandra Ganser, and Alex Boutros.

Many thanks to my editor, Richard Morrison, for his advice and vision for this book, and to Adam Brunner, for taking the time to respond to all my questions over the course of the book's production. Kathy Delfosse, thank you for your sharp eye in editing the manuscript. Thanks also to Kristina Kachele for her beautiful work on the cover design. I am grateful to the artists, curators, gallery directors, and assistants who kindly helped me acquire reproduction permissions and images: Cristin O'Keefe Aptowicz, Marta Fodor, Lowell Bassett, Maggie Fleming, Basia Irland, Aviva Rahmani, Betty Beaumont, Emily Ruotolo, Helene Lundbye Petersen, James McKee, Amy Plumb, Dennis Oppenheim, Richard Long, Chris Drury, Berit Potter, Jeanne Dreskin, Daniel Cheek, Stephanie Joson, Kim Tischler, Jackie Brookner, Ichi Ikeda, Newton Harrison, Christopher Rawson, Liesbeth Nieuwenweg, Helen Little, Naomi Potter, Nancy Fulton, Aurora Aspen, and Alexis Sutton.

This research was generously funded by the Social Sciences and Humanities Research Council of Canada (SSHRC) and the Fonds québécois de la recherche sur la société et la culture (FQRSC). I am also grateful to those who gave me the opportunity to present this work publicly in its formative stages: Daniel Adler and Jeanette Redensek, Ronald Bernier, and the Department of History of Art at Ohio State University.

I would like to extend my sincere gratitude to my family, especially to my parents, Elisabeth Gedge and Gus Boetzkes, and to my grandfather, Lloyd Gedge, for their unfailing support.

And finally, a special recognition to the artists featured in this book. Your work has been both challenging and rewarding to write about.

The Ethics of Earth Art

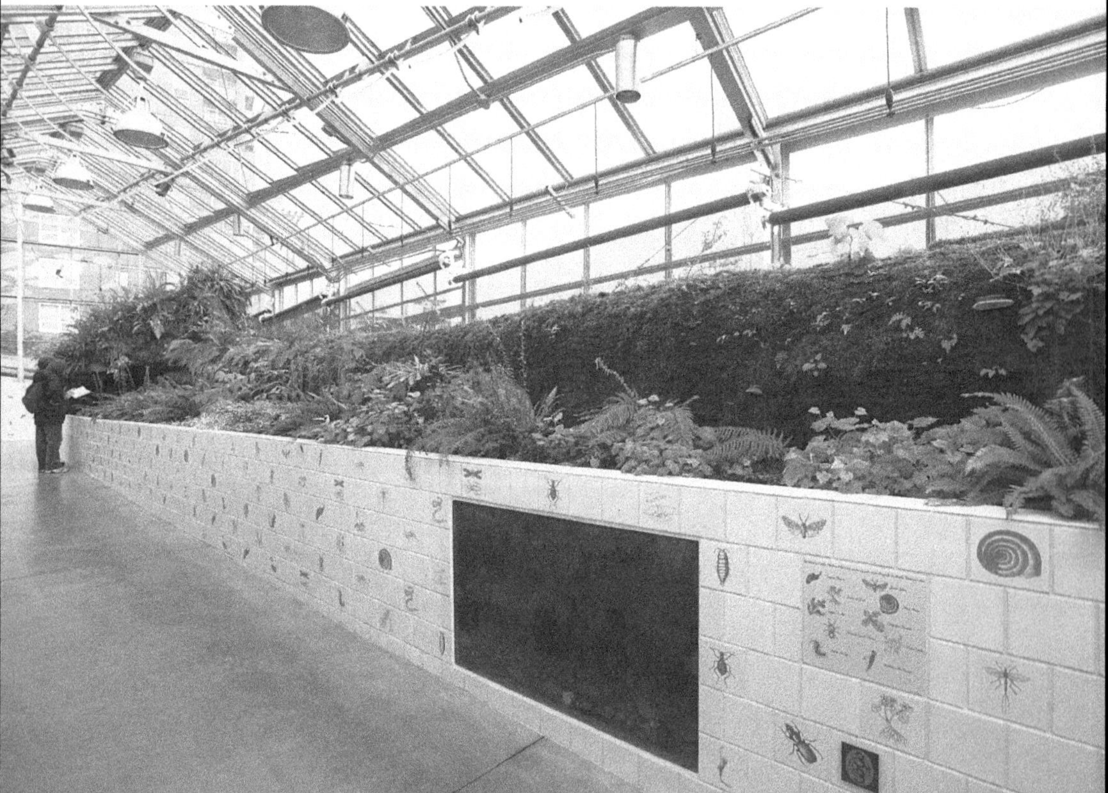

FIGURE 1. Mark Dion, *Neukom Vivarium,* 2007. Mixed-media installation. Greenhouse structure, eighty feet. Installation view at Seattle Art Museum, Seattle. Photograph by Paul Macapia. Courtesy of the artist; Tanya Bonakdar Gallery, New York; Seattle Art Museum, Seattle. Gift of Sally and William Neukom, American Express Company, Seattle Garden Club, Mark Torrance Foundation, and Committee of 33 in honor of the seventy-fifth anniversary of the Seattle Art Museum.

INTRODUCTION

# At the Limit of Form

At the Olympic Sculpture Park in Seattle, Washington, a giant hemlock tree lies entombed in an eighty-foot-long greenhouse. Having fallen over a ravine in a protected watershed area not far from the city, the tree was recovered by the contemporary American artist Mark Dion and installed in a conservatory that attempts to replicate the conditions of the old-growth forest from which it came. Now an artwork titled *Neukom Vivarium* (Figure 1), the tree rests underneath an elaborate system of water sprinklers, lights, and drains in a bed of soil, humus, and leaf litter. Though the tree is dead, its decomposition gives rise to a host of animal and insect species, vegetal growth, and single-cell organisms. Indeed, the base of the tree bed is decorated with tiles illustrating the different life forms that can be found in the ecosystem that the dead tree nourishes.

Dion's work mobilizes the double bind of ecological ethics at the beginning of the twenty-first century. In its strictest sense, ecology is the study of the interaction of organisms with their environment. It is predicated on the principle that every creature is connected to every element that composes the environment, so that all living things depend on the balance of a complex system of growth and decay. On the surface, Dion's work demonstrates this balance in action. Though there is a melancholic dimension to the fact that the hemlock tree has died, at the same time its death provides the basis for a vital and diverse natural world. But there is more to the artwork than a simple narrative of ecological balance. Dion insists that the artwork is, in many respects, an abomination. Not only has the tree been violently torn from its original site, but it has been relocated to a space that technologically reproduces the natural environment. The system lives only because of a significant investment of equipment, labor, resources, and scientific expertise. Needless to say, the vivarium is anything but natural. Dion states that the piece is perverse because it shows that despite all our technology and money, when we destroy a natural system, it is virtually impossible to get it back. He writes, "In a sense, we're building a failure."[1]

*Neukom Vivarium* thus speaks to the fact that ecology is not just a scientific discipline but a discourse about the human relationship to the planet, a discourse that is always accompanied by an awareness of environmental crisis, be it the extinction of species, the contamination of the biosphere, or the stripping of resources, to name only a few of the many distressing environmental upsets caused by humans. For this reason, the term "ecological" often implies an ethical commitment to preserve or reestablish the balance of ecosystems, to promote biodiversity, and to counteract the exploitation of resources. As Dion shows, however, these efforts are inextricable from technology and industry. Thus, he explains, though the hemlock appears to be a Sleeping Beauty, a romantic image in which natural splendor is preserved and protected, the tree is actually closer to an inert body on life support, kept alive only through the supreme efforts of a team of scientists, donors, workers, interpreters, and of course, the artist.

In this respect, art has a part to play in critiquing the ways we frame nature through representation as well as through science and technology. Moreover, it does so by forging an aesthetic awareness of how nature exceeds these discourses and representations. Though *Neukom Vivarium* behaves like a natural history museum in which specimens have been extracted and recontextualized for the purposes of display, it is also a memento mori of a spontaneously occurring ecosystem, impressing upon the spectator a sense of the loss of the natural world. Through the replication of the forest, one that is doomed to fall short, Dion illustrates "the uncanniness of nature—the wonder of the vast complexity and diversity within a natural system . . . [and] how difficult that is for us to grasp."[2] This perhaps best summarizes the ecological impetus of the artwork: it acknowledges that nature exceeds the scope of human knowledge and systems of representation. More pointedly, an ecological stance involves revealing the limits of an anthropocentric worldview and recognizing these limits as thresholds to the excess of the earth.

Dion's work also shows how the aesthetic and ethical concerns of the early earthworks movement of the late 1960s have come to fruition in the multimedia strategies of contemporary practices. Since the inception of the earth art movement, there has been a proliferation of new aesthetic strategies that make nature visible in terms of its spontaneous changes, its temporality, and the intangible qualities that constitute the environments in which we live. More than using the land as a sculptural medium, earth art initiated an interrogation of how the elusive presence of nature problematizes the drive to represent. The broad field of contemporary earth art now includes a range of media, from postminimalist sculpture to body art performances, installations, photographic interventions, biosculptures, public protest art, and community-based projects. This book seeks not merely to explain the diversification of new media in the contemporary era but, more profoundly, to identify the roots of a particular preoccupation with nature at the beginning of the earthworks movement and to examine this pivotal time through the lens of ecological ethics in order to cast new light on contemporary practices. What concerns me, then, is not just the transition from modernist objects to postmodern practices; it is the question of how the earth prompts this redefinition of art and art historical analysis. More strongly, though it would seem that the monumental land-based sculptures of the late 1960s and the diverse media used in more-recent contemporary art are so different as to warrant separate aesthetic and art historical categorizations, I would argue that these two generations are connected by their elucidation of the earth as a domain of ethical concern. This is not to suggest that there are not distinctions to be made between the most recent art and the original earthworks movement. Nor is it to claim that all earth art has a simplistic ecological agenda that involves restoring the balance of an ecosystem or promoting sustainability. Rather, it is to investigate how, since the sixties, artists have challenged our assumptions about the earth and, more strongly, how they propose an ethical relation to it.

In the works considered here, the earth is not a closed system that can be balanced, restored, studied, and effectively reintegrated into an "eco-friendly" global capitalism. Instead, the artworks mediate contact with elemental forces that overwhelm the senses and confound the stability of one's perceptual apparatus. This approach, which considers the tenor of one's encounters with natural phenomena, and specifically how nature troubles representational form, corresponds to what in eco-philosophy is known as recessive ethics: a stance of retraction from and receptivity to the earth that foregoes the propensity to actively subsume it within the parameters of our preexisting logic.[3] Through the withdrawal from representation, in gestures that mobilize a fundamentally recessed subject, artists create the conditions of possibility for the earth to appear at the limits of intelligible form and to deliver a sense of it at the point at which it overflows the field of perception. In this way, contemporary art counters two deeply flawed but nevertheless pervasive stances toward the earth: the instrumental view, which seeks to master the planet through an exclusively human-centered knowledge of it, and the romantic view, which holds that we can return to a state of unencumbered continuity with nature.

## The Limits of Site-Specificity

Recent scholarship in art history frames earth art under the rubric of "site-specificity." Though certainly earth art is sometimes defined by the parameters of its spatial and temporal location, the category "site-specific" is perhaps not precise enough to express the ethical stakes of the artworks. Indeed, the notion of site-specificity is now so ubiquitous to contemporary art as to be only a rudimentary description of earth art's theoretical concerns. Though the discourse of site-specificity has contributed much in terms of evaluating the economic, phenomenological, aesthetic, and ideological structures that situate an artwork, or more subtly, the inextricability of the artwork's form from the paradigm of site it espouses, it often equates the notion of the earth with the most literal interpretation of "site"—a geographic place or geological foundation. In fact, this simplification of the earth is a new development, for when the earthworks movement began, the idea of siting artworks in deserted landscapes was a means of breaking out of the spaces and economy of the gallery system. The limit*less*ness, and not the limit*ed*ness, of the earth was the basis of its radicality.

It is paramount in approaching the question of "site" that we resist the tendency to understand the earth only in terms of its most base material properties or that we avoid the question of nature altogether—as is more often the case—lest it betray a nostalgic desire to return to an imaginary Eden underpinned by latent conservatism and traditional gender and ethnic identities. This book takes issue with the assumptions that the earth is a stable foundation of banal matter onto which conservative ideology can easily be projected and that any artistic concern for nature abandons a deterritorialized global orientation in favor of a uniform local subjectivity. In order to evaluate the validity of the discourse of site-specificity and ultimately develop it further, it is important to ask how the earth informs our discursive knowledge and, most importantly given the context of global environmental crisis, how artistic practices elaborate an ecological stance toward the planet.

In an interview with Montreal critic John Grande, the British artist David Nash explains of his work, "'Site-specific' is not a good enough term. It is too loose. The land is absolutely fundamental and has to be in the front."[4] Nash has been active since the 1970s and is known for works that are integrated into the environment, revealing its ecological particularities, but that also involve laborious processes of structuring and manipulating that environment. *Black Dome* (Figure 2), for example, is a protruding dark mound made from the charred ends of nine hundred larch poles and installed in a hole twenty-five feet in diameter and eighteen inches deep, in the Forest of Dean. Originally a pronounced shadowy presence when it was installed in 1986, the work was built to slowly rot back into the ground, leaving only a slight alteration on the forest floor.

Nash's comment raises two important issues regarding the place of earth art in relation to the discourse of site-specificity. First, although some earth art is bound to a geographic site, the mere fact of its locatedness is not the core issue of the work. An artwork may be instantiated in the land but upstage or intervene on its environ-

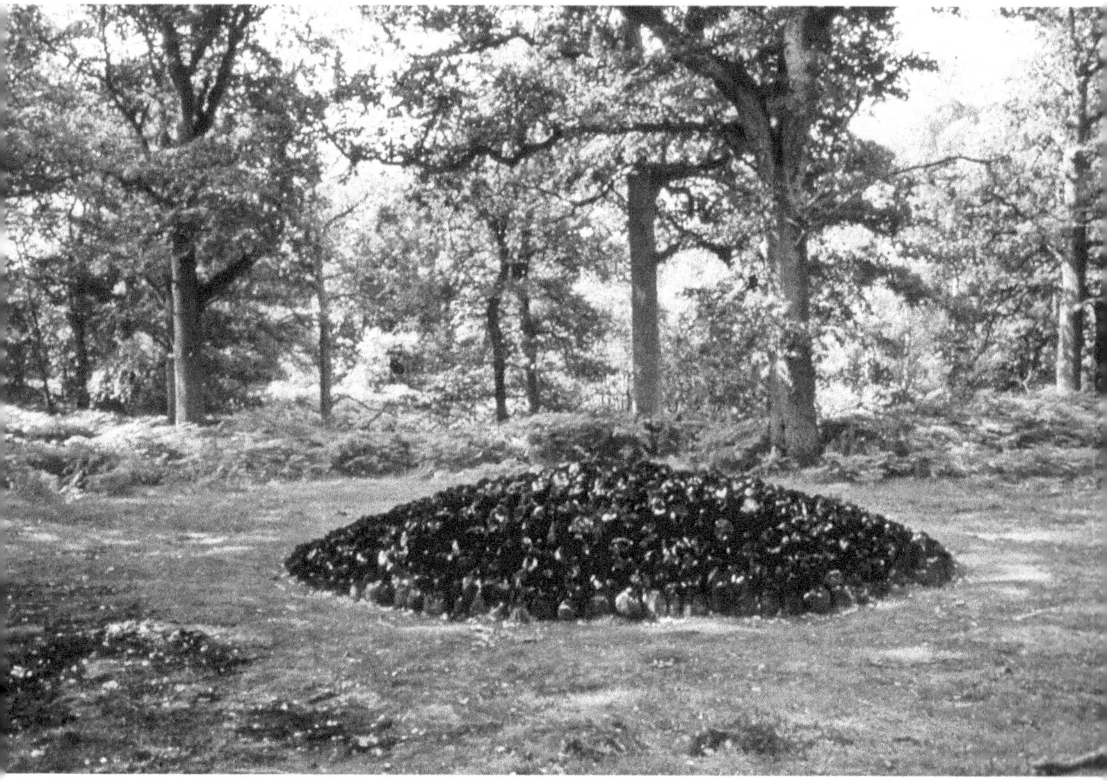

FIGURE 2. David Nash, *Black Dome,* 1986. Charred larch. Copyright David Nash. Courtesy of Annely Juda Fine Art, London.

ment. Furthermore, though many artists, such as Nash, continue to practice outdoors, many others now bring natural phenomena into studio and gallery settings or into urban environments, as in the case of Dion's *Neukom Vivarium.* They thus challenge the notion that nature must be rooted in a particular place. Second, the term "site-specific" has become so generalized that when applied to earth art, it distracts from the central role that natural activity plays in creating the work. In other words, for many artists, the concept of "site" is not interchangeable with "earth" or "nature." The characteristics that define the locus of an earth artwork sometimes overlap with those of site-specific art but cannot be reduced to them.

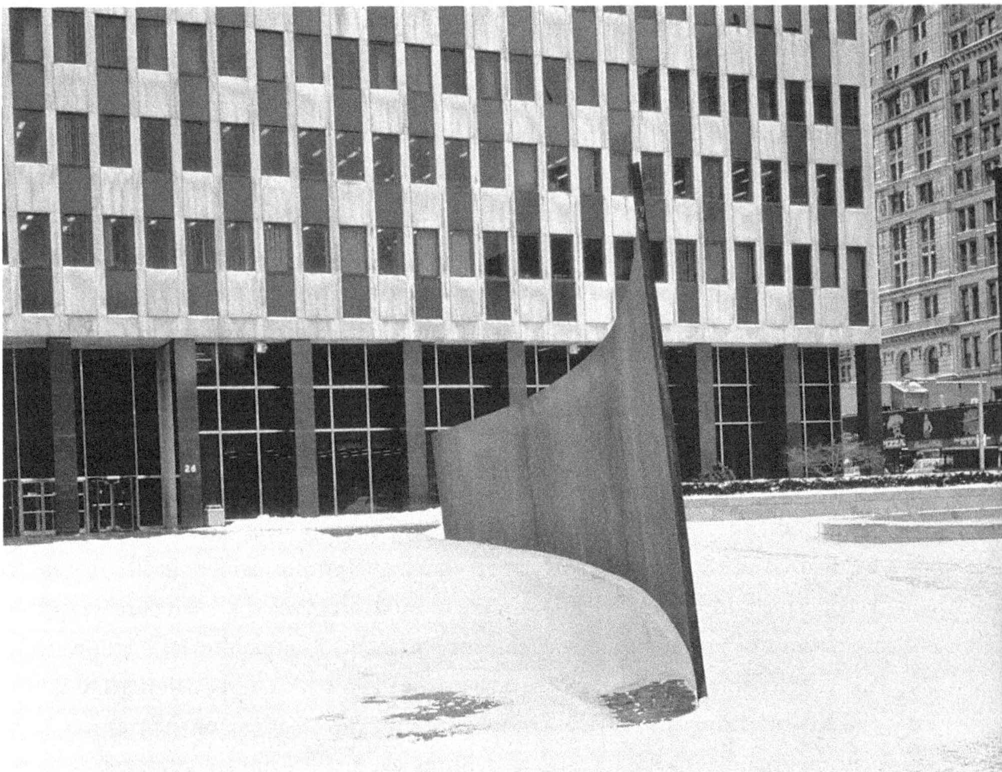

FIGURE 3. Richard Serra, *Tilted Arc,* 1980. Corten steel, 12 × 120 feet. Federal Plaza, New York. Copyright 2009 Richard Serra/Artists Rights Society (ARS), New York.

The now-famous debates surrounding the removal of Richard Serra's public sculpture *Tilted Arc* (Figure 3) from the Federal Plaza in New York City in the early 1980s stimulated a wealth of discussion, both within and beyond academia, on the concept of site-specificity. At 12 feet high and 120 feet long and made of hot-rolled steel, the sculpture was for some a critical appropriation of public space, and for others an aesthetically displeasing and disruptive intervention into the plaza. Not only did the Serra controversy foreground the idea first initiated by postminimalism and early earthworks that art responds to and garners meaning from its location, but it also sparked debates about what defines the notion of "site" in the first place. In his 1987 essay on Serra's public sculpture, for example, Douglas Crimp argues that Serra's work redefines the space of a work of art as the site of political struggle.[5] The site is not a preexisting neutral space; it is the locus of a political or historic tension that the artwork exposes and materializes. Likewise, in her book *Evictions: Art and Spatial Politics,* Rosalyn Deutsche describes how art navigates urban spaces and the operations of social control.[6] In a rigorous discussion of public art, inflected by Henri Lefebvre's *The Production of Space,* Deutsche cautions against a presumed separation of the concepts of space and society, for not only do social relations then appear to be unsituated and to exist apart from material forms, but one also risks overlooking the fact that spatial organization is the seat of hegemonic ordering and political strife.

Just as *Tilted Arc* uncovered the way social relations and political struggle are realized in the production of space, contemporary earth art exposes and redefines the social and political forces that define our environments. It does so, however, by incorporating natural activity as an equally determining force in the way space is conceived. Moreover, what is at stake in earth art is the disclosure not simply of operations of power, but also of the entwinement of human social relations with the terrestrial realm. Through the enactment of an ethical responsiveness to space, the artwork brings this earthly component into view, evidencing the way in which natural phenomena are integral to defining the sites of human conflicts, politics, and social formations.

If one assumes that the earth is merely a geological support for human activity, it might appear that the recourse to nature results in the stabilization of the site of art and a restriction of the parameters of artistic practice. Earth art would therefore run against the supposition that contemporary art is undertaking the dematerialization of the object, a hypothesis originally posed by Lucy Lippard in the early seventies.[7] Earth artists, however, have been at the forefront of the movement to challenge the definition of art according to either its objecthood or the fixity of medium. It seems, though, that some confusion remains between the notion of the dematerialization of the art object and of dematerialization *tout court.* Lippard's argument responds to the emergence of ephemeral media such as performances, happenings, or otherwise transient events. Yet not only did these practices heighten awareness of the material and temporal conditions of space, intersubjective relations, and the aesthetic experience, they also relied heavily on tangible forms of documentation, such as photography, written texts, and film. Lippard's argument was not an absolute claim that contemporary art was on a virtual trajectory. However, in her recent book *One Place after Another: Site-Specific Art and Locational Identity,* Miwon Kwon suggests exactly that, arguing that the concept of site has evolved from a grounded physical location to a discursive vector that is virtual.[8] Kwon's hypothesis thus assumes a drive to sever art from its material contingencies and betrays a presumed dichotomy between the physical and the discursive constructions of art, leading to a certain privileging of the latter over the former as an art historical concern.

Kwon outlines a genealogy of site-specificity through three categories of analysis: phenomenological, social/institutional, and discursive.[9] These categories provide a nexus of ideas that present the site as the main tenet around which art, the artist, and the spectator are organized. Thus, the emphasis on the site of an artwork does not necessarily implicate the work in fixed locales. To the contrary, Kwon notes, the growing attention to social and discursive sites in recent decades has stimulated new forms of allegedly discursive artworks. Artworks geared toward subverting the institutions and structures of power that determine particular social groups, be it on the grounds of class, race, gender, or sexuality, have reinvented the definition of site. What we consider to be a site may not be defined by a particular place but might instead be determined by a virtual community of people united by an infinite variety of circumstances. The artwork may gather together a group of people on the basis of their ethnicity, or it may assemble a temporary community to draw attention to a particular social issue.

The notion of a discursively determined site stems from a more widespread intellectual movement that began in literary criticism and took hold in other disciplines largely under the influence of Michel Foucault's writings. The principle of discourse emphasizes that our language is thoroughly permeated by apparatuses of power that structure knowledge and that we reproduce in all aspects of cultural production. Locating art at a discursive site involves exposing and possibly attempting to reorganize the valences of power and knowledge that subject us—that is, that both make us into subjects and subjugate us. Not only is discourse intimately tied with subject formation, but it is also a constantly shifting conceptual network that is not localizable and is inextricable from our shared language and knowledge, and thus from linguistic media, such as text.

However, Kwon positions physical locations against virtual sites, assuming that the virtual is an extension of the discursive and that both are extracted from the actual and material. That is to say, the more the concept of site is defined in terms of discursive categories, and particularly as subject formation becomes the focus of artistic practices, the more art has allegedly become dematerialized, no longer appearing as an object rooted in a place but instead responding to its imagined public, taking a variety of forms, from temporary installations to performances, public interventions, and net art. There is an implicit suggestion in this analysis, though, that fixed locations are antithetical to complex deterritorialized subjectivities. While it may be true that in contemporary art, the notion of site has come to be understood as discursively determined and that art is now interpreted as a mechanism that reveals the terms of knowledge production, the boundaries of a community, or the politics of a cultural debate, we must be wary of the potential dualism perpetuated by the drive to unhinge the notion of site entirely from living environments. Does the drive toward the virtual realm that Kwon diagnoses eject the important work of earth artists from the contemporary scene? Does a redefinition of the site of art as a purely discursive formation foreclose ecological imperatives by positioning the earth itself as retrogressively limited in time and space?

The latent dichotomy between nature and culture has long been the target of ecological criticism. According to eco-critics, within the prevailing logic of domination, humans distinguish themselves from nature on the basis of their ability to reason and to acquire knowledge independently of physical circumstances; that is, our transcendence of the natural world is the basis for our dominion over it. As Val Plumwood writes in her provocative book *Environmental Culture: The Ecological Crisis of Reason:*

> The ecological crisis can be thought of as involving a centric and self-enclosed form of reason that simultaneously relies on and disavows its material base as "externality," and a similar failure of the rationalised world it has made to acknowledge and to adapt itself adequately to its larger "body," the material

and ecological support base it draws on in the long-denied counter-sphere of "nature."[10]

Inevitably, the disavowal that Plumwood describes leads to the hyperseparation of nature and culture, whereby nature is construed as being fundamentally detached from the cultural sphere.[11] Similarly, the denial of the material basis of knowledge, language, and social and technological development could easily be the premise for a false understanding of the virtual vector of discursive sites as opposite and exclusive to grounded physical locations.

What remains understated in Kwon's prognosis of the virtual trajectory of contemporary art is that the very notion of a discursively determined artwork has its roots in early earthworks, which were designed to break out of the limits of the gallery. Earth artists had a mandate to overturn the modernist ideal that the spectator can achieve a centralized and singularly located perspective of an art object. They consistently showed that situating an artwork outside the gallery leads to a displaced spectatorial experience and subverts the continuity of perception. Indeed, this was in no small part due to the particularities of the geographic locations the artists chose. Robert Smithson, whose massive earthwork *Spiral Jetty* I address in chapter 2, was one of the first generation of artists to demonstrate the correlation between an artwork's incorporation in the earth and its consequent reliance on "displaced" or discursive media, such as textual narratives, maps, photographs, and film. The art historian Craig Owens related Smithson's work to the dizzying experience of decentering that occurred, in Jacques Derrida's words, "at the moment when language invaded the universal problematic, the moment when, in the absence of a center or origin, everything became discourse."[12] What deserves to be considered, then, is how contemporary art's discursive malleability becomes apparent through its recourse to the earth. Indeed, precisely because these locations were so unwieldy in scale, atmosphere, and many other environmental contingencies, earth art challenged the assumptions that a fixed location has a predetermined significance and that it could ever be the basis of an essential identity.

This book therefore posits that earth art has a critical role to play in showing how interactions with, and sensations of, the earth happen at the edges of the discursive realm of culture. In contemporary practice, nature is not a site that is subjected to human signification; it is present to the senses and, most importantly, it appears in its resistance to being subsumed into representation. Since it cannot be contained within, or reproduced as, an artwork, the earth appears as a temporal or sensorial excess at the limit of representational form. The various practices that mediate natural activity therefore demand a more nuanced approach than the notion of site-specificity, particularly one that does not frame the earth's materiality pejoratively, as a restriction to the potential malleability of the postmodern subject.

## The Earth as Elemental

Insofar as it foregrounds the spectator's bodily contact with, and sensorial experience of, natural phenomena, earth art defines itself through the terms of both aesthetic experience and ethical encounter. The ambition is not just to translate a local knowledge of place into an artwork that claims to speak universally about nature, but rather to mediate a visceral contact with nature in order to suggest a way of interacting with it. At the same time, earth art resists delivering nature as a thematic image, such as a landscape, or a tangible object, such as a specimen in a natural history museum. Earth art navigates the shifting territory between sensation and perception, nature and culture, and the material and the discursive, as well as between the local and the global. Yet in framing earth art through the concepts of ecology, ethical encounter, perceptual excess, and aesthetic experience, a host of conflicting terms arise, with regard to both what distinguishes earth art within the broader field of contemporary practice and how it fits in with a growing environmental consciousness. It is therefore worthwhile to elaborate on some key concepts, such as "ecosystem," "earth," "elemental," and "land," each of which has a part to play in upsetting the view of the planet as a "standing reserve" of resources for human consumption, to use Martin Heidegger's phrase. It is important to stress, however, that earth art is not always commensurate with the conceptual framework of ecology (taken either as a scientific discipline or as strict environmentalism).

The terminology surrounding the notion of "ecology," though useful for understanding the multifarious workings of the planet, has recently come under scrutiny. The philosopher Stephen David Ross, for example, makes a valid criticism of some of the foundational principles of the environmental movement. Specifically, Ross argues, the ideas of "biodiversity" and "sustainability" privilege the order and boundaries of an ecosystem and aim to restore the environment to a presumed original state of stability, endurance, and reliability.[13] James Lovelock's model of Gaia, elaborated in his now-renowned 1979 book *Gaia: A New Look at Life on Earth,* for example, frames the planet as a self-regulating living creature whose complex system is analogous to an ordered democracy. Lovelock writes:

> From a Gaian viewpoint, all attempts to rationalize a subjugated biosphere with man in charge are as doomed to failure as the similar concept of benevolent colonialism. They all assume that man is the possessor of this planet; if not the owner, then the tenant. . . . The Gaia hypothesis implies that the stable state of our planet includes man as a part of, or partner in, a very democratic entity.[14]

Though Lovelock is rightly critical of the subjugation of the planet, he counters the ideology of mastery with the logic of an internally regulated system of which humans are only a part. Ross's critique, however, is that nature is wild and disorderly, and that while it may at first appear that the principles of biodiversity and sustainability celebrate nature, in fact they betray a certain conservatism, whereby nature is patterned on human ideals of order.

This convincing argument exposes the tendency to merely apply an anthropocentric model to the earth's activity. Similarly, in artistic practice, "land restoration" or "land reclamation" projects may seem to be the most obviously aligned with environmental ethics. However, their value does not necessarily lie in the fact that they revivify ecosystems, which does not in itself provide a deeper understanding of the human relationship to the earth. In replacing the art object with a living yet stable system that is couched in the vocabulary of political democracy—or more often for this kind of artwork, the rubric of the science laboratory—reclamation projects risk being complicit with a sociopolitical order responsible for pollution and the overzealous harvesting of resources. This is why many artists see their role as cultivating a different attitude or stance toward natural activity that acknowledges its existence beyond the parameters of human control.

It is evident, then, that an account of ecology's ethical commitments, which is also critical of anthropocentrism and a utopian desire for order, is necessary to deal with contemporary earth art in its various forms. As I have been arguing, it is crucial to recognize that the discursive world and the material earth are intertwined but also discrete. Edward Casey summarizes this position, basing his model in phenomenology. He outlines the coexisting realms of the human world and the earth.[15] "World," he suggests, is the communal, historical, and linguistic domain of human speech and action. To operate in the world is to seek out a place and orientation in the human order. The human world is by no means static; however, it is constituted on a fundamental base. "Earth," or what Edmund Husserl calls the "original ark" or "basis-body," subtends the world. Not only is it the ground from which all organic matter, organisms, and life issue, but it also determines one's sense of movement, stillness, space, and other bodies. Husserl argues, "Bodies are given as having the sense of being earthly bodies and space is given as having the sense of earth-space. The totality of We, of human beings or 'animate beings,' is in this sense earthly—and has no contrary in the nonearthly."[16] The earth is therefore neither just a globe (a body among many celestial bodies) nor just a spatial container for human life, but the horizon of the world and the precondition for sensation. It is an endlessly shifting parameter that can never be reached or outstripped. Thus, earth does not stabilize the world but rather stands as an enigmatic presence that continually drives the world to reorient itself.

The philosopher John Sallis further explains that as a constitutive basis, the earth remains closed off from human knowledge.[17] This is not simply because its literal matter is impenetrable but, more profoundly, because the earth withholds itself from being known; it is an irreducible elemental. Heidegger observes this withdrawn quality of the earth by making an analogy to a stone: "The stone presses downward and manifests its heaviness. But while this heaviness presses against us, it denies us any penetration into it. If we attempt such a penetration by breaking the rock into pieces, it still does not display in its pieces anything inward and opened."[18] The stone withholds because it, like the earth, "shatters every attempt to penetrate into it." Heidegger's analogy suggests that to conceive of the earth as "elemental" is to take into consideration its unyielding quality.

An elemental cannot be analyzed by dividing it into constituent parts, nor can it be summarized as a single entity. Likewise, the earth for us is not a mere thing with clear boundaries, but rather the essential terrain that orients all perception. As Husserl suggests, though we may know in the abstract that the earth is a planet, we experience it, in Fred Kersten's words, as having its own inherent "spatial and temporal spreadoutness" in relation to the body.[19] It is the way the earth manifests as an infinitely spreading and omnipresent ground for the body and posits an enigma to the imagination that is of particular interest here. As much as the earth is the starting point for any phenomenological understanding of space, its resistance to a totalized concept continually reveals the limits of the human world, as well as the point at which natural activity exceeds those limits.

It is for this reason that the earth can be considered the basis from which we experience all natural phenomena such as water, air, light, the growth and decay of organisms, mists, or hurricanes. These phenomena could also be considered elementals, since they, as Husserl argues, compose spatial fields that become visible in relation to the earth. Thus, he gives the example: "The 'sky' is also necessarily constituted as the field of what is outermost, yet which can be spatially experienced for me and all of us—with respect to the earth-basis."[20] Not only is the earth an original standpoint from which other elementals come into view, but they in turn occasion a sense of the evanescence of the earthly realm. Significantly, many artists have turned their attention away from land sculpture as such and toward the aesthetic dimensions of elementals. In chapter 3 I discuss how artists such as James Turrell, Chris Drury, and Olafur Eliasson, for example, deploy light as a medium. As I will argue, insofar as their use of elementals revives the phenomenological condition of the body's contingency on the earth, it seems appropriate to consider their work for its relevance to the earth art movement and ecological ethics.

Where, then, does the notion of "land" enter? Edward Casey defines land as an intermediary zone between earth and world that brings the earth into visibility in the realm of language and representation. He claims, "Land turns the earth inside out, as it were, putting its material contents on display, setting them out in particular places, so as to become subject to articulation in language and to play a role in the history of those who live on it."[21] It is not surprising, then, that the term "land art" has been applied to so much art from the late sixties to the present. But perhaps this category is too easily associated with the medium of sculpture, as though to emphasize the substance out of which the work is made, such as soil, mud, or rock. It is clear that many artworks that address the condition of the earth and the human relationship to it cannot be categorized as sculpture. To reiterate an earlier point, earth artists work in urban settings, making installations both outdoors and indoors. They employ film, digital images, and the Internet. Indeed, as I show in chapter 1, earth art was born as much of performance and conceptual art as it was of postminimalist sculpture. Considering that many artists deal with other elementals as well, such as light, water, wind, and so forth, it seems that land is only one of many intermediaries between the earth and the human world. There are two risks in employing the category "land art," then. First, it lends itself too easily to an interpretation of art as a surface marking, as though the earth itself were merely a textual archive of human history and events. Second, "land art" does not necessarily address the earth's quality of withholding and its resistance to representation that Heidegger identifies and that has been compelling for so many contemporary artists since the sixties. It seems appropriate, then, to use the term "earth art," in this study, not only because ecology has brought a renewed interest in the state of the planet as a whole, but also because what is most striking about the range of artworks I deal with here is the way their use of elementals awakens a sense of the human world in relationship to the earth's ineluctable presence.

Earth art need not be pitted against "land art," for indeed, many of the artworks that appear in this study do feature the terrestrial surface and its role as a bridge between the earth and the artwork's meaning. But instead of focusing on the use of land as a sculptural material, I maintain that land is one of many elementals that reveal the earth's resistance to form, image, and structure. The artworks I analyze highlight two complementary features of elementals: their sensorial plenitude and their unrepresentability. The persistent question of how to present the unrepresentable earth has driven both early land-based art and more recent intermedia strategies that deal with the sky, light, water, and weather. It is this continuity between the generations of artistic practice that deserves analysis now.

## Sensation and the Excess of the Elemental

Earth artists are sometimes misunderstood as romantic or essentialist for taking their encounters with nature as the principal tenet of their artworks. This might be said of landscape painting in the Western tradition, which often showcases "virgin" wilderness as a way to imagine the earthly realm as radically separate from the human world. As Robin Kelsey argues, a traditional landscape can be defined as a fantasy of not belonging to the totality of terrestrial life. Further, this fantasy of not belonging is underwritten with a desire to take precedence over the earth, to see it as a territory belonging to us.[22] Earth art departs from this idealistic and ideologically charged visual vocabulary. Though the claim that the earth exists beyond representation may appear to hark back to the fantasy of untouched nature, in fact earth artists attempt to overturn the disavowal of our terrestrial basis and to reestablish an awareness of both our ecological condition and our inability to control the totality of natural life. To demonstrate the earth's alterity from the human world is neither to presume its purity nor to deny that we are in a mutually constitutive relationship with it. Rather, it is to insist that the parameters of the human world are limited and that the whole of natural phenomena cannot be contained within them.

In contrast to landscape painting, which attempts to mask human presence or naturalize human dominance, earth art explores the point of contact between the body and the earth. The British artist Richard Long, for example, has spent his career executing long walks as a form of performance, documenting his excursions with photographs and short written descriptions of the areas. As part of the walk, Long marks the land with a trace of his presence. To make *A Line and Tracks in Bolivia: An Eleven Day Walk Crossing and Re-crossing a Lava Plain* (Figure 4), the artist repeatedly walked a line in a lava field, thereby clearing away the sedimented rock and creating a straight line, which he then photographed. Far from showing an untouched landscape, the image is organized around Long's intervention at the site. Yet the intervention is of a considerably more demure scale then Richard Serra's *Tilted Arc*. The line is only a precarious index of the performance, a mark that is eventually effaced and reabsorbed. Long's performances reinforce the distinction between an idealized image of nature and the artist's bodily experience of the earth, which can only be delivered as a textual document that fails to reproduce the same experience for the spectator.

What is crucial here is that sensations of the transient natural conditions of the site—sounds, smells, and changing light and weather conditions—cannot be delivered through visual representation. By making bodily contact with the earth the prime focus of the performance, and by foregrounding his own withdrawal from the site, Long alters both the landscape tradition that is bound to a fantasy of not belonging and its counterpart, a desire to colonize territory. Long distinctly marks his withdrawal from the place with ephemeral traces—a path worn into the dirt, or in other cases, a line in the snow or a row of upturned rocks—slight modifications on the land that are bound to be destroyed, covered over, or otherwise wiped out over time. In marking himself as simultaneously present and absent, the artist opens a new space between the fiction of pure nature and an acknowledgment of the fact that the earth is an endlessly shifting ground that precedes and will continue beyond human history.

Long's work is an example of how contemporary artists stage the inability to represent the earth as such. This is not to suggest that earth art does not use representational media. Rather, the artists disclose the failure of images and words to capture natural phenomena and the fullness of sensation when the body comes into contact with them. Instead of picturing nature, then, contemporary artists are constantly watching and waiting for a way to reveal the earth without thematizing it through preconceived notions of what nature is (or should be). In this way, the artwork is developed out of the friction between the artists' attempts to make the earth visible and its resistance to signification. This tense encounter is the onset of a dialogue about how we perceive the earth and how it thwarts our perceptual expectations.

Maurice Merleau-Ponty's phenomenological paradigm, first established in *The Phenomenology of Perception* and further developed in *The Visible and the Invisible,* was highly influential in the analysis of early earthworks, particularly in elaborating how the artwork invites a multisensorial or bodily perception of the environment.[23] In light of more-recent feminist and ecological criticism of Merleau-Ponty's phe-

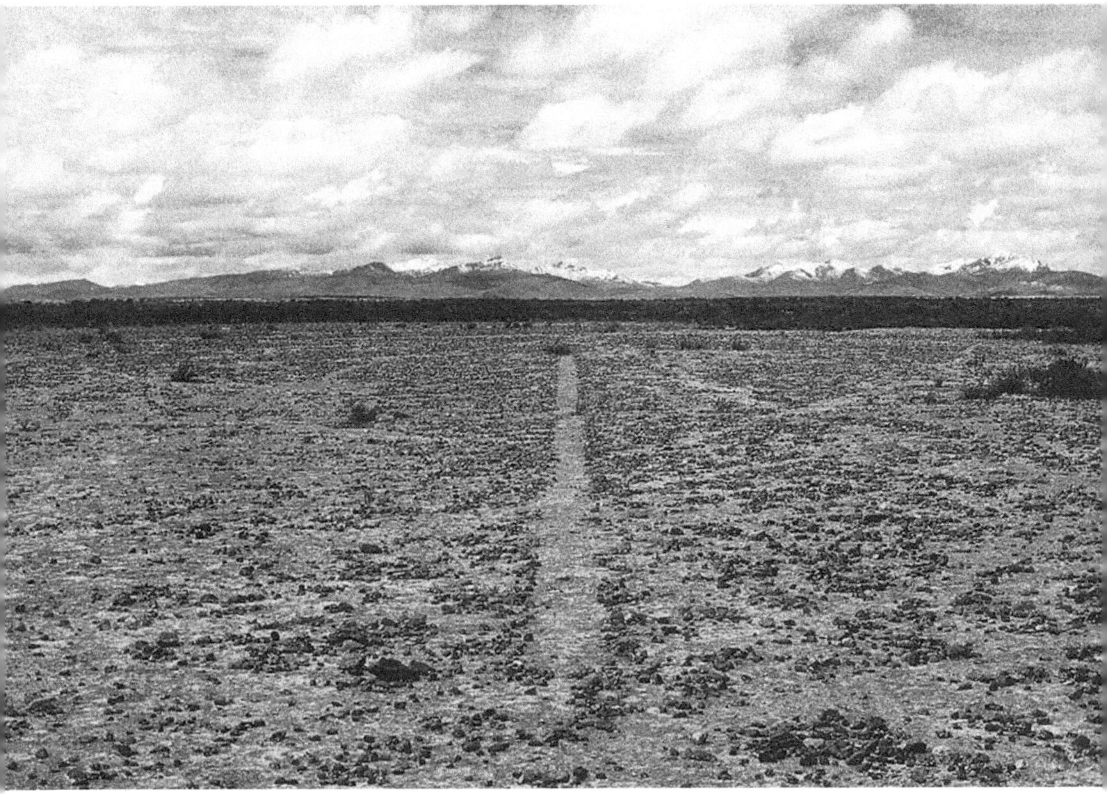

FIGURE 4. Richard Long, *A Line and Tracks in Bolivia: An Eleven Day Walk Crossing and Re-crossing a Lava Plain,* 1981. Copyright 2008 Richard Long. Courtesy of the artist and Haunch of Venison Gallery, London.

nomenology, it is now also important to investigate how earth art exposes the inability of the spectator to subsume natural activity into her or his perceptual field. That is to say, though an artwork may open the senses to natural activity, it also confounds perceptual certainty, revealing how elementals overflow at the limits of visual form. In this regard, Luce Irigaray's critique of Merleau-Ponty's presumed reversibility of the senses of visuality and tactility in *An Ethics of Sexual Difference* is particularly important.[24] For Merleau-Ponty, visuality develops out of our tactile sensations of the world, and in turn vision organizes bodily sensations into a coherent perception. For Irigaray, by contrast, tactile sensations never completely register in visual perception. Tactility may inform how one sees the world, but this is not to suggest that what one sees is all there is. Irigaray's work is therefore pertinent to this study, which foregrounds both the physical contact with nature and the way the artwork consistently signals aspects of nature that exist beyond our perception and knowledge of it.

This is not to suggest that earth art is exclusively concerned with tactile sensation; rather, it exposes the divergence of tactile sense from the visual field and the loss of the former as it registers in the latter. Though an artwork attempts to mediate subtle impressions of the temporality, rhythms, and materiality of elementals, often it is ephemeral and requires some form of documentation, be it a narrative, a photograph, a film, or some other textual record. Indeed, the documentation of the artwork is an integral part of much earth art practice. Artists such as Richard Long formulate an artwork out of an aggregate of representations that are suggestive of a complete aesthetic experience of nature but that nevertheless fail to deliver its sensual fullness. Like Dion's *Neukom Vivarium,* the textual document points to the inability to re-create nature.

Contemporary artists expose this failure to coalesce natural activity into a visual representation by marking it as an absence of, or an obstacle to, coherent sight. The loss of the site as elemental phenomena escape the parameters of the artwork therefore becomes an insistent aspect of many of the works in this study. More subtly, earth art expresses the loss of *site* as concomitant with a loss of *sight* that accompanies the sensual contact with elementals. My claim is that earth art's insistence on troubling vision and revealing the lapses in signification are cues to a practice of withdrawal from the impetus to represent nature.

## Ethics and the Withdrawal from Representation

Irigaray defines ethics as a commitment to preserving the other's difference from oneself. This is achieved in a twofold manner. First, the ethical relation is born of the persistent question, who art thou? that arises in recognition of the other's irreducibility to one's own solipsistic orientation. Second, it is forged through sensual contact, and more precisely, through an open and receptive mode of touch that does not attempt to enclose but reinforces the parameters of difference. Irigaray's provocative account of the relationship to the other is relevant both in the exploration of new possibilities for ecological ethics and in analyzing the aesthetic territory of earth art.

Ultimately, I argue that earth artists develop an ethical stance by positioning the artwork as a receptive surface. I take the notion of receptivity to mean both a literal surface of visibility, on which elementals appear without being formalized into a pictorial image or stable object, and a distinct stance of recession and openness to the excess of sense that elementals deliver. The receptive surface—be it the shadowy image projected on the wall of a camera obscura, film footage of glaring sunlight, an aperture in a chamber that opens to the sky, or a porous armature on which vegetation grows—articulates a withdrawal from representation and an exposure of the fundamental differentiation between the human world and the earth. The artwork is the threshold at which elementals exceed the limits of perception. In simultaneously making contact with natural phenomena and withholding the drive to unify them in the viewer's field of vision, the artwork offers itself as a medium on which the earth manifests and asserts its irreducibility to human signification. In this way, the aesthetic strategies of earth art are coextensive with its ethical statement.

In chapter 1, I track the evolution of the paradigm of earth art I am developing here. Since the sixties, there have been many diverse strategies of redirecting art toward an ecological consciousness. Art that is normally associated with ecology, namely, site restoration and activist art, has its roots in postminimalist sculpture, process art, performance art, and conceptual art. As I will show, these precedents, in their decided rejection of modernist ideals and institutions, opened the way for an ecological orientation in artistic practice. This brief history will also, I hope, challenge any erroneous presumptions that earth art is confined to sculpture in the land or that these early practices have no connection to our current environmental concerns.

In chapter 2, I undertake an in-depth analysis of Robert Smithson's *Spiral Jetty*, an iconic earthwork that has not often been considered in terms of its ecological trajectory. Indeed, it has been critiqued for its complicity with a masculinist industrial aesthetic. I argue that *Spiral Jetty* was a turning point in the history of earth art for a number of reasons. Not only is it divided into several different media, including a sculpture, an essay, and a film, but it also thematizes its own inability to represent the natural site in which the sculpture is located. This chapter emphasizes the ways in which Smithson encodes his various modes of representation with lapses in signification. Although he expresses the loss of the site that results from the process of representation, he nevertheless gives evidence of the persistence of the artwork's connection to it. At different points, the site appears to permeate the text as an amniotic fluid, stimulating in the artist an imagined descent into primordial amorphousness. Smithson therefore reinforces the idea that the texts harbor an indexical relation to the site and are perpetually oriented toward those points at which the site's dynamic forces have been evacuated. It therefore encapsulates the coexistence of the discursive and material spheres of art, as they surge up within one another.

Other earth artists have sought different means of mediating sensations of natural excess. Chapter 3 addresses three artists, James Turrell, Chris Drury, and Olafur Eliasson, whose works position the spectator in an immersive situation, be they earthen enclosures or installations saturated by light, colored filters, or reflective mirrors. Though these works appear to offer unencumbered access to natural phenomena, in fact they are all structured to restrain the viewer at the threshold of elemental manifestations, such as sky, light, atmosphere, water, and color. The artworks are thus born of two seemingly contradictory trajectories: a gravitation into the earth and a retraction from it. I argue that the phenomenological positioning of the spectator as surrounded by, but also separated from, elementals expresses a necessary withdrawal from the earth that opens the senses to the dynamism and plenitude of the earth.

Chapter 4 addresses artworks that feature the contact between the artist's body and the earth, in order to demonstrate the body's role in generating and supporting the friction between transient sensations of natural phenomena and the perceptual closure of representational form. Here, the human body (or alternatively, specific body parts) appears as the representational limit of the artwork and the surface on which elementals become visible. The artists Ana Mendieta, Susan Derges, and Jackie Brookner demonstrate the intermingling of the body and the earth, but most importantly, they perform the separation of the body in order to offer it as an exteriorized plane on which the earth can be sensed as other. In their works, elementals appear in various forms on the body, whether as an influx of activity, a sudden spectral shape, a flourish of growth, or a flood of water and reflections. However, while these manifestations are sensorially rich, they are not coherent images. Following the recurrent figure of "the face" in phenomenology, I define these spectral appearances as face-to-face confrontations between the earth and the body.

The concluding chapter concerns water, both as it is incorporated into contemporary artistic practice and as the prime focus of environmental concern in the first decade of the twenty-first century. The Japanese artist Ichi Ikeda mobilizes water as a medium that is antithetical to permanent form. More than this, however, his installations, performances, and activist events, which revolve around the topic of global water supply, show how this elemental epitomizes an ethical paradigm by which relationships are reconfigured across geographic boundaries and national borders. Likewise, with her two series *Hydrolibros* and *Receding/Reseeding,* the American artist Basia Irland sets water in tension with written text, staging the erosion of books, as though to enact the ruination of history. This undoing of text as it is impacted, marked, and dissolved by water clearly shows how contemporary earth art repositions text as a receptive surface. Moreover, for both Irland and Ikeda, water is an elemental that addresses the imagined future of the planet. Whether it be to relay water to future inhabitants, in the case of Ikeda's work, or to dissolve the past and forge new social networks, in the case of Irland's projects, ecological imperatives are parlayed into gestures of purifying and offering water. The implicit future trajectory of these ecological gestures is expressly pursued in *Greenhouse Britain,* by Helen Mayer Harrison and Newton Harrison. Anticipating the rising water levels due to global warming, the Harrisons created an installation and accompanying online exhibition that imagines the displacement of millions of people over the next hundred years due to flooding. The artwork also proposes an entire reorganization of urban space and communal dwelling based on ecological sustainability.

It is impossible to ignore the fact that environmental crisis has become a central concern in contemporary art. My goal in addressing a variety of earth art practices from the 1960s to the present, then, is not to conflate early artworks with more recent multimedia art under the rubric of a single movement; I am not interested in ascribing a stringent classification to what is obviously a very diverse group of artistic practices. Rather, it is to suggest that the ethical awareness of the earth that emerged in the late sixties has continued to evolve as artists have conceived of new ways of perceiving and addressing the natural environment. The continuity between the generations lies in the artists' impetus to challenge definitions of both art and nature, to reveal the limits of human conceptions of nature, and to open art to the congregation of elementals that give rise to a sense of the earth.

ONE

# Contemporary Art and the Nature of Site

Though the systematized exploitation of natural resources now seems unstoppable, there has been no lack of vision on the part of artists of how to reinvent our relationship to the environment. A plethora of strategies have surfaced with a view to, in Robert Smithson's now-famous phrase, "mediating between the ecologist and the industrialist."[1] It is therefore worth examining the diverse approaches that orient art toward an ecological consciousness, as well as the political, social, and aesthetic issues that these new forms address. My introduction to earth art through debates about site-specificity responds to the risk of reiterating a binary between the actual and the virtual—between earth and world—at a time when historians of contemporary art are accounting for the global mobility of ideas and the deterritorialization of subject positions. What must be established is that historically, an insistence on the materiality of the discursive sphere, and conversely on the discursive malleability of our earthly condition, was the basis of a rejection of positivist definitions of both site and subjectivity through art. Since the late sixties, sculpture, site restoration, activist art, process art, and performance have advanced the notion of a dislocated artwork—art that is no longer defined by medium-specificity, objecthood, or an assumed position in the museum or gallery space. Thus, the paradigm of site-specificity does not lead to a strict dematerialization of art. Rather, it signals an upset in the dichotomy between the artwork's meaning and the material conditions of its production and reception, a shift that opened the door to a reconsideration of our ecological predicament.

## Surfacing Sculpture: Phenomenological Encounters with the Earth

In the late sixties, the early earthworks movement lodged a critique of the modernist ideal that the artwork should transcend its literal environment. The first contemporary earth artists called upon the seemingly limitless horizon of the earth's topographic and temporal conditions in order to infiltrate the spectator's aesthetic engagement with the singular art object. Many of these early projects reenact or thematize the phenomenological experience of space, opening a reconsideration of the earth itself not merely as a spatial envelope for the art object but as an active component of it, and more precisely, as an assembly of volatile forces that pose a dilemma to the self-enclosure of the modernist art object and equally to the self-determination of the spectator's perceptual experience.

In his 1967 essay "A Tour of the Monuments of Passaic, New Jersey" Robert Smithson used the term "earthworks" to draw a parallel between the industrial debris of Passaic (a New Jersey suburb) and the ruinous landscape of the 1965 dystopian novel *Earthworks* by Brian Aldiss.[2] Not long after, the term "earthworks" was commonly used to describe an entire genre of immense sculptural objects built out of and into the land. Artists such as Smithson, Alice Aycock, Suzanne Harris, Michael Heizer, Nancy Holt, Walter De Maria, Mary Miss, and Richard Serra (among others) expanded the scale of minimalist sculpture, often situating their works in obscure, deserted landscapes. Because these projects were unwieldy in size and inaccessible to the museum space by design, they refused a straightforward categorization according to medium. The term "earthwork" was more suitable, or at least more descriptive, than "sculpture," "architecture," or "monument." The artists' evasion of traditional media and institutions demanded a theorization that would give precedence to new spaces of experience in lieu of a formal analysis of the artists' mastery of a particular medium.

The art historian Rosalind Krauss advanced such a theorization, examining the works of Smithson and Heizer in her book *Passages in Modern Sculpture.* Krauss reads earthworks as a continuation of minimalism's break from the Greenbergian model of aesthetic judgment that had been, during the prime of abstract expressionism, the philosophical foundation of modernism's valorization of the purity of medium and the distinctiveness of vision from the other senses. She argues that minimalist sculpture consistently propels meaning to the surface of the artwork rather than cultivating a sense of inherent significance from within. Minimalism, she argues, rejected the easy association between the meaning of an artwork and the interior life of the artist, posited by the sense that the artwork houses its own quasi-psychological interior. A key aspect of Krauss's project was to sever a patrilineal history of art indebted to the mythology of the artist's "inner, inviolable self." In denying the private life of the artist, the minimalist art object reveals meaning as originating from a public audience.[3] This conclusion led Krauss to borrow from two theoretical frameworks in her later interpretations of earthworks as a postminimalist movement. First, she understands the proliferation of new hybrid forms of art-making in semiotic terms, a point to which I shall return. Second, she draws from phenomenology, since in the excision of interiority and the embrace of surface, minimalist and postminimalist art invites a direct relationship to the viewer's body and to the surrounding space.

Phenomenology inspired artists and art historians alike to view artworks in terms of the contingency of the body and the surrounding space of exhibition. A central part of the critique of modernism that earth art inherited from minimalism was the way in which it rooted the aesthetic experience in bodily perception. According to Krauss, minimalism assimilated the principles of Merleau-Ponty's *Phenomenology of Perception,* so that artists revealed what sculpture had previously hidden: that the perceived stability of a sculpture happens not in spite of the variability of the spectator's perspective but precisely through that variability.[4] Minimalist sculpture, for

Krauss, foregrounds the idea that apprehending an object is synonymous with inhabiting the entire space around it, so that the object is perceived as thoroughly instantiated in that space. Minimalism's project was therefore to divest the object of interiority and to see it in relation to the space that it occupies.[5]

In the late sixties, earth art also collapsed the boundaries between the object and space but did so by producing works that would break out of the limited space of the museum or gallery. Instead of producing a discrete object designed for visual apprehension, earth artists constructed works that required the spectator to be fully immersed in them in order to perceive their dimensions, thereby exemplifying Merleau-Ponty's argument that vision and orientation stem from the body's motility, actions, and tactile senses, which produce a "lived experience" of being absorbed in the spaces and intertwined with the objects one sees. In expanding the boundaries of the art object into the broader space of bodily experience and in changing the conditions of that experience from the museum to the infinite horizon of the desert panorama, earth art finalized minimalism's departure from the disembodied visual mode of modern aesthetic judgment.

For Merleau-Ponty, embodied sight entails a reciprocal relation between oneself and the object or other person in the visual field, and this relation constitutes perception. He explains:

> The perceived world is not only *my* world, but the one in which I see the behaviour of other people take shape, for their behaviour equally aims at this world, which is the correlative not only of my consciousness, but of any consciousness *which I can possibly encounter.* . . . It is true that I see what I do see only from a certain angle, and I concede that a spectator differently placed sees what I can only conjecture. But these other spectacles are implied in mine at this moment.[6]

Early earthworks demonstrate two essential aspects of perception as explained by phenomenology: first, a visual field is informed by the bodily sensation of being surrounded in a space, and second, one is equally constituted within that visual field from other perspectives that inform one's own perceptual experience. To assimilate a Merleau-Pontian model meant that earth artists had to simultaneously

FIGURE 5. Richard Serra, *Shift*, 1970. Cement, six rectilinear sections, each 60 × 80 inches. Copyright 2009 Richard Serra/Artists Rights Society (ARS), New York.

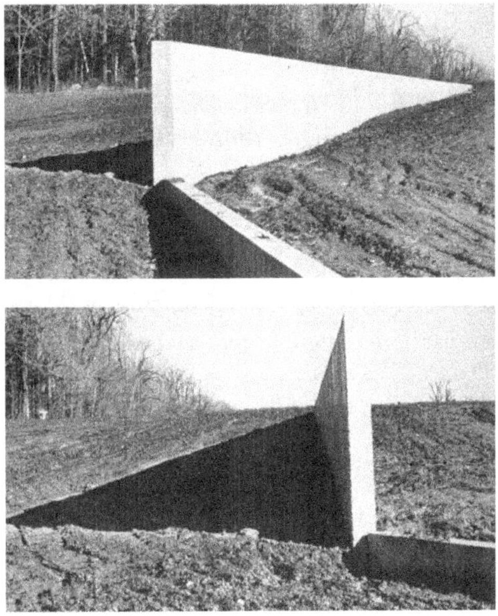

locate the spectator in a space and arrange her or his visual field in relation to that space, which resulted in a decentered spectatorial experience.

Richard Serra choreographed a performance-sculpture that demonstrates this kind of sited vision by enacting the formulation of perspective through the interlocking of looks between two people moving across the land. In *Shift* (Figure 5), Serra and artist Joan Jonas positioned themselves on either end of a three-hundred-yard-long field and walked across the land on opposite ends, always keeping each other in view despite upsets in the topography, from swamps to hills and trees. As Serra explains, "The boundaries of the work became the maximum distance two people could occupy and still keep each other in view. . . . What I wanted was a dialectic between one's perception of the place in totality and one's relation to the field as walked."[7] Short concrete walls were placed at the points where the artists' eye levels were aligned, functioning like orthogonal lines leading toward a horizon. However, in contrast to the fixed orthogonal of a centralized Renaissance perspective, these stepped elevations confirm that one's horizon is continually shifting, or in Serra's words, it is "totally transitive: elevating, lowering, extending, foreshortening, contracting, compressing, and turning."[8]

Serra and Jonas show that one is forever experiencing the world from within the particularities of one's physical surroundings. The variability of the land generates a continually moving horizon. The boundaries of the artwork are produced from the contingency between the transience of the environment and the subsequently changing horizons. By introducing a scenario dependent on the spectator's movement through space and the reciprocal gaze of another person, *Shift* breaks with the ideal of a singular, centered orientation toward an art object.

It is important to recognize, however, that Merleau-Ponty's question is, why do we experience the world as unified and consistent *in spite of* constant changes in our body's orientation? His project is to break with Immanuel Kant not by showing how bodily perception results in disorientation and a fractured knowledge of the world, but rather by showing that the bodily experience is precisely that which gives us our orientation and knowledge of the world. As Yve-Alain Bois explains, Serra's work eliminates the presumption of a gestalt and recalls to the spectator's body its indolence, weight, and material existence.[9] Accordingly, *Shift* does not abandon all parameters of the art object; rather, its parameters are determined by the bodily experience of space. The artwork's frame emerges from the relation between oneself, the other, and the geographic shapings of the external space. *Shift* clearly speaks to Merleau-Ponty's response to Kant in the *Phenomenology of Perception* that "in so far . . . as I know the relation of appearances to the kinaesthetic situation, this is not in virtue of any law or in terms of any formula, but to the extent that I have a body, and that through that body I am at grips with the world."[10] Moreover, works such as Serra's show how, through the body, one also strives to be at grips with the earth.

## From Earthworks to Site Restoration

Earth art's initial break with modernist institutions opened an attentiveness to the spatial environment in which art is viewed and, particularly in its acceptance of a phenomenological paradigm, foregrounded the continuity between the body and that environment. I shall return to the issue of bodily contact, but first it is important to examine how practices of site restoration entered the trajectory of contemporary art and how the notion of being "at grips" with the earth coincided with an awareness of our ecological condition. Site-restoration projects, otherwise known as "reclamation art," emerged not long after the initial earthworks of the late sixties. These endeavored to revive natural sites, particularly those that had been exhausted by strip mining, by turning them into public green spaces. Over the course of the seventies, artists were concerned not merely with the aesthetic revitalization of space but also with ecological resuscitation. To this end, they joined forces with scientists, landscape planners, engineers, environmental specialists, activists, and local communities to create art projects that would overhaul degraded sites and quite literally bring them back to life.

Betty Beaumont stands out as one of the first artists to launch a large-scale reclamation project. For example, her work *Ocean Landmark,* begun in 1978 (Figures 6 and 7), is an underwater habitat made out of coal fly-ash blocks, an industrial byproduct that has undergone a planned transformation into a productive new ecosystem. Beaumont collaborated with scientists who had recently discovered how to use this material to stabilize the toxicity of water and proposed using their materials to create an underwater sculpture. The artist imagined that fishing the new structure would feed people, and the work would regenerate the area located in the Atlantic Ocean forty miles from New York Harbor and three miles off the coast of the Fire Island National Seashore. The work transformed a potential pollutant into an underwater sculpture that generated a flourishing ecosystem teeming with fish.

To present the work, Beaumont exhibited a video of the project, underwater photographs, and a replica of the fly-ash reef. Though the artist insists that underwater photography cannot capture the entire body of the work because of the limited visibility of the ocean's water at the work's depth, she is now working with global positioning satellite technology to create images using remote sensing and side-scan sonar.[11] The fact that the work requires a variety of imaging techniques, however, points to the very necessity for a different approach to presenting the project as a work of visual art. Beaumont remarks on the project, "Fundamental to the original concept of the work was the belief that its integrity resided in its invisibility—it could only be imagined."[12] Interestingly, her point is that while the project itself has a real impact on the ecosystem, *Ocean Landmark* is also an

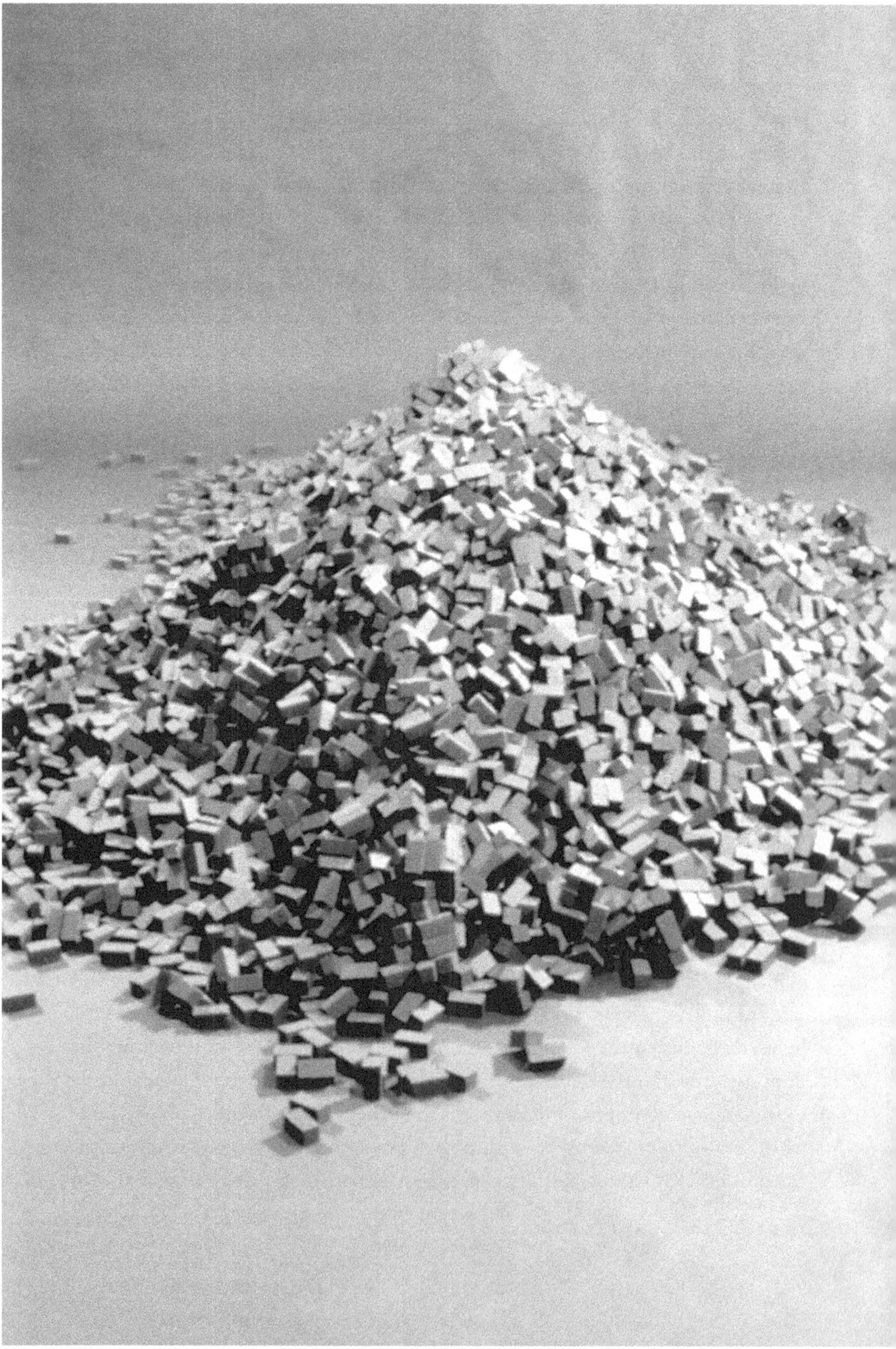

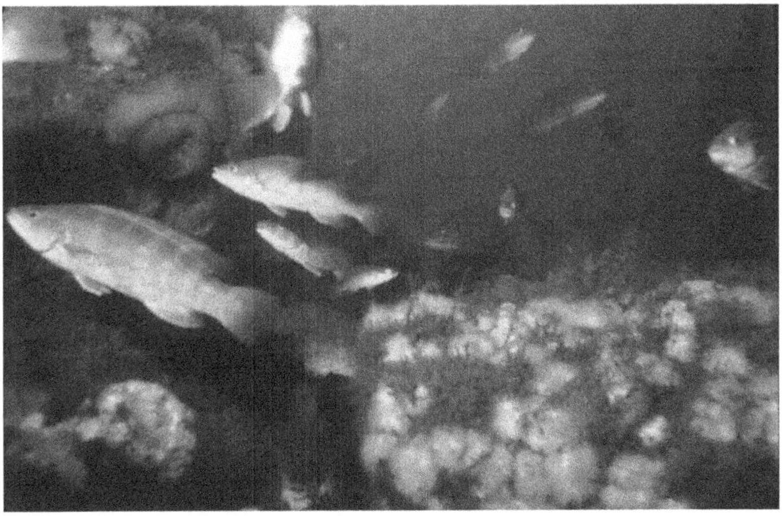

*opposite*
FIGURE 6. Betty Beaumont, *Ocean Landmark* (surrogate), 1978–80. Dimensions vary; approximately 30 × 180 × 60 inches. A simulation to scale of the materials used for the armature has become a surrogate for *Ocean Landmark*: seventeen thousand blocks were fabricated on a one-inch-equals-one-foot scale to give the artist a sense of the potential volume of five hundred tons of coal waste material. Courtesy of the artist.

FIGURE 7. Betty Beaumont, *Ocean Landmark* (detail), 1978–80. *Ocean Landmark* has grown and developed into a thriving marine ecosystem and continues to evolve. It is listed as a fish haven on the National Oceanographic and Atmospheric Administration (NOAA) Approach to New York Harbor coastal navigational chart. It is a realized living sculpture that suggests a new industry that makes use of recycled coal waste with the potential to revitalize coastal fishing industries. Courtesy of the artist.

assembly of images and objects that have been abstracted from the literal environment and yet call attention to it in such a way that we might reconsider its value. Thus, *Ocean Landmark* can be appreciated not through the pleasure of natural beauty, but rather through reflection on the concealed natural activity that exceeds vision and requires the use of a host of tactics to bring it into view.

Beaumont's project was among the first of its kind to posit restoration as a way of securing the connection between the visual media of site-based art—including photographic images, maquettes, maps, and scientific data—and a growing awareness of ecological imperatives. This legacy continued to develop in the works of the American artist Aviva Rahmani in the nineties. As one example, Rahmani organized a reclamation project in which she restored a degraded wetland habitat. Begun in 1991, *Ghost Nets* (Figure 8) was not simply an exercise in recycling materials; rather, it involved an entire lifestyle change in which the artist, as she describes, took ten years to weave her life into the local fishing culture and become an activist in the community of Vinalhaven, Maine. Like Beaumont, Rahmani collaborated with bioengineers to arrange the transformation of sixteen tons of granite debris into a viable saltwater wetland ecosystem. The artist was concerned with reversing ecological damage, but just as important, she crafted the restoration project into a visual narrative.

The restoration, which involved planting four hundred saplings in order to revegetate the wetland, fortifying the shoreline to prevent erosion, and constant monitoring of animal, plant, and organic life, took seven years to prepare but only three days to implement. Indeed, the varied forms of labor, from the meticulous mapping of the area, to researching the site's geomorphology, to time-consuming assessments of the progress of specimens, on top of fund-raising and getting permits to reclaim the site, signal the fact that restoration is not simply a branch of landscape design but a highly demanding political and scientific endeavor. Yet Rahmani explains that, above and beyond the restoration, she wanted to show how the degradation of the salt marshes and their subsequent rescue both influenced the lives of the local people and made a statement about how care of the natural environment is inextricable from the history of a community. The title of the piece, *Ghost Nets,* refers to the invisible and indestructible monofilament nets used by fishermen; when lost overboard, the nets drift into the ocean, trap fish, and ultimately strip-mine the area.[13] Rahmani uses the metaphor of the ghost net to illustrate the way familiar habits of production and consumption can lead to our own entrapment and ultimately our own peril. Interpreting the restoration project as a microcosm of global change, Rahmani presented *Ghost Nets* in several media, including video, photographs, paintings, journals, and installations.

Though this kind of collaboration could be considered an example of what Miwon Kwon calls a "sited community art project," it is clear that the trajectory of

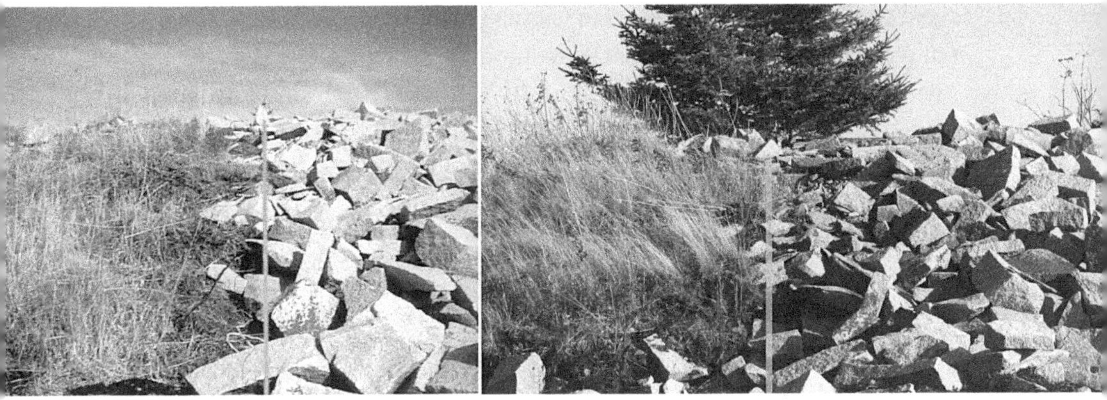

FIGURE 8. Aviva Rahmani, *Ghost Nets*, 1991–2001. Line of demarcation between restored and unrestored uplands with new spring growth emerging. *Left*, 1998; *right*, 2008. Copyright 2009 Aviva Rahmani.

Rahmani's practice is larger than the specific site and the local community.[14] Indeed, the ecological paradigm by its very definition is global in scope. Rahmani explains, "I have spent ten years trying to see how very small things relate to very big things: for example how what is typically a very small source of forage, spawning and nesting in the fly zone and fish migration avenues, incrementally lost, fits in a pattern of global restoration our lives depend on."[15] Certainly, the reclamation project is bound to a specific site, but its ecological consequences, political statement, and aesthetic resonance have a reach far wider than the local community.

## Social Sculpture, Activism, and Ecology

The idea of art as a means to effect social change on a global scale was a driving force behind the work of the German artist Joseph Beuys, who was active from the late 1950s to the 1980s and was well-known for his sculptures made of such raw materials as fat, fur, wood, and felt, as well as for his work as a performance artist. Beuys was also particularly concerned with the ways art could address the natural world. In the sixties, he had made contact with the international artist group Fluxus and staged several performance events in Germany, which, like those of his New York counterparts, aimed to revolutionize traditional art practice.

Beuys's initial forays into the intermedia practices characteristic of Fluxus led the artist to conceive of more democratic forms of art. In 1974, Beuys went to the United States on a month-long tour, during which he lectured and performed at galleries and universities in New York, Chicago, and Minneapolis. Indeed, Beuys considered the tour itself to be a performance in its own right, one that he entitled *Energy Plan for the Western Man.* It was at this time that the artist advanced his conception of "social sculpture," the engine behind his "energy plan." Essentially, Beuys took the view that everyone should participate in the shaping of society, and in so doing every person could realize her or his potential to be an artist. This vision of society as sculpture, as itself an artwork that was ever in the process of being shaped by the public, also aimed to reintegrate nature into the human social structure. Otherwise put, Beuys's energy plan was to redefine art as a public dialogue that included all citizens, as well as animals and elemental forces. This dialogue would be an energy source, a sort of battery that would not only heal the traumas of the increasingly barbaric wars of the twentieth century but would revitalize the natural environment as well.

As part of his 1974 American tour, Beuys performed his now-famous *Coyote, I Like America and America Likes Me* (Figure 9), in which the artist spent seven days with a coyote, locked in a space in the Rene Block Gallery in New York. Beuys arrived at the gallery by ambulance, having arranged to be transported from the airport wrapped in felt and carried in a stretcher. Once in the caged space, an encounter with the coyote ensued. To Beuys's mind at least, the performance was a negotiation with the invisible wild and natural energies of America. It acted as both a reckoning for the harms of European colonization and a lifting of that trauma.[16] Over the course of the performance Beuys engaged the coyote through various actions, such as wrapping himself entirely in a large swathe of felt and holding out a shepherd's crook above his head, then slowly bowing to the coyote. The coyote ripped at the edges of the felt, tugging off bits at a time and ultimately exposing the artist concealed underneath. Beuys offered his brown leather gloves, throwing them to the coyote, which retreated with them to smell, lick, and otherwise investigate them. The artist also slept in the coyote's straw, leaving the animal the

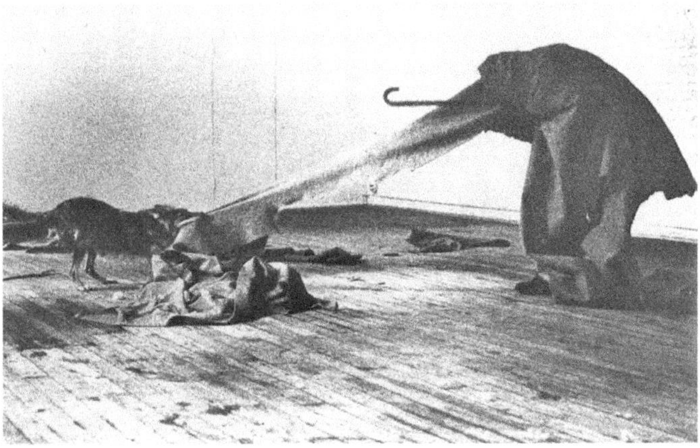

FIGURE 9. Joseph Beuys, *Coyote, I Like America and America Likes Me,* 1974. One-week performance for the opening of the Rene Block Gallery, New York. Copyright 2009 Artists Rights Society (ARS), New York/VG Bild-Kunst, Bonn.

ripped bolts of felt to sleep in, thus exchanging their respective spaces in the cage. At times tense and at times relaxed and comfortable, the drama between artist and coyote did indeed encapsulate the intricacy of confronting natural forces under the auspices of dialogue. Far from attempting to tame the animal, Beuys was instead attempting to discover a form of communication in spite of the animal's wildness. He even describes the coyote as a kind of elemental force: "The spirit of the coyote is so mighty that the human being cannot understand what it is, or what it can do for humankind in the future."[17]

While Beuys has been criticized for his obscure symbolic references and his fabrication of a loose metaphysics in which he mythologizes himself by performing the role of shaman or priest, his vision of art as a means of developing a politics of ecology has nevertheless had a significant impact.[18] Not only did the artist in 1973 found the Free International University for Creativity and Interdisciplinary Research, which included in its infrastructure an Institute of Ecology and an Institute of Evolutionary Science, but he also became a founding member of the Green Party in Germany in 1979.[19] His political, aesthetic, and ecological goals found fruition in *7,000 Eichen (7,000 Oaks)* (Figure 10), his project for Documenta 7, held in 1982 in Kassel, Germany. The work is a social sculpture that involved the planting of seven thousand oak trees, each accompanied by its own monument, a basalt column. Not only were the trees planted, but the project was also extended to

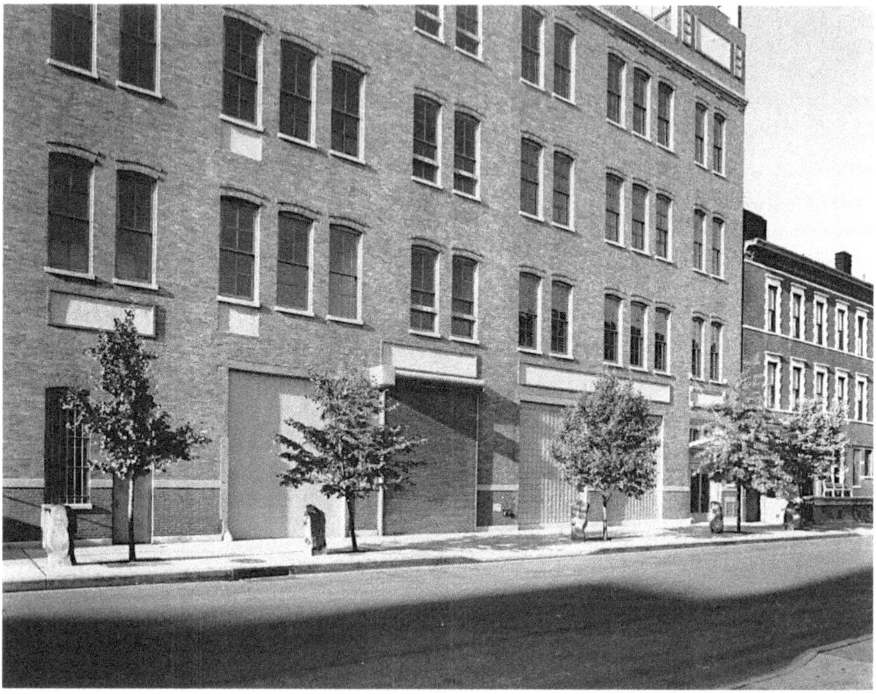

FIGURE 10. Joseph Beuys, *7,000 Eichen (7,000 Oaks)*, 1982– (ongoing). Installation view at West Twenty-second Street, New York City, between and including Tenth and Eleventh avenues. Copyright 2009 Artists Rights Society (ARS), New York/VG Bild-Kunst, Bonn. Photograph by Bill Jacobson. Courtesy of Dia Art Foundation.

different sites, including, in 1988, the Dia Foundation for the Arts in New York City. Beuys imagined *7000 Oaks* not only as a way to integrate natural growth in urban spaces but also as a symbolic beginning for a new ecological orientation. The basalt stones were thus installed to mark the beginning of the social transformation that would perpetuate the project far beyond the seven thousand trees. That is, each installation of an oak and stone column in a "planting event" signaled the starting point of a more profound regeneration of the earth and human social structures. Beuys explains, "This will be a regenerative activity; it will be a therapy for all of the problems we are standing before. . . . I wished to go completely outside and to make a symbolic start for my enterprise of regenerating the life of humankind within the body of society and to prepare a positive future in this context."[20]

Activist art such as Beuys's shows that an ecological orientation in art is not founded on an antimodern nostalgia but rather opens new possibilities for social organization. Indeed, it runs counter to the legitimate concern that an ecological society is tantamount to a fetishization of local community. Kwon raises precisely this argument in her critique of Lucy Lippard's book *The Lure of the Local: Senses of Place in a Multicentered Society.* Lippard outlines the troubled relationship between a seemingly conservative desire for rootedness and permanence, and the nomadism of the contemporary art world. In Kwon's view, Lippard betrays "a reinvestment in connecting with the uniqueness of place."[21] She accuses Lippard of neglecting the importance of a dialectical relationship between place and the malleability of identity. Yet, in her favor, Lippard is conscious of the interests of non-Western positions that stem from the intimate connections between identity, history, and territory. She poses the question of site-specificity, not from a definition of art tied to the mainstream international art scene but from a more general notion of creative production that is integrated into the land, history, and culture of a place.[22]

Lippard argues that the cosmopolitanism of the art industry demands the homogenization of localized interests and the perpetual production of new art forms that deny a historical link to place. She thus argues for a "place ethic" by which what is at stake in art production is the actual place where artists and viewers find themselves, rather than the abstracted space of the museum or gallery. Whereas Kwon sees the potential of virtual media to counter the fetishization of communities as authentic and timeless, Lippard argues that the move toward the virtual disregards the importance of the local environment. She thus posits the local as an anti-institutional and anticorporate stance. Artists should, she argues, "innovate not just for innovation's sake, not just for style's sake, nor to enhance their reputation or ego, but to bring a new degree of coherence and beauty to the lure of the local."[23]

As I suggested in my introduction, however, in the midst of this debate between the virtual trajectory of art and the subversive potential of a reinvestment in the local, a false dichotomy emerges between the particular concerns of the environment and the complex identities that stem from global interconnectivity. Does the cosmopolitanism of the contemporary art world necessarily foreclose an ecological mind-set? Is deep local knowledge incommensurate with a global orientation?

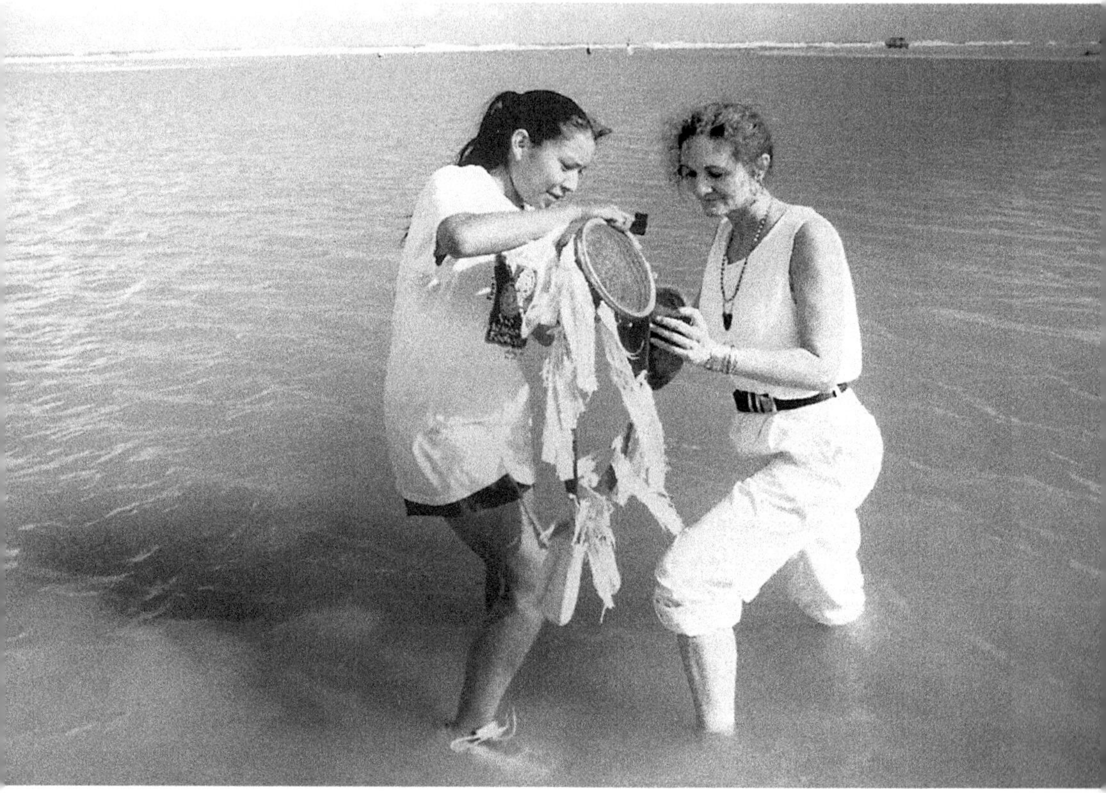

FIGURE 11. Basia Irland, *A Gathering of Waters: Rio Grande, Source to Sea,* 1995–2000. Copyright Basia Irland.

Beuys's "symbolic performances" show that this dichotomy does not have to determine artistic production or its ethical commitments. Moreover, in the eighties and nineties, other artists organized strategies that similarly assembled new configurations of community to respond to specific instances of ecological endangerment. In these projects, the artwork aims not only at consciousness-raising about environmental degradation but also at reorienting social structures as a means of addressing the problems. Basia Irland's performance *A Gathering of Waters: Rio Grande, Source to Sea* (Figure 11) united diverse groups of people, including artists, members of government agencies, Native American leaders, private water us-

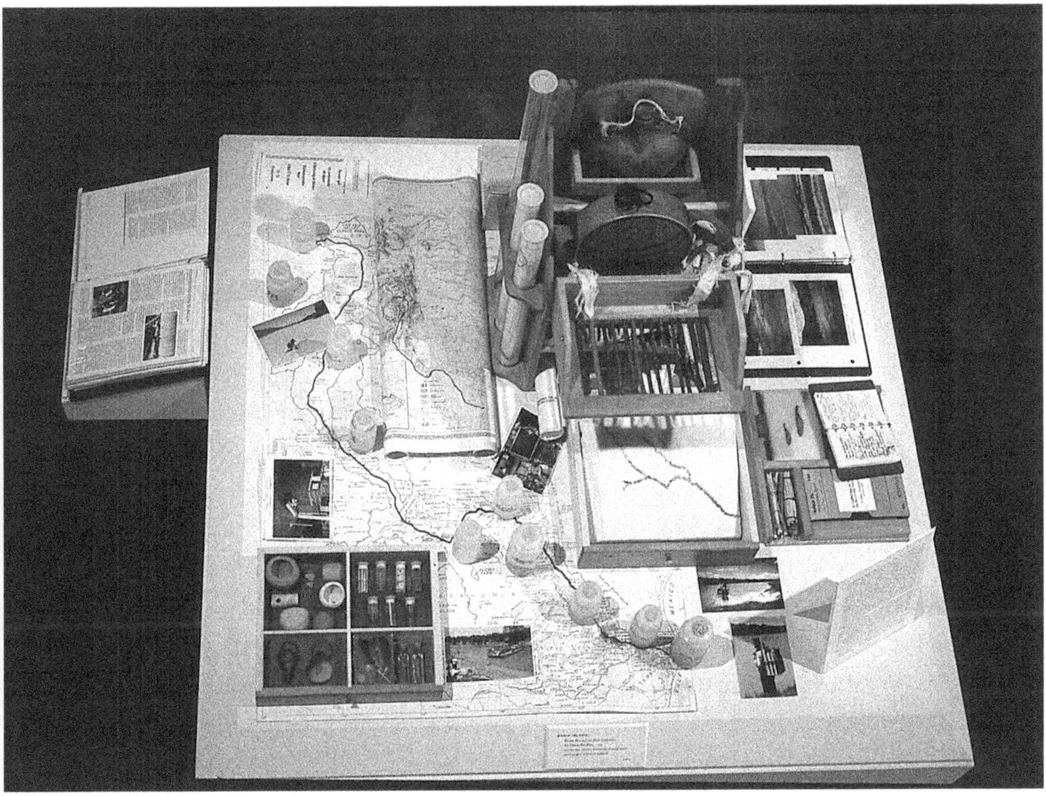

FIGURE 12. Basia Irland, *A Gathering of Waters: Rio Grande, Source to Sea,* 1995–2000. River repository with contents. Copyright Basia Irland.

ers, farmers, and ranchers, all of whom live near and rely on the 1,885-mile-long Rio Grande/Rio Bravo basin that rises in Colorado, passes through New Mexico, crosses the border, and flows into the Gulf of Mexico.[24]

Beginning at the source of the river in Colorado, Irland initiated a performance by asking participants to collect river-water samples in a canteen and write their experiences in a logbook. The canteen and logbook were then passed from one group of participants to the next, traveling by boat, raft, canoe, hot-air balloon, car, van, horseback, truck, bicycle, mail, and foot, joining the range of people in the common project of focusing awareness on the condition of the river and the integral role it plays in the lives of everyone who depends on it.[25] One part of the performance included a 150-mile relay, run by members of the Pueblo villages in New Mexico, in which the water was transported in a baton made of cattail reed and passed at one-mile intervals over a two-day period. Insofar as it joined a cross-section of social groups that live on the vast stretch of river, the artwork consolidated a virtual community, forging new networks. This social reformulation was secured through the hand-to-hand contact between participants, so that the artwork did not merely revolve around a discursive topic but rather pitched activism as the central tenet of a community of otherwise disparate people.

Essentially, Irland remaps social relations as ecological ties, a concept that becomes evident in the "river repository," the artist's archive of the project. The repository, an art object in its own right, holds a variety of objects that form a record of the performance (Figure 12). Along with the logbook and the canteen that traveled down the river, Irland included a video documentary, samples of flora from the riverbanks, sticks that were chewed by beavers, small canteens made from river clay that were given as gifts to the participants, vials of water from each section of the river where a transaction took place, and a variety of charts, including a wooden atlas covered in salt and inlaid with a tracing of the river in turquoise and a foldout map that chronicles the scientific data of the river's precarious condition, showing, for example, the area where the river has dried up and the places where biologists have discovered that fish eggs will not hatch due to impossible spawning conditions. The repository thereby weaves the river into a tangible record of a new socio-ecological arrangement.

The Rio Grande/Rio Bravo gathering was the first among many. Irland executed gatherings along the Don River in Ontario, Canada, in 2000; on the River Dart in Devon, England, in 2005; on Boulder Creek, Colorado, in 2007; and most recently, in 2008, on the Nisqually River in Washington State. What began as an experiment in consciousness-raising about ecological conditions thus became a modus operandi by which Irland mobilizes the arteries of the planet to draw out the dormant histories of rivers, the elemental sources that determine the patterns of human settlement, the way in which water has traditionally oriented artistic and cultural practice, and, most important, how all of these are keyed into larger systems of animal and organic life.

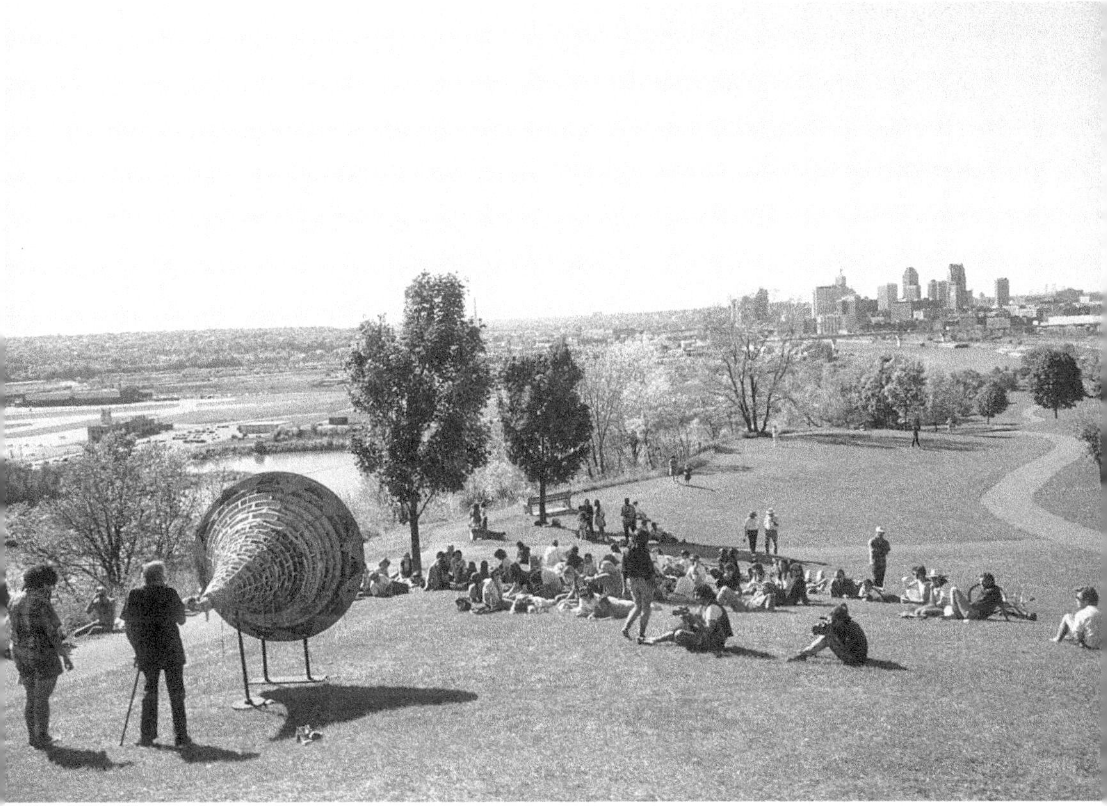

FIGURE 13. Rebecca Belmore, *Ayumee-aawach Oomama-Mowan: Speaking to Their Mother,* 1991. Gathering, St. Paul, Minnesota, 1992. Photograph by Michael Beynon. Courtesy of the Walter Phillips Gallery, The Banff Centre.

Political activism in art also comes from communities whose interest in the environmental crisis is inextricable from a larger context of structural oppression. A significant critical voice in contemporary art that has consistently drawn attention to the correspondence between colonization and environmental exploitation comes from First Nations artists. At the Land, Spirit, Power exhibition at the National Gallery of Canada in 1992, artists exposed the interlocked offenses of ethnic and ecological abuse that began during the colonization of North America by western European countries and that have since been perpetuated by the Canadian and

U.S. governments. Along with these critiques of systemic racism and environmental negligence, First Nations artists have coordinated interventions that revitalize their cultural claim to the land.

For her performance *Ayumee-aawach Oomama-Mowan: Speaking to Their Mother* (Figure 13), the Ojibwa artist Rebecca Belmore invited a gathering of leaders, writers, poets, and social workers to speak to the land through a giant carved wooden megaphone. Among the more interesting and politically charged locations where the artwork toured was a spot near the Canadian prime minister's private residence.[26] The protest affirms the primacy of the earth to the discursive site that the artwork formulates, namely, the assembly of First Nations activists. Its weaving of land to cultural heritage and to the fraught history of imperialism thus allows the performance to double as a critique of government policy.

## Process Art and the Manifestation of Elementals

Whereas activist art links ecology to political action, in the sixties artists developed other forms of art that emphasized the all-pervasiveness of natural forces, designing artworks that incorporated elementals such as light and water. Hans Haacke's condensation boxes (Figure 14), for example, were the inverse of works such as Serra's *Shift,* in that rather than embedding art in the land, Haacke activated natural processes within the gallery space. Using the gallery as a science laboratory, Haacke made Plexiglas boxes containing water. The water turned to vapor and then condensed, dripping down the sides of the cube to eventually turn again to vapor and repeat the cycle. A very basic natural process thus becomes highly aestheticized as the water drops thicken on the walls of the cube, growing heavy and eventually dripping in rivulets to the bottom. Minimalist in appearance, the condensation boxes were also subtle in that the condensation process itself was slow, and to see any visible transformation demanded fixed attention. This different "timescale," as the critic Jack Burnham describes it, subverts the way the cube seemingly contains the water and instead delivers a juxtaposition of mechanical and organic systems. Accordingly, Haacke instructs in his own short manifesto, "Make something which experiences, reacts to its environment, changes, is nonstable. . . . Make something sensitive to light and temperature changes, that is subject to air currents and depends in its functioning, on the forces of gravity. . . . Make something that lives in time and makes the 'spectator' experience time. . . . Articulate something natural."[27]

Haacke's work sensitizes the viewer to the otherwise hidden dimensions of natural activity. In its insistence on staging transient natural events, moreover, his practice invites the unpredictability and fundamental impenetrability of the elemental. It is in this sense that the art could be considered ethical: rather than presenting the spectator with information (scientific facts about ecosystems or environmental

FIGURE 14. Hans Haacke, *Condensation Box,* 1965. Plexiglas, water. Copyright 2009 Artists Rights Society (ARS)/VG Bild-Kunst, Bonn.

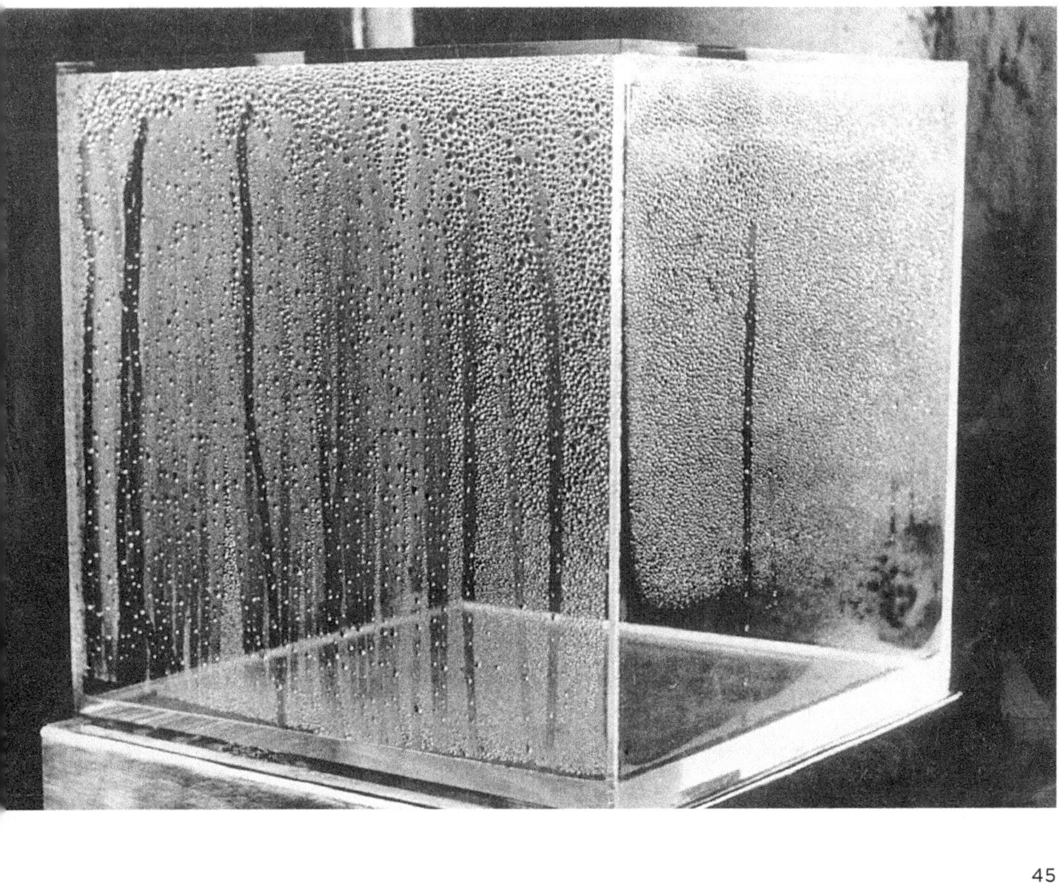

degradation), it requires the spectator to stand, watch, and wait for elementals to reveal themselves. It is through retraction, then, and not a penetrating intention that the artwork opens the viewer to the earth.

For the British artist Andy Goldsworthy, natural processes come into the viewer's trajectory precisely in their disarticulation from the formal structure that the artwork would impose on it. Much of his work sets temporal limits on the production of the art object, in this way staging the incompatibility of artistic intention with natural flows. For example, Goldsworthy will initiate an elaborate ice sculpture at the crack of dawn, thus incorporating the pressure of the sunlight that melts the form he is attempting to consolidate. Or he will attempt to build an egg formation out of rock on a beach before the tide comes in and destroys the construction. In his work *Black Stone/Rain Shadow* (2001), he filmed a two-part performance that captures the way the earth fundamentally defies thematization. He begins by describing a stone in a site near his home in Dumfriesshire, Scotland:

> This stone is one that I am drawn to, but it's one that I always feel . . . almost . . . not a fear, but a certain reluctance to work on. . . . Yesterday afternoon I spent several hours walking around all these stones that are on the other side of the river, knowing all along that *this* stone was here, and it was almost as if I was trying to avoid coming here. . . . At the end of the day, the last stone I come to see is this one, and it's there with its incredible shape and I have to do it, I have to work with it. . . . There is something which drives me to make works on occasions even though I'm telling myself in my mind, "No, don't do that."[28]

For Goldsworthy, the stone is compelling precisely because it triggers a sensation that he cannot quite put his finger on, that drives him both toward it and away from it. He expresses this experience by blacking out the stone with black moss, in this way turning the stone into an invisible presence that upsets a seamless view of the landscape (Figure 15). Though earth art is often described as "sculpting with natural materials," in fact Goldsworthy's project is often to disjoin elementals from his touch and to show how the earth resists artistic intention. It is therefore important to underscore the way the point of contact between the artist and the site becomes the focal point of the artwork and the fact that the artwork does not

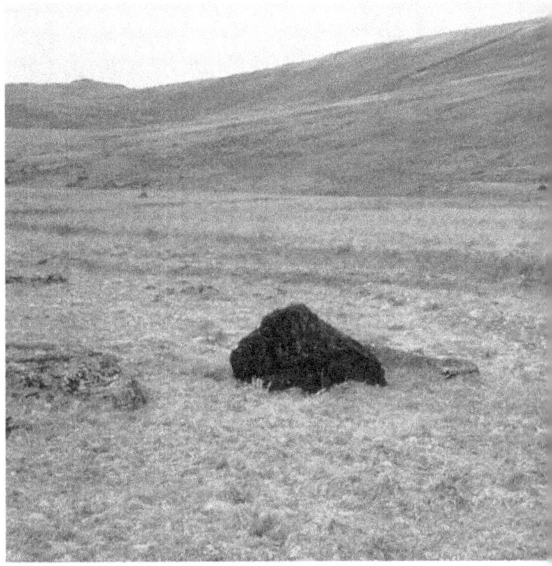

FIGURE 15. Andy Goldsworthy, *Black Stone, Dumfriesshire,* 1994–95. Unique Cibachrome print, framed, 33¾ × 32¾ × 1½ inches. Copyright Andy Goldsworthy. Courtesy of Galerie Lelong, New York.

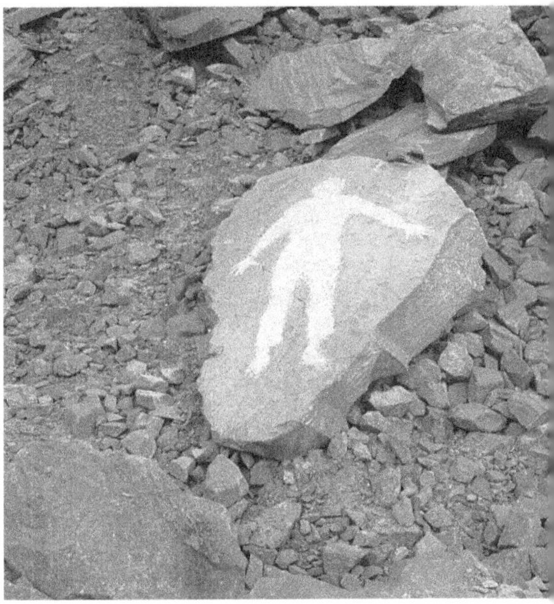

FIGURE 16. Andy Goldsworthy, "A stone / laid on previously for several hours / low rain / dried as quickly as it wetted / returned in summer / sun and showers / five shadows in three days / Getlaw Bridge, Dumfriesshire / July 1993" (detail), 1993. Two unique Cibachrome prints, framed, 48½ × 30¾ × 1¾ inches and 20½ × 16⅝ × 1½ inches. Copyright Andy Goldsworthy. Courtesy of Galerie Lelong, New York.

provide unfettered access to "nature" but rather upsets perceptual assumptions. For the second part of *Black Stone/Rain Shadow,* Goldsworthy enacts his retraction from the site, thus conveying his encounter with the earth as an enigmatic trace. On a road near the stone, he lay on the pavement during a rainfall and then, after removing himself, photographed the silhouette of his body. By blacking out the stone, the artist communicates its withdrawal from the parameters of his knowledge. With the rainfall performance, the artist answers the stone with an inverse gesture, marking the site with his shadow, an index of his presence in, but most importantly his withdrawal from, that place (Figure 16).

Though the conspicuous absence of the body is a recurrent theme in earth art, this is not to suggest that the artworks make an erroneous statement about the absolute division between the human world and the earth. Rather, they express the friction that arises as we grapple with the enigma that the earth poses for us. To even express this relation as friction says something about the importance of sensation to earth art. Retraction, then, is not to be equated simply with absence; rather, it is a device by which artists interrogate our modes of sensory contact with the earth. By staging the body's separation out from the earth's substance, and indeed by positioning the body as the emblem of that partition, artists identify a rupture between sensation and intelligibility. That is to say, instead of using sensation to confirm our perceptual expectations of, and intentions toward, the earth, artists express sensation as a deliberate act of passive receptivity. Or otherwise put, the performative act in earth art is the passive receiving of sensation across the limits of the body.

## Performance and Body Art

An attentiveness to the mode of encounter that Haacke's and Goldsworthy's works promote is also at the heart of another important branch of early earth art, namely, performance and body art. Artists such as Ana Mendieta, Dennis Oppenheim, Jan Dibbets, Richard Long, and Hamish Fulton were not simply preoccupied with exposing the fallacy of the centrality of the spectator. Instead, they were forwarding another agenda that, like earthworks, foreclosed the gallery system through the staging of transient interventions rather than monumental sculptures. Their performances were ephemeral, small-scale gestures that caused negligible disruptions to the land and usually involved some form of documentation, most often a written text, a photograph, or a film. In these performances the earth begins to register more definitively as a living, changing elemental force and less as a host for a massive art object. Earth performances and body art took their cue from the merging of the artwork and the site and developed it further in the act of inscribing the artist's bodily presence.

The art historian Nick Kaye argues that earth art performances and body art do not simply position the artist in relation to a specific place; rather, the artist's body actually becomes the site of the artwork.[29] Thus, in the performance the artist's body becomes, by Dennis Oppenheim's description, the "material . . . the sole vehicle of the art, the distributor, initiator and receiver simultaneously."[30] More than

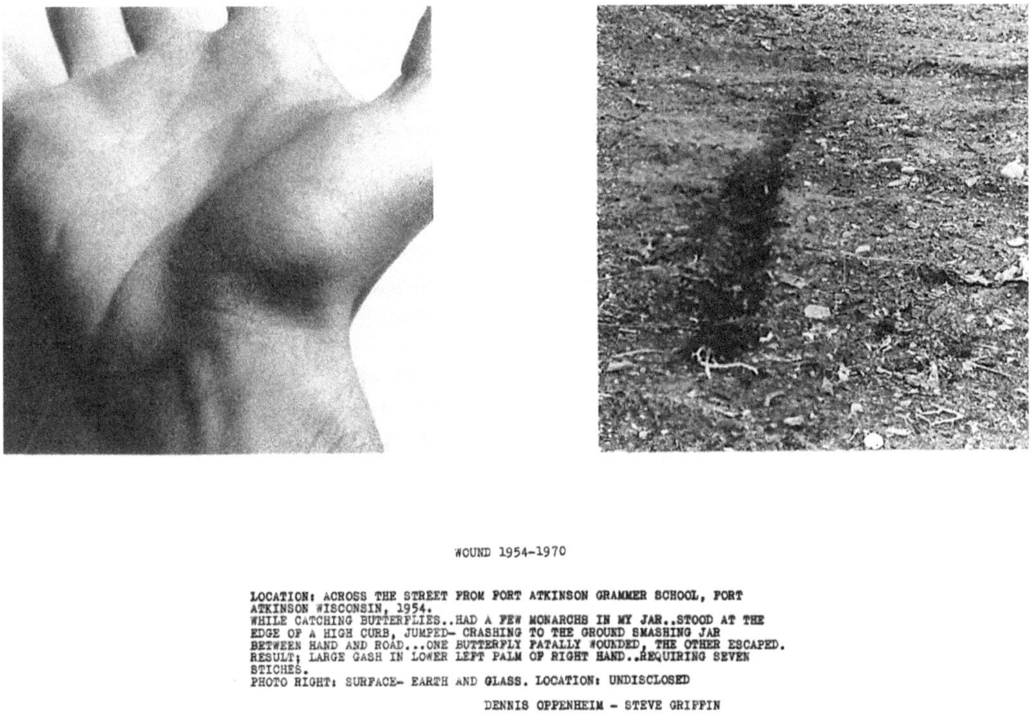


FIGURE 17. Dennis Oppenheim, *Wound,* 1954–70. Photodocumentation, 45 × 60 inches. Courtesy of the artist.

simply replacing the art object, however, the use of the body as an artistic medium cultivated a heightened physical engagement with the earth. In his *Wound* series, for example, Oppenheim correlates the surface of his body to the earth's surface by cutting or otherwise marking his skin and then photographing both his wounded body and an area of altered land. In one performance of the series, Oppenheim smashed a jar between his hand and the road, leaving a large gash that required seven stitches (Figure 17). He then mounted a photograph of his scarred hand next to an image of land with a line of overturned soil. In this visual parallel, the scar and the marked land each record the transaction between body and earth.

More than simply making this visual analogy between skin and land, however, Oppenheim's performances in the 1970s signal a particularly new receptivity to elementals. In his performance *Reading Position for Second Degree Burn* (Figure 18), for example, Oppenheim lay in the sand with an open book spread on his chest. Over a five-hour period, the artist sunburned his skin, leaving a white square where the book had covered him. He explains his early body performances, such as this one, as a reversal of energy expenditure. That is to say, rather than forming material in the manner of a sculptor or painter, the artist presented his body as the recipient of natural energies. "I allowed myself to be painted, my skin became pigment.... Not only would my skin tones change, but its change registered on a sensory level as well—I could feel the act of becoming red.... It's like plugging into the solar system, communicating with an element."[31] Interestingly, Oppenheim describes the sensorial experience when the body is touched by light. In this way, not only does the artist change the conception of the artwork, from an active process of drawing out form from matter to a passive process of being formed (or transformed), but he also links this to an opening of sense that occurs where contact between the body and elementals is made. Furthermore, in *Reading Position,* the artist inserts his body at the juncture between elementals—the point at which sunlight meets the earth. Here, the body is located at the horizon where elementals become sensible while nevertheless remaining concealed from visibility or tangibility as such. The earth is not structured into an object or landmark, and the sunlight is not reflected or otherwise directed; rather, the body is reformed by its specific positioning between earth and sky, revealing the specificity of each. In its resolute closedness, the earth both supports the body and leaves it utterly exposed to the sky and sunlight, which envelop and burn the body in their unrestricted expansiveness.

Earth art performances since the late seventies are derived from early experiments such as Oppenheim's in the sense that they are concerned with the artist's physical intervention. However, other artists came to alter the interaction between the earth and the body by focusing more on the body's impact on the earth's surface. Often, artists conspicuously rendered themselves physically absent by making an indexical mark on the land. As in Oppenheim's *Wound* series, the act of marking generates an artwork that is constituted by the contact between the body and the earth. Furthermore, as artists such as Ana Mendieta demonstrate, as natural activ-

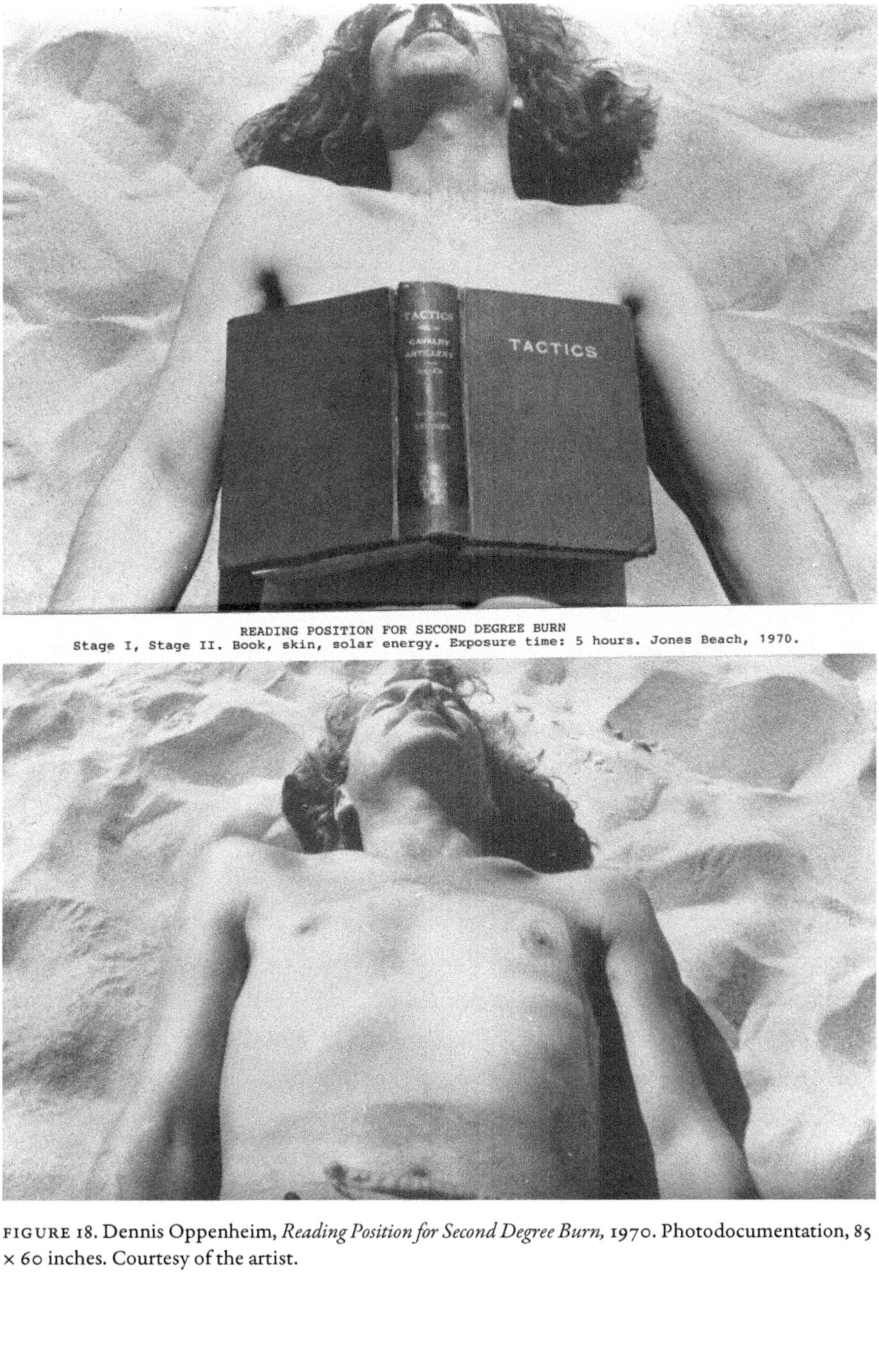


FIGURE 18. Dennis Oppenheim, *Reading Position for Second Degree Burn,* 1970. Photodocumentation, 85 × 60 inches. Courtesy of the artist.

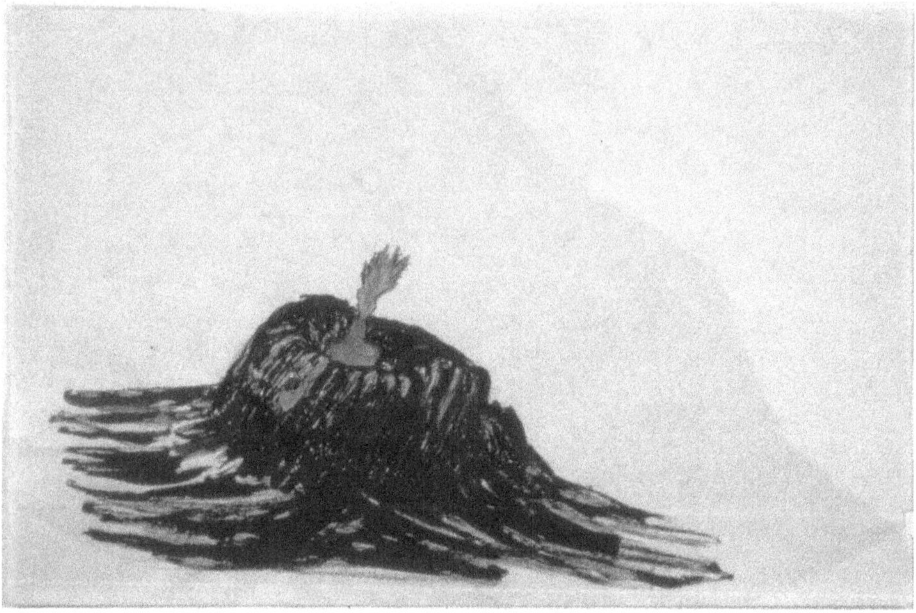

FIGURE 19. Ana Mendieta, *Untitled,* circa 1980–84. Oil and marker on paper. Copyright The Estate of Ana Mendieta Collection. Courtesy of Galerie Lelong, New York.

ity interacts with that mark, the performance subverts the very notion of materiality as a fixed condition.

In Mendieta's "earth-body sculptures" of the late seventies and early eighties, for example, the artwork enacts a fluctuating relation between the body and the earth. Her *Silueta Series* (which I discuss in detail in chapter 4) could be seen as the inverse trajectory of Oppenheim's *Reading Position for Second Degree Burn,* in that rather than marking the body, Mendieta imprinted her bodily form on the land and then photographed the transformation of the land as the *silueta* melted, burned, filled with water, or blew away (Figures 40–43). That is to say, the earth is the recipient of the performative action, and the imprint is an ephemeral mark of that contact. More than drawing an analogy between the body and the land, Mendieta's *Silueta Series* stimulates an appearance of elementals, opening a threshold for the earth to become visible and sensible in its excess of perception.

We could read Mendieta's volcano studies as figures of the threshold to the un-

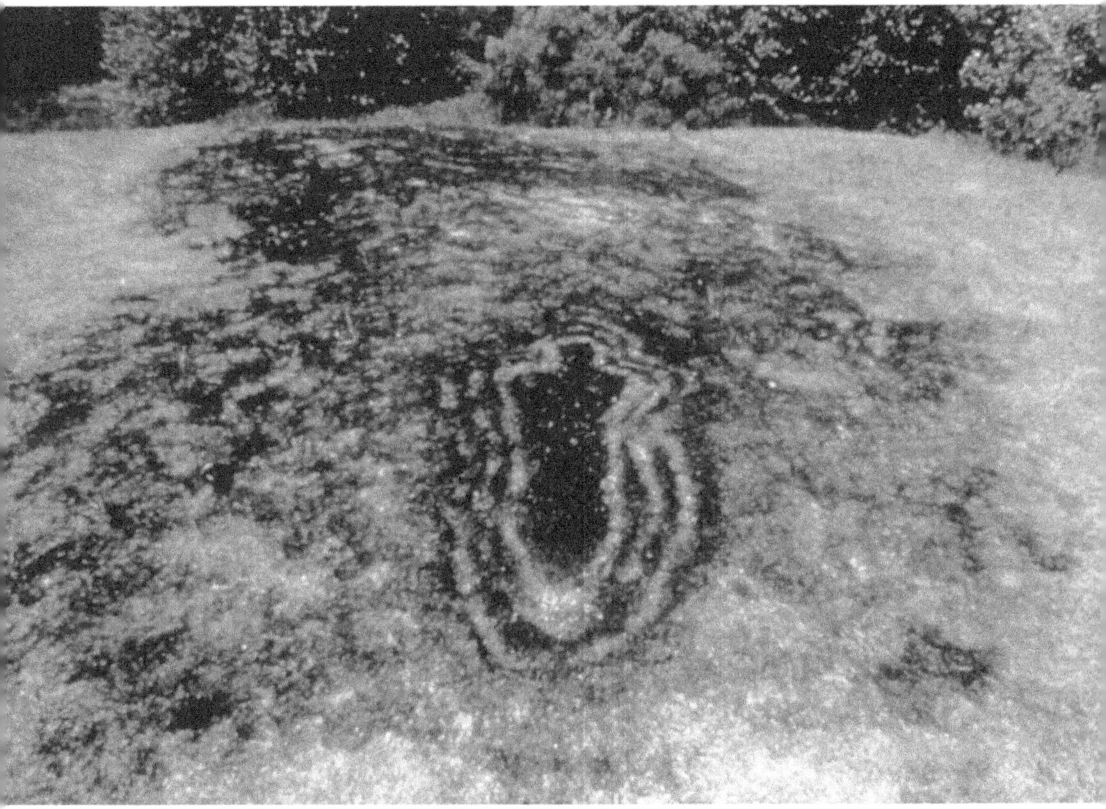

FIGURE 20. Ana Mendieta, *Untitled (Silueta Series, Iowa)*, 1977. Copyright The Estate of Ana Mendieta Collection. Courtesy of Galerie Lelong, New York.

derlying fluid that courses beneath the earth's withdrawn exterior (Figure 19). In her sketches, lava, fire, and smoke burst through concentrated masses of land, breaking apart the earth's semblance of solidity. The earth's resistance appears as both a dispersal of its materiality and the foreclosure of tangibility. Rock gives way under the pressure of elementals whose dynamic qualities—of burning heat, spreading liquidity, dissipating smoke—prevent perceptual definition, though they nevertheless evoke a wealth of sensation. Sensation of the earth, then, appears at this threshold; it is both raised and deferred at the point where the opaque surface opens up to an uncontainable spectacle of vital substance.

Mendieta revisits the volcano figure in a *silueta* made of gunpowder in 1977 (Figure 20). Laying successive lines of gunpowder around one original silhouette, she enacts an outburst of natural force that originates from the outline of the body and then expands past the repeated outlines. The fire stems from and appears on the division between the body and the earth. As the fire diffused, it left the index of the body as well as the visible traces of the overrun of sensation beyond its perceptual field. Mendieta locates the sensorial dimension of the performance at the body's limits, demonstrating the overflow of elemental force. In this way the imprinting of the body, a distinct act of withdrawal, enables an excess of sensation. The *siluetas* do not simply reveal the earth's "otherness," then; rather, they are preoccupied with the limits of perception and the mobilization of the body *as* that limit.

Mendieta's performances have sometimes been misunderstood as essentialist gestures that reproduce the patriarchal association of women with nature and by extension with reproduction. However, it is now generally accepted that the figure of the *silueta* problematizes the coherence of the female body as "natural." In her book *Body Art: Performing the Subject,* Amelia Jones suggests that the interplay between the body and its absence expresses the coding of the female body as loss within patriarchal artistic practice.[32] Where in the masculinist paradigm of modernism, the art object is coded as solid, universal, permanent, and closed, the artist's body and actions are coded as fluid, particular, interactive, and transient. Jones's reading of performance art as an alternative and feminized history of art opens the possibility of analyzing bodily actions as ways of problematizing biological determinism through intersubjective engagement.

In her analysis of Mendieta's work, however, Jones does not question the essentializing function of the earth. Indeed, she emphasizes that the artist viewed the earth as a maternal body. She argues that the performance ultimately overrides the association between the earth and maternity, emphasizing that the performance enlists an intersubjective engagement between the absent artist and the viewer. I would argue further, however, that Mendieta refutes biological essentialism by showing how the unstable signification of the body is achieved precisely because of the instability of the elementals, which wash over, grow through, or otherwise disrupt the *silueta.* The chiasmic tie, which, Jones argues, decenters the "Cartesian subject of modernism" in performance art, does not only exist between the artist and the spectator. In Mendieta's case, it is forged between the artist's body and the earth.

Jones's stance on the potential of body art to trouble the self-containment of the art object is in part inspired by her reading of Merleau-Ponty's *The Visible and the Invisible.* In this unfinished manuscript, Merleau-Ponty counters definitions of the body as an object pure and simple with his model of the chiasm. He maintains that the body is both object to others and a lived reality for the subject, which is defined by its relations with other beings and with the world itself. Subjectivity is organized through the perception gleaned by the body's active and expressive movement in the spatial world of objects, others, and elementals. What we know of ourselves and others is thus created by a sense of the body's flesh as intertwined with the "flesh of the world": "The presence of the world is precisely the presence of its flesh to my flesh, that I am of the world and that I am not it."[33] Merleau-Ponty's chiasm is an intercorporeal sense of being, where the contact of flesh folded back upon itself characterizes the interaction between the seer and the visible, between the subject and the object, between oneself and the other.

Art historians such as Jones see the potential of Merleau-Ponty's phenomenology to challenge essentialist categorizations by theorizing that the body is constituted in intersubjective exchanges. Though Merleau-Ponty's work has been raised in feminist art history as a means to dismantle logocentrism and phallocentrism, the possibility of an eco-phenomenology that would take up the relationship between the body and the earth in art has not yet entered the purview of the discipline. Earth art is open to just this kind of analysis. However, phenomenology itself is not without a troubled ethical ground. Luce Irigaray criticizes the dormant feminization of the earth and the body in Merleau-Ponty's metaphorics of the world as landscape of the maternal body. In her rewriting of Merleau-Ponty's essay "The Chiasm—the Intertwining," Irigaray harnesses the potential of the model of the chiasm to forward an ethics of sexual difference. Irigaray argues that perceiving the other's essential alterity is a fundamental aspect of ethical encounter. In her view, we are always already constituted in relation to the other, but by the same token, it is our fundamental difference from that other that evokes the primary passion of wonder. Wonder at this difference prevents us from the solipsistic tendency to assimilate the other into ourselves and into the "sameness" of our own perspective.

The sensation of the other's excess, thus, is the primary condition for an ethical attitude.

Irigaray's countermodel of an ethics of sexual difference is equally pertinent to cultivating an ethical relationship to the earth that both recognizes the historic duality between humans and nature and takes seriously the responsibility to remedy that situation. As the philosopher Mick Smith elaborates in his book *An Ethics of Place: Radical Ecology, Postmodernity, and Social Theory,* an ethical feeling for the earth counters the instrumental view of the world as a fixed and inert storehouse of materials awaiting manipulation. Global modernity abstracts the particularities and vitality of our geophysical environment, degrading the history of local relationships to the earth by replacing them with an economy of sameness—a universal space devoid of the earth's irregular intrusions.[34] An ethics of place is an explicit disruption of the homogenizing force of modernity that would mechanize all natural energies for human purposes, because the power of ethical feeling lies in the excess that transcends self-interest and refuses to force nature to fit into the categories of one's own symbolic order.[35]

Smith's radical ecology differs from other ecological theories—social or deep ecology, for example—in that it posits a constitutive relation to the earth. Smith takes the view that our ethical tie to the earth precedes the ontology of the modern subject. His position stems from the work of theorists such as Irigaray, Emmanuel Levinas, and Judith Butler, who argue that the subject is constituted in and through its relation to the other, and we might extend, to the earth as well. For Levinas, the other makes a demand on the subject—a call that stems from basic need—that inaugurates the subject's differentiation and self-recognition. Self-awareness is actually precipitated by the other's call to responsibility. Subjectivity is a response to the other's command, so that subject formation functions as an offering to the other of a recognition of differentiation that occurs in order to support that other. Whereas Merleau-Ponty positions the subject and the other in a precognitive and reciprocal chiasmic tie, Levinas founds the emergence of the subject on ethical responsibility to the other. Because the ethical feeling precedes the ontology of the subject, ethics exceeds the discursive world into which the subject is subsequently initiated. As Smith explains, the ethical is not an alien infringement on the autonomy of a separable and pregiven self, but rather a constituent and primary passion at the heart of a relational self.[36]

Levinas's paradigm of the "face-to-face" encounter with the other inflects many aspects of Irigaray's ethics of sexual difference, though, as Tina Chanter argues, she criticizes Levinas for abstracting sexual difference into nonexistence. Nevertheless, Irigaray draws from Levinas's work in her insistence on the irreducibility of the other, and especially in her consideration of how to relate to otherness without submitting it to the demands of logic.[37] For Irigaray, the ethical relation is negotiated through a mode of corporeal interaction. This relation caresses and embraces, but never grasps or envelops, the other. It is also important not to overlook the fact that in Irigaray's work ethics is coded as fluid and elemental. As Smith argues, the ethical appears as a surprising flow of emotion in contrast to the solidity of reason's instrumental principles. Because the ethical is a "'never-surfeited sea' that tends toward *infinity* rather than *totality*, it cannot be fixed, frozen or fully accounted for."[38]

This elaboration of ethics as an excessive sensation links it to body art and performance insofar as these practices are founded on spatial, temporal, and intersubjective conditions that are not reproducible and cannot be encompassed by the documents that record them. That is to say, like performance, the ethical cannot be sufficiently pictured or thematized; it can only be felt. Yet it is precisely because performances are lost in time that they are supplemented by text and enter into discursive modes of circulation and interpretation. In performing the body's interrelationship with the earth in encounters that are inherently transient, practices such as those by Oppenheim and Mendieta are only available through a host of textual paraphernalia. The priority of earth art is thus to demonstrate the dilemma between the loss of the intertwining of the artist and the earth, and a failed recovery through texts that betray the expenditure and loss of the elemental forces they attempt to represent. A crucial aspect of the textual artwork is therefore to reveal the impossibility of subsuming the earth into representational form. Like the body in performance art, the visual text in earth art stands as a threshold to the excess of the earth.

## The Text as Limit: Expressing the Earth

Rosalind Krauss's essay "Sculpture in the Expanded Field" was one the most influential treatments of late-sixties earth art.[39] Krauss outlined the rise of hybrid forms of artistic practice, which she called "the expanded field of sculpture," according to a semiotic diagram called a Klein group. Her essay maps out the oppositions and mutual implications of landscape, architecture, and sculpture to explain the production of artworks that escape categorization according to a single medium. Krauss proposes three new terms to advance the classification of site-specific works that appear at the periphery of the categories of landscape, architecture, or sculpture, namely, "site constructions," "marked sites," and "axiomatic structures." Understood semiotically, the conditions for a redefinition of artistic practice in the postmodern era are set by the way an artwork exceeds, combines, and redifferentiates the parameters of media in the same way that, in language, meaning exceeds the terms that hold it together and is actually expressed through the relationship among words.

Krauss's work propagated considerable discussion on the semiotics of earth art, most notably, Craig Owens's theory about the increased textualization of art. In his 1979 essay "Earthwords," Owens argues that Robert Smithson's works are symptomatic of an eruption of language into the visual arts that has made language a material entity and art interchangeable with writing.[40] Much of Owens's theorization can be attributed to the increased use of documentary or textual media in contemporary art. For example, in Smithson's site/nonsite works of 1968, the artist exhibited photographs, aerial photographs, and maps of an area, usually a remote one, alongside piles of rock and sediment taken from the site (see Figure 24, in chapter 2). The artist deemed these traces of the site as "nonsites," highlighting the absence of the place from which the material and images were extracted. The exhibition of nonsites drew attention to the site as a distinct place, and equally, the nonsite could not exist without being defined in virtue of the absent site. Smithson's site/nonsite dialectic enacts a congruence between language and visual art; like a word that substitutes for the object it signifies and consequently decenters that object,

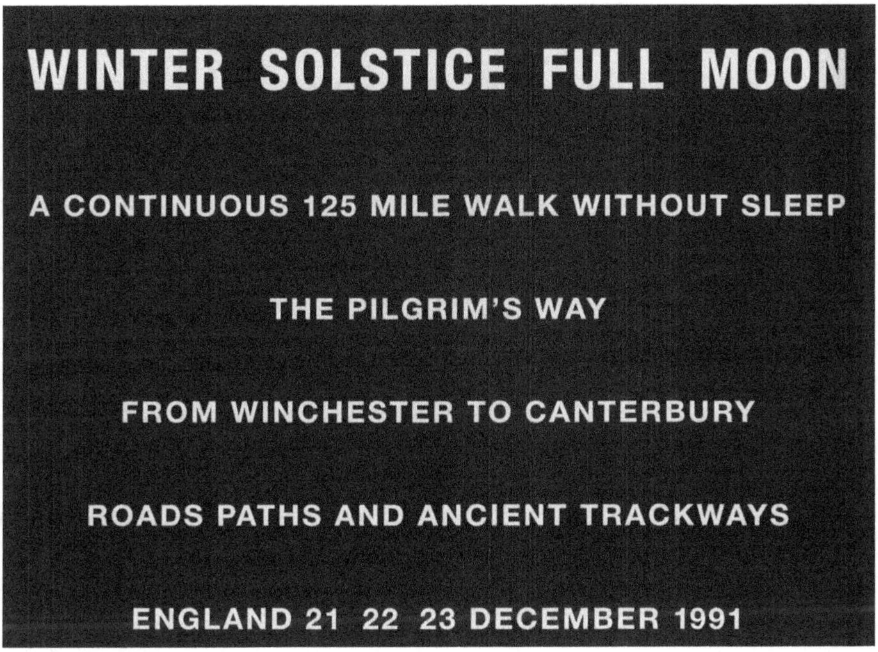


FIGURE 21. Hamish Fulton, *Winter Solstice Full Moon . . .*, 1991.

Smithson's art object is displaced from the gallery by being presented as text, a signifier of an elsewhere.

The convergence of text-based practices and earth art, not only in Robert Smithson's artworks but in later generations of earth art as well, initiates a recurrent theme, specifically, the tension between the pursuit of physical sensations of the earth and a loss of its coherence as it enters into signification as a textual artwork. Contemporary earth art thus revolves around the dilemma between the phenomenological engagement with elementals and the representation of that interaction. For Owens, earth art is always in some sense textual: the artwork either emblematizes the earth allegorically—that is, the artwork overwrites the earth with meaning—or it represents the earth with a supplementary document, an empty signifier that stands in for the "real" art object and betrays its own loss of inherent meaning. However, it is the emptiness of the textual signifier that earth art challenges.

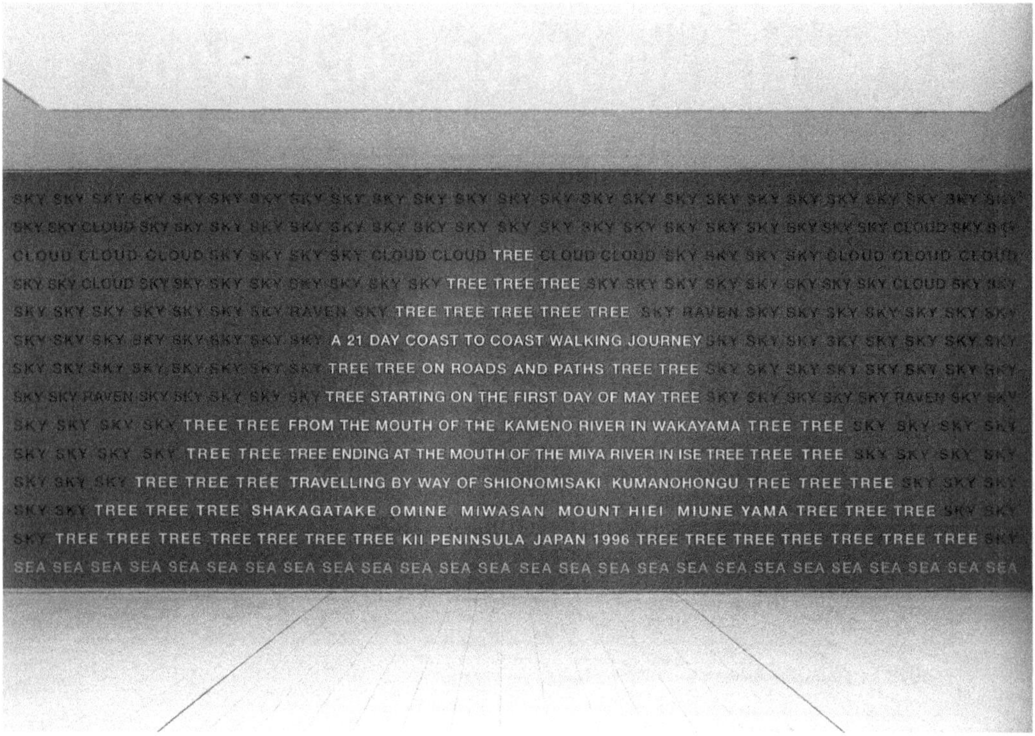


FIGURE 22. Hamish Fulton, *A 21 Day Coast to Coast Walking Journey on Roads and Paths . . .*, 1998. Installation view at the Kunsthalle in Kiel, Germany.

The textual mode is particularly noticeable in Hamish Fulton's oeuvre. Since the seventies, Fulton has presented walks in largely uninhabited landscapes as a kind of performance art. Much like Richard Long, Fulton documents these often extensive and laborious ventures, exhibiting the performance in the form of photographs and textual descriptions. Unlike Long, Fulton does not necessarily mark the land as part of the performance. Often, the artwork is defined simply as the experience of the walk itself. Fulton conveys this, however, through visual and written accounts of the journey. For example, *Winter Solstice Full Moon* (Figure 21) is composed simply of a textual record of the walk in white lettering on a black background. The text simply states the performance—a 125-mile walk without sleep—

and the location and date. The bodily experience of this exercise in endurance is presented as a straightforward list of facts. Occasionally, Fulton superimposes text on a photographic image taken on one of his walks. Yet the recourse to text signals the impossibility of capturing the performance, in terms of both its duration and the full extent of its sensorial dimensions.

Curiously, in Fulton's work, text itself takes a visual form, so that the act of supplementing the earth with words becomes explicit. At an exhibition at the Kunsthalle in Kiel, Germany, in 1998, Fulton constructed a massive tableau, in which words were the visual components of a landscape scene (Figure 22). The background was covered in dark grey text reading "SKY" over and over again and occasionally reading "RAVEN" or "CLOUD." The center area, whose edges delineated the outline of a tree, was composed of white lettering repeating the word "TREE." Embedded in the middle of the tree was a description of the walk: "A 21 DAY COAST TO COAST WALKING JOURNEY ON ROADS AND PATHS . . ." The bottom line consisted of the repeated word "SEA" in light blue lettering.

Through the textualization of the visual image of the landscape, Fulton exacerbates the impossibility of representing the fullness of sensation of the performance he describes. He nevertheless suggests that the performance made a residual imprint, for the text does not only outline the contours of the landscape; it infers the temporal dimension of the walk. The viewer must discern words that describe the walk from the visual text that pictures it. As the eye travels from left to right, and as the words "TREE TREE" give way to "ON ROADS AND PATH," the landscape image transitions into a narration. Interestingly, the repetition of the pictorial words produces a sense of duration as though to mimic each step of the long walk. To this end, both modes of text function together to reproduce the visual and temporal experience of the performance.

Text-based artworks such as Fulton's disclose the loss of immediate contact with the earth; however, they also implicitly raise the question of what has been lost. Earth art must not be understood only in relation to its "discursive trajectory"—the fact that it is generally experienced in sets of textual representations; rather, it must be understood to be posing the question of what escapes when the artist touches, pictures, and writes about the earth. The textual work is constituted not by meaning inhering in a formed art object but by the expression—quite literally, the expulsion, evacuation, propulsion, and radiation—of elementals. It is precisely because textual representation is underpinned by the "expression," the simultaneous projection and loss, of natural force that the work coincides with the artist's ethical goal of evidencing the earth as irreducible to form. Thus, the phenomenological scenario that the artist frames in terms of the earth's excess registers in the textual document as an obstacle to meaning, an obstruction of visual coherence, and ultimately a question of the earth's otherness that has escaped signification. The sensation of elementals and perceptual intelligibility are thereby severed and reconstituted in the textualized artwork as this very enigma of the earth's alterity.

Insofar as the texts in earth art present natural phenomena as raw expression and refuse to represent that expression as a theme, they withhold themselves from their signifying function. This holding back is what I am relating to the project of recessive ethics—the very same move that Levinas describes as the differentiation *from* the other in response to that other's need, and that for Irigaray is a retraction from the mistaken presumption that one knows the other, in order to let the other present itself on its own terms. In other words, within the intimacy of the ethical relation, an inward recession appears as an outward differentiation. Irigaray explains, "Porosity, and its fullest responsiveness, can occur only within difference. A porosity that moves from the inside to the outside of the body. The most profound intimacy becomes a protective veil. Turns itself into an aura that preserves the nocturnal quality of the encounter, without masks."[41]

It is significant that Irigaray describes the ethical relation as simultaneously an intimate porosity and a move from the inside to the outside of the body. This exteriorization allows the formulation of a protective veil or aura that preserves the intimacy of contact and the wonder of difference. The spectral forms of the "aura" or the "protective veil" are distinct from "the mask," or plastic representations that distort the other into a comprehensive totality. I am suggesting that the textual artwork is the locus of discursive limits—the mask that cloaks the earth—but that it is also a reconfiguration of the medium of representation into a surface on which the earth can be inferred. The trajectory of earth art can be seen in this slightly altered approach to textualization, for as works such as Fulton's show, text does not function merely to communicate but instead becomes a surface that suggests an underlying visual sense, while nevertheless foregoing a penetrating view of the earth as strictly an idealized landscape. It is important to note that sense, for Irigaray, is not just associated with touch; it is also conferred through light: "Light is the chance for emergence out of chaos and formlessness . . . the light that shines through discourse, that filters through words, that bestows a sense of the cosmos."[42] Light is that liminal zone that touches and breaches one's ordered framework. As we shall see, in the multimedia practices of earth art, light, color, atmosphere, and other elemental events appear in contradistinction with words, objects, and architectonic shapings.

While it would seem that in the context of ecological crisis, we need to "get back to nature," the paradigm of recessive ethics suggests the opposite—that we should withdraw from it. This is not to say that we should no longer see ourselves as embedded in the ecosystems we inhabit (to the contrary), but rather to say that we should step out of our characterizations of nature, our idyllic images, and our desires for homeostasis and open a space for that which exists beyond our self-enclosed and self-serving worlds. What is required, as far as earth art is concerned, is an acknowledgment of our limits and an offering of that limit to what lies beyond, namely, the irreducible earth. In this way the limit of representation is the locus of contact with the earth—where it touches us as it exceeds that limit. As early as the sixties, the earthworks movement reformulated text into a surface that would be receptive to elemental manifestations. I now turn to Robert Smithson's *Spiral Jetty,* a work that was keenly preoccupied with the potential of material texts to withdraw from representation and, consequently, to intertwine with the elemental activity at the site in which the sculpture is located, the Great Salt Lake in Utah.

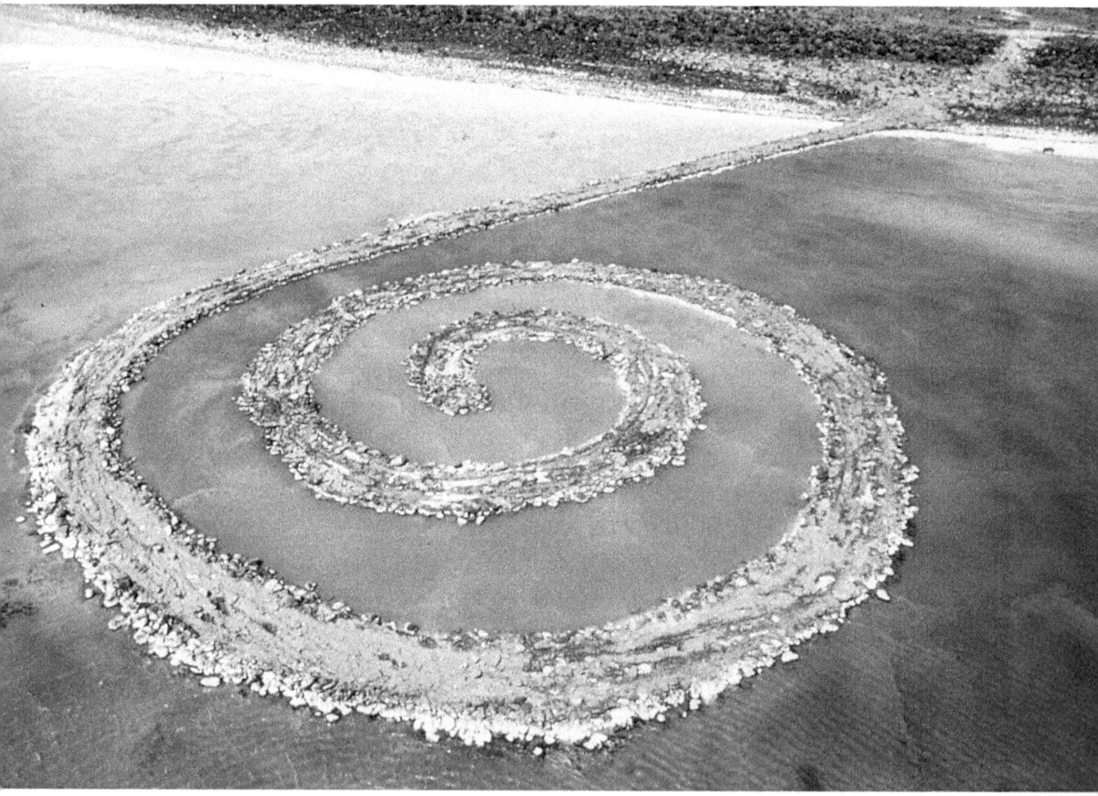

FIGURE 23. Robert Smithson, *Spiral Jetty,* 1970. Great Salt Lake, Utah. Black rock, salt crystals, earth, red water (algae), 3 × 15 × 1,500 feet. Copyright Estate of Robert Smithson. Licensed by VAGA, New York. Courtesy of James Cohan Gallery, New York. Collection of DIA Center for the Arts, New York. Photograph by Gianfranco Gorgoni.

TWO

# *Spiral Jetty:* Allegory and the Recovery of the Elemental

In two essays published in *October* in 1979 and 1980, the art historian Craig Owens developed a theory of the merging of language and visual art read through the concept of allegory.[1] An allegorical impulse, in Owens's view, explained the decentering characteristics of early earthworks and site-specific projects, namely, the fragmentation of the artwork into multiple texts and, correspondingly, its aesthetic of ruination. Furthermore, he understood the textualization of the artwork, and correspondingly the materialization of text as an object, as the primary indicators of a shift from a modern to a postmodern paradigm. By reconsidering these essays in relation to Robert Smithson's *Spiral Jetty,* I am returning to a pivotal moment in the history of art when the possibility of a complex synthesis of art and earth was established. I am suggesting that more than simply forging a dialectical tie between a specific site and its representation (a process that involves the petrification and fragmentation of the unified art object into multiple texts), early earth art such as Smithson's showed how textual forms could be affected by and were ultimately receptive to elementals. In this way, he brought the earth to bear on the discursive malleability of the artwork.

*Spiral Jetty,* begun in 1970 and located in Utah's Great Salt Lake, stands out as one of the earliest examples of an earthwork that is not defined solely by its oppositional stance toward the museum or the gallery (that is, in terms of its inaccessibility to spectators and its unavailability to the art market) but rather pointedly elaborates the theme of dislocation through the historic and geological particularities of the site (Figure 23). With a team of construction workers, Smithson manufactured *Spiral Jetty* out of black basalt rock and soil. The sculpture, which is still intact, is a 1,500-foot-long and 15-foot-wide coil that extends from the shoreline at Rozel Point into the lake.

The spiral shape alludes to the site in two ways. First, it references the local folklore that there was a treacherous whirlpool in the Great Salt Lake. Smithson was piqued by this myth since the whirlpool, because it has no unifying center and instead spins around a hollow core with no beginning or end, connotes a disruption in the continuity of time and space. Second, and perhaps most important for Smithson, *Spiral Jetty* is a macrocosm of the molecular structure of a salt crystal. Because the lake is a body of saline water, its shore is encrusted with salt crystal deposits. This detail of the site triggered the artist's knowledge of crystallography. Smithson noted a parallel between the irregular structure of a salt molecule, which grows in the shape of a screw around a fissure on a surface, and the structure of a whirlpool, which orbits around an empty center. The spiral was an ideal form to advance Smithson's project of creating an artwork that would respond to the conditions of the site and also disrupt the central orientation associated with the modernist paradigm of spectatorship. Not only was the art object in a decidedly remote location, but because it was a decentered sculpture, Smithson's jetty also epitomized a dislocated spectatorial experience. Weaving together its allusions to local mythology and to the salt crystals that accumulated on it, the work internalized the historic and geological resonances of the site into its aesthetic critique of modernism.

It is important to note that Smithson did not build *Spiral Jetty* as a discrete object but rather executed it in at least three mediums—as a sculpture, an essay, and a film.[2] The work is thus dispersed and located in the interaction between the site and the textual media that represent it. I would suggest, however, that the texts do not substitute for the site as empty signifiers; rather, their materiality indexes their connection to the site. Thus, where Owens argues that *Spiral Jetty* thematizes the gaps in signification that occur between the texts, I am arguing further that the artwork deploys these gaps as a means to disclose a residual elemental tissue that binds them to the Great Salt Lake.

Though Owens's analysis of *Spiral Jetty* is important to my discussion of more recent earth art that is both born of the temporal fluxes of natural phenomena and, equally, relies on various forms of textual documentation, I bring up his essays to highlight certain ambiguities about *Spiral Jetty*'s relationship to its site and to suggest an alternative interpretation of the sense of loss that it enacts. I propose that Smithson did not intend for the art object to be absorbed by the site, but that he instead designed the sculpture to behave as sediment that would reference its own emergence, and extrication, from the site's temporal volatility. The sense of loss that Owens attributes to the semiotic distance between the text and the site is not just a device to dislocate the spectator from the site of the artwork, then, but the means by which the site's unrepresentability becomes the subject of the artwork itself. The many empty centers—or "dislocation points" as Smithson calls them—that repeatedly arise in the essay and the film do not reveal an abstract space between site and text. Rather, these voids glean a visceral quality, as though the absent site remained as a dormant fluid underlying the text. The recurrent theme of the empty center in the artwork can therefore be understood as an important commentary about the way in which the discursive trajectory of an artwork is generated by and through elementals. Indeed, Smithson repeatedly describes the work's empty centers as thresholds to amorphous substance, or as palpable holes that are replete with fluid. Each textual medium of the work is thus shaped, textured, and visually inflected by these points at which the site is lost and subsequently recovered as dynamic fluid. The texts do not "represent" the site in motion; they are receptive to, and imprinted by, its volatile materiality. Through the emblem of the whirlpool, Smithson reveals the site as a simultaneous absence and presence—as a current that has been evacuated from the text but that periodically surges back into it. The artwork is thereby tethered to the site by its lapses in representation.

## Beyond Textual Matter(s)

Art historians who, in the seventies and eighties, analyzed the emergence of postmodern art in relation to semiotics were considerably influenced by Roland Barthes's essay "The Death of the Author," in which he considers the way the meaning of a text is produced not by the author but by the reader. "Writing," Barthes says, "is the destruction of every voice, of every point of origin. Writing is that neutral, composite, oblique space where all identity is lost, starting with the very identity of the body of writing."[3] While a text for Barthes does not originate in its writer, its unity lies in its destination—the reader: "The reader . . . is simply that *someone* who holds together in a single field all the traces by which the written text is constituted."[4] The idea of a "death of the author" in visual art underpins much of the theorization of postmodernism as a rejection of the modernist valorization of the heroic male artist, its association of the artwork's meaning with the artist's psychological interior, and its idealization of the unification of meaning and matter in the art object. The spectator of postmodern art, like the reader, "is the space on which all the quotations that make up a writing are inscribed."[5] Like their espousal of phenomenology in the 1960s, artists' explicit use of text inspired a shift in emphasis from the inherent meaning of an artwork to the way meaning is produced by the spectator in the space of experience or exhibition. Accordingly, the move to site-specificity was an acknowledgment of the artwork's contingency on varying spatial and social contexts, whereby the artwork is defined by, and made meaningful through, the spectator and the location of experience.

This contingency, however, also raises the possibility that a site-specific work might possess conflicting or opposite meanings. That is, if one views a site as emerging through its articulation in an artwork, one must concede that in its reliance on a context of performed practices, the artwork, like language, is left open to ambiguous interpretations and possibly even to a complete degeneration of meaning as such. It is precisely the coexistence of two mutually exclusive concepts within the same artistic practice that concerned Robert Smithson's site/nonsite works of the late sixties. The site/nonsite dialectic demonstrates that not only are sites defined through artistic practice, but the site and the artwork also define one another through mutual exclusion.

Smithson identified a fissure between a site that he would visit—usually an abandoned area on the periphery of an urban center or an otherwise deserted landscape—and a nonsite, the maps, aerials, photographs, piles of rock extracted from the site, and other textual documents that represented it in the gallery. *A Nonsite, Franklin, New Jersey* from 1968 (Figure 24), for example, presents the spectator with a series of trapezoidal wooden bins filled with ore from the site, each of which corresponds to sections of an aerial photo-map of the area that are likewise cut into trapezoids. By matching the trapezoidal objects with the aerial photos of the same shape, Smithson makes an analogy between his delimitation of the area of the site, which he depicts on the map, and the ore containers in the gallery. It is precisely the artist's intervention of extracting the nonsites that defines the site as such. The photomaps carve out the limits of the site, and the ore corroborates its materiality. Yet the nonsites deny the site to the spectator as a coherent presence. Despite the ore containers' imposing density, Smithson empties them of any implicit significance by declaring them nonsites, recognizing that to bring the site to the spectator in the gallery is to split it apart as a totality. Thus, the objects in the gallery do not encompass the site; they are only the sum of its parts—a pile of debris. The site is pictured and is physically tangible through the nonsites, yet it exists to the spectator only as disjointed fragments. The wholeness of the site is foreclosed from the gallery by the very objects that constitute it.

Though the nonsites represent the site to the spectator, the artist strips them of inherent meaning and instead uses them to orient the spectator elsewhere, away from the objects and from the gallery. The nonsites point to, but are polarized from, the site. Smithson thus decenters the artwork, locating it on a dialectical fracture rather than embodying the site as a unified object. Moreover, insofar as the nonsite represents the site as an absence—it encompasses that which the site is not—it functions as a signifier, replacing the object that it signifies. As the critic Lawrence Alloway argues, the relation of the nonsite to the site is "like that of

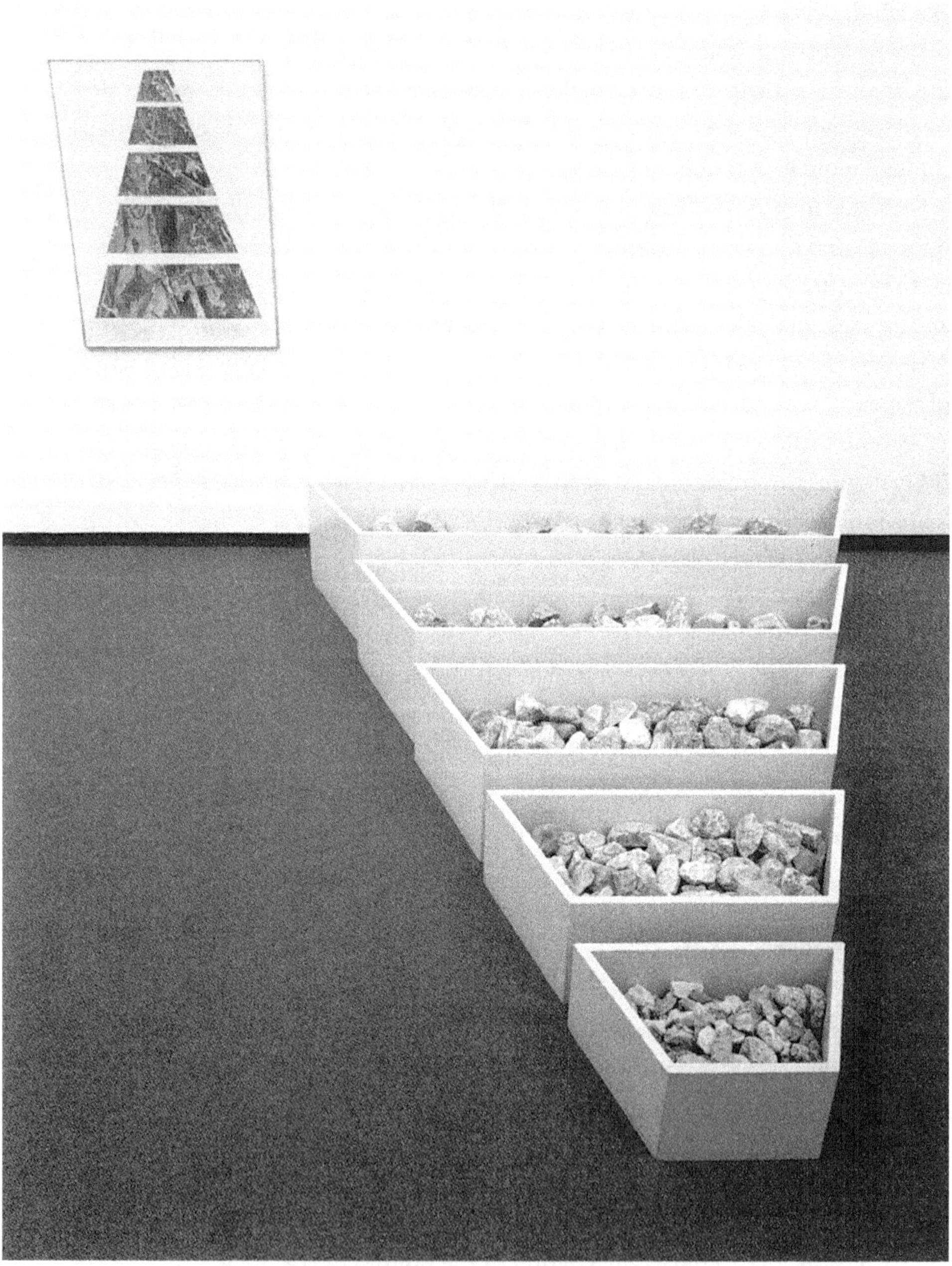

FIGURE 24. Robert Smithson, *A Nonsite, Franklin, New Jersey*, 1968. Wood, limestone, aerial photographs, 16½ × 82 × 110 inches. Copyright Estate of Robert Smithson. Licensed by VAGA, New York. Courtesy of James Cohan Gallery, New York. Collection of Museum of Contemporary Art, Chicago.

language to the world: it is a signifier and the Site is that which is signified. It is not the referent but the language system which is in the foreground."[6] The presence of the nonsite thus propels the site to the periphery. Only a supplementary text is in the foreground of the gallery and at the center of the spectator's focus. Craig Owens further explains that whenever Smithson invokes the notion of the center, it is to describe its loss. Similarly, language, "which proposes the potentially infinite substitution of elements *at the centre,* destroys all possibility of securely locating any centre whatsoever."[7]

Through the site/nonsite dialectic, Smithson exemplifies the upsurge of language into visual art and the consequent effect of dislocating the artwork and making the limits of the gallery apparent. Moreover, Smithson's choice of deserted postindustrial landscapes as the sites with which to distinguish the gallery as the nonsite of art is not coincidental. In positioning the artwork in a site where the earth is starkly apparent, closed and yet unfolding infinitely against the sky, Smithson summons an equally persistent tension between nature and culture. His chosen sites are the antithesis of the abstract space of the gallery, long upheld as a neutral environment for spectatorship. To be sure, Smithson disdained an idealized notion of nature; indeed, he describes "nature" as a modern fiction.[8] Yet he turns to a notion of the irreducible earth, which manifests in the temporally charged geology of a location, as an alternative to that ideal. It is this chaotic aspect of the site—precisely the fact that it is never whole or still—that he unleashes on the gallery. The artist chose his site in Franklin, New Jersey, for example, because it was replete with discarded and unusable industrial byproducts such as ore. The sediment of refining processes, materials such as ore and slag connote the fracture of the earth's foundation, which Smithson opposes to the wholeness of the art object. He writes, "The breakup or fragmentation of matter makes one aware of the sub-strata of the Earth before it is overly refined by industry."[9]

By pairing the unwieldy "geologic chaos" with the art object, Smithson upsets the unity of form and matter. He explains of his art objects, "Solids are particles built up around flux.... All chaos is put into the dark inside of the art."[10] Although objects such as *A Nonsite, Franklin, New Jersey,* are characterized by seemingly inert material, careful delimitations, symmetry, and stillness, Smithson secures a dialectical tie to the site by implanting the nonsites with the earth's tendency toward disarray. The statement is not just that the site is absent but that its totality is not, and never was, possible. This realization is corrosive and breaks apart the apparent order of the nonsite object. The artwork cannot be stabilized in a single location, for it is always moving between the site and the nonsite. Smithson reveals the site in its evasive movement away from the texts that attempt to represent it as an image or object. The unavailability of the site inspires a fractured artwork that acquires significance through the spectator's ever-shifting orientation.

Craig Owens attributes the impasse of the artwork between the site and the nonsite to a general trend toward the textualization of visual art. This hypothesis does not suggest that textualization corresponds to the dematerialization of the artwork. Rather, it marks a shift in emphasis from the presence of the artwork as object to a presentation of it through the movement that it undergoes as it splits into representations. Objects and images that are visually and materially manifest for the spectator remain; moreover, there is a real site "out there." The artwork, however, cannot reconcile the two and instead remains split between them.

In the same way that meaning shifts and changes through the use of a word but cannot be reduced to the word itself, the site cannot be reduced to the nonsites that stand in for it in the gallery. For Smithson, a work of art emerges precisely out of that fracture between meaning and word, site and nonsite. Whereas in a modernist paradigm, the artwork unites object and meaning so that the work's significance can be read through the object's form and materiality, Smithson pries meaning and matter apart and locates meaning elsewhere, at the site, leaving only empty form and fractured matter: the nonsite. The artwork thereby elaborates the instability of language as a material brittleness; words are substantial but are tenuously held together and likely to break apart. Smithson likens text to geological strata or layers of verbal sediment. He remarks, "The names of minerals and the minerals themselves do not differ from each other, because at the bottom of both the material and the print is the beginning of an abysmal number of fissures. Words and rocks contain a language that follows a syntax of splits and ruptures."[11]

The text, as a material fragment voided of implicit meaning, is thus vulnerable to being appropriated and rewritten by new meaning. In drawing a parallel between words and rocks, text and earth, Smithson presumes that the actual sites were unstable in the first place and thus vulnerable to being overwritten. Interestingly,

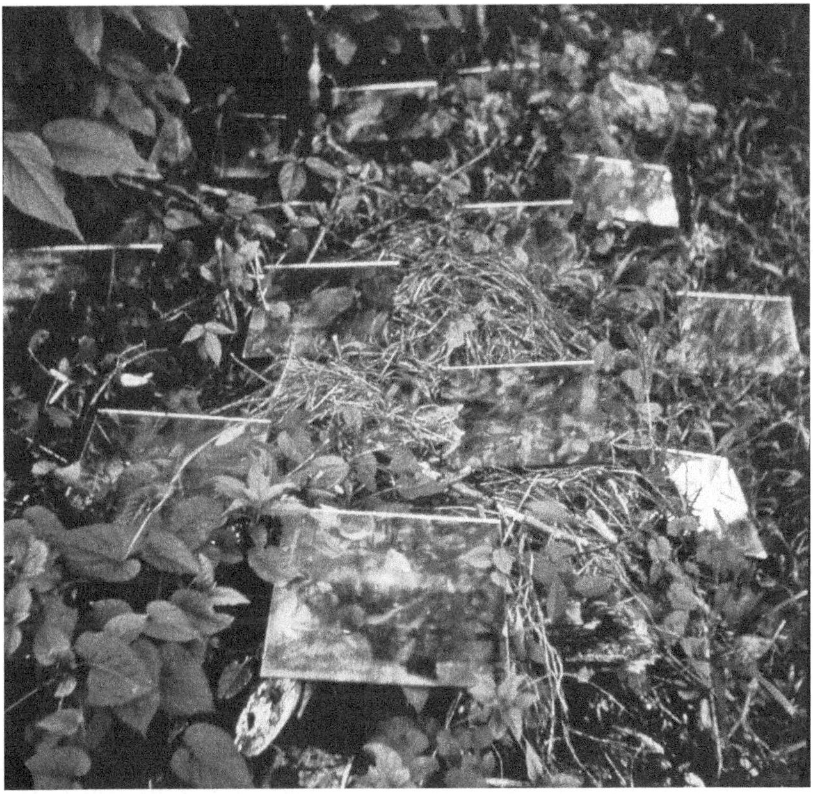

FIGURE 25. Robert Smithson, *Fifth Mirror Displacement* from "Incidents of Mirror-Travel in the Yucatán," 1969. Nine locations on a trail, Yucatán, Mexico. Copyright Estate of Robert Smithson. Licensed by VAGA, New York. Courtesy of James Cohan Gallery, New York. Collection of Solomon R. Guggenheim Museum, New York; purchased with funds contributed by the International Directors Council and Executive Committee members Edythe Broad, Henry Buhl, Elaine Terner Cooper, Linda Fischbach, Ronnie Heyman, Dakis Joannou, Cindy Johnson, Barbara Lane, Linda Macklowe, Brian McIver, Peter Norton, Willem Peppler, Denise Rich, Rachel Rudin, David Teiger, Ginny Williams, and Elliot Wolk, 1999.

Smithson's mirror-displacement artworks in Yucatàn, Mexico, in 1969 alter the site/nonsite binary by deploying the artwork as a dialect between light and earth. In this way, he introduces the play of elementals, their fluctuations and overlaps, to the site/nonsite dialectic. He therefore did not adhere to a predictable polarity between nature and art or between actual sites and discursive (non)sites. In his essay "Incidents of Mirror-Travel in the Yucatán," the artist describes nine mirror displacements: works in which he wedged twelve mirrors in the ground at nine different locations. He then photographed the mirrors, which were partly covered in soil, sand, or vegetation (or, in the case of the seventh displacement, supported against a tree) and which partly reflected the surrounding site. The mirror was a device for Smithson to cut across the division between the site and the nonsite. That is, his goal was to consider the mirror both as an object and as the reflection it creates. The twelve-inch-square mirrors signaled the rational dimensions of painting and the ordered space of the gallery. The mirror was "an ongoing abstraction that is always available and timeless." The reflections, on the other hand, were "fleeting instances that evade measure."[12] Not only was the mirror both nonsite and site (mirror and reflection), but it also repatterned the dialectic onto the encounter between earth and light. Tilted between horizontal and vertical planes, the mirrors occupied a middle ground between capturing light and reflecting the land and vegetation. At times, as in the case of the *Fifth Mirror Displacement,* this resulted in the refraction of abundant color, a sensuous and fluid product of the meeting of earth and sky (Figure 25). As Smithson describes the work:

> In the jungle, all light is paralyzed. Particles of color infected the molten reflections on the twelve mirrors, and in so doing, engendered mixtures of darkness and light. Color as an agent of matter filled the reflected illuminations with shadowy tones, pressing the light into dusty material opacity. Flames of light were imprisoned in a jumbled spectrum of greens. . . . The word "color" means at its origin to "cover" or "hide." Matter eats up light and "covers" it with a confusion of color.[13]

The mirror displacements provided a means to recover a sense of the elemental without representing it. Instead, the mirror is "an abstraction, absorbing and reflecting the site in a very physical way." Rather than merely absenting the site, then, the mirror is receptive to it, while nevertheless rebuffing penetrability. It therefore instigates a relation of simultaneous contact and polarity between the site and the nonsite. Moreover, the mirror allows Smithson to demonstrate the reversibility of site and nonsite. In his *Eight-Part Piece (Cayuga Salt Mine Project),* the artist

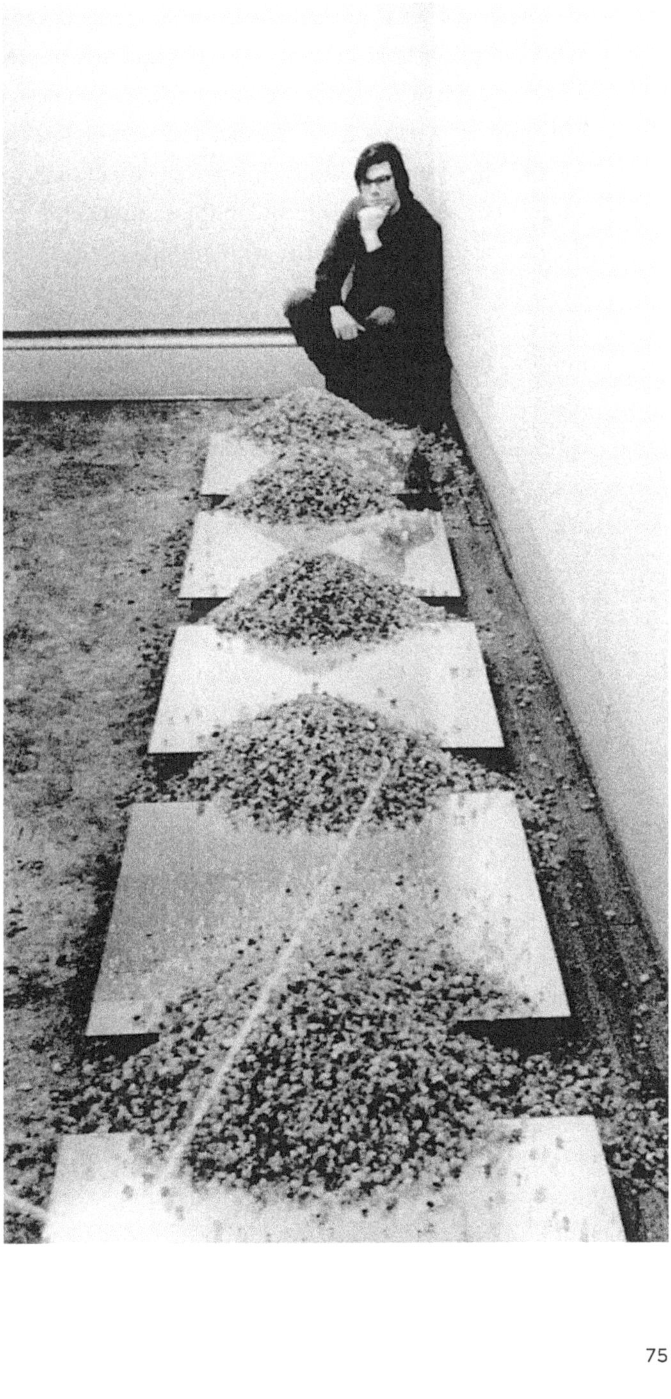

FIGURE 26. Robert Smithson, *Eight-Part Piece (Cayuga Salt Mine Project)*, 1969. Rock salt/mirrors, 11 × 30 × 360 inches. Copyright Estate of Robert Smithson. Licensed by VAGA, New York. Courtesy of James Cohan Gallery, New York. Collection of Statens Museum for Kunst (Villads Villadsen).

executed a mirror displacement that took place in the interior of an underground mine at Cayuga Lake and that was subsequently re-created in the space of the gallery in the Earth Art exhibition at the Andrew Dickson White Museum in 1969. This project marks a more distinct reversal, or intertwining, of the site/nonsite, for the initial mirror displacement was visually inert because it was isolated underground, whereas the nonsite in the exhibition, *Eight-Part Piece,* came to life in the gallery as it reflected the white lighting (Figure 26). Setting the mirrors in a row, linked to one another by piles of rock salt, the nonsite positioned the earthly matter as a binding agent, whereas the rectangular mirror flashed reflections and blinding light. Thus, Smithson explains, whereas in his previous nonsites, such as *A Nonsite, Franklin, New Jersey,* the earthly matter was amorphous and held together by a rigid container, here the earth is the container for the mirror.[14] Earth, then, both binds and splits the succession of volatile "signifiers": the mirrors that recover the site ("absorbing it in a physical way") and present it as a scattering of reflections that are impossible to grasp.

## Allegory and the Evacuation of Site

Both the impenetrability of light and the fragmentation of earth enact the instability of signification; the site's discursive meaning is precariously strung together in a "syntax of splits and ruptures" that threaten to scatter. Yet though the site cannot be represented, it is recovered as a volatile elemental that appears on the surface of the textual abstraction (the reflections of the mirror). Perhaps this subtle transition in Smithson's work has been overlooked in favor of a more straightforward explanation: that the site is merely overwritten by text. For Craig Owens, the destructuration of the artwork into fragments secures a kinship between Smithson's work and the concept of allegory.

A general definition of allegory in literary terms would be the use of a metanarrative to prescribe the direction of a primary narrative. In art, allegory frequently appeared in the domain of history painting when an artist depicted a tale from antiquity or another historical event in order to comment on a parallel situation in contemporary life. Allegory retrieves the past as a fragment, an emblem, or an image. But the past does not interject meaning onto the present; rather, the allegorical image infuses the past with a significance that is particular to its contemporary setting. The fragment of the past is thus decontextualized; it loses its original meaning, and meaning is affixed to it through the act of retrieval. Owens closely follows Walter Benjamin's exposition of allegory in *The Origin of German Tragic Drama,* seeing in it a common element with Smithson's conception of text as geological sediment. In allegory, Owens explains, language is "broken up, dispersed, in order to acquire a new and intensified meaning in its fragmentation." Because the allegorical emblem overwrites the fragment, it condenses the past into a single image but deploys that image as written text. On this point, Owens cites Benjamin, who observes that allegory "opens up a gulf in the solid massif of verbal meaning and forces the gaze into the depths of language. . . . At one stroke . . . [allegory] transforms things and works into stirring writing." The task of the allegorist, Owens explains accordingly, is not to uncover the meaning of the historical object but to acquire and assemble fragments. The allegorical work is "the calculable result of the process of accumulation."[15] Owens's description recalls Smithson's boxes of accumulated ore and the carefully arranged trapezoidal photo-maps in *A Nonsite, Franklin, New Jersey.* The reasoning behind his reading of Smithson's works as allegorical is thus clear; the artworks accumulate and arrange fragments, under the guise of acquiring meaning, but in so doing they surface their own vacancy.

The resurgence of allegory in visual art was a significant enough break from modernism to warrant Owens's identification of it as the most definitive characteristic of a postmodern trend. Outlining the history of allegory since the eighteenth century, Owens details the reasons why allegory transgressed modernism's aesthetic and disciplinary boundaries. The crux of his argument is that allegory's combination of the visual and the verbal, of spatial simultaneity and temporal contingency, is symptomatic of its hopeless confusion of all aesthetic categories.[16] For the semiotician Roman Jakobson, the linguistic formula of allegory was the projection of metaphor, the static axis of language, onto metonym, the temporal dimension of language.[17] Joel Fineman relates the differences between the metaphoric and metonymic dimensions of language to the distinction Ferdinand de Saussure made between *langue* and *parole.* Metaphor is the "synchronic system of differences that constitutes the order of language (*langue*)," whereas metonym is the diachronic principle of combination and connection by means of which structure is actualized in time in speech (*parole*).[18] That is to say, metaphor is the static, abstract structure of language, and metonym is the particularization of language through its expression in time. In addition, Jakobson associated metaphor with verse and romanticism, whereas he identified metonymy with realism and prose. However, according to Fineman, allegories combine these divisions; they "cut across and subtend all such stylistic categorizations, being equally possible in either verse or prose."[19]

In the division of the spatial and temporal orders of language (metaphor and metonym, respectively), Owens recognizes a corresponding polarization of the visual and discursive arts, which, he argues, began in the late eighteenth century with the French Revolution and was inherited by modernists. In order to distinguish the relative merits of the two disciplines, Denis Diderot defined them according to their temporality.[20] He located poetry and all the discursive arts along a dynamic axis of temporal succession—the narrative of a work of literature, for example, unfolds over time. Visual arts, on the other hand, were identified with the axis of spatial simultaneity. Like metaphor, they are static and immediate, whereas the discursive arts, like metonym, develop in temporal succession. These categories were strictly adhered to, such that the visual arts were, in Owens's words, "denied access to discourse," with the sole exception being a literary text that might accompany a work but never be incorporated into it.

Moreover, allegory's association with history was violently opposed by artists who were trying to spearhead an art form that was concerned with the modern. As the nineteenth century progressed, it was condemned as antithetical to Charles Baudelaire's modernist credo, "Il faut être de son temps."[21] Allegory, it was reasoned, always looked backward in time, conceiving of the present with respect to the past and veiling the contemporary situation in historical references. In its very theoretical origins, modernism distinguished itself against historicism and tradition. Thus, allegory, as the prime vehicle of the historical in art, had to be ejected from the modernist project. Owens argues at length that allegory was never completely abandoned by modernists but was merely repressed until its uprising in the sixties. The appearance of text in and as art in the sixties marked a rejection of the long tradition of separating the discursive arts from the visual arts. In its combination of the art object and text, allegory creates hybrid forms of spatial simultaneity and temporal succession. New artistic strategies such as appropriation, performance, body art, conceptual art, and site-specific art imply a cross-fertilization of disciplines and media that had formerly been segregated.

The challenge that Robert Smithson waged against modernism with his site/nonsite works, then, was not just geared toward the limits of the gallery space; it was also a confrontation with modernism's strict adherence to the aesthetic categories of painting and sculpture and its denial of the relationship between visual art and discursive practices. Smithson positioned the object component of art (the nonsites) as descriptions, texts, or signifiers voided of a signified. Some nonsites were pictorial but were not painting, as in the case of the photo-maps in *A Nonsite, Franklin, New Jersey.* Others, such as the trapezoidal boxes of ore, were three-dimensional objects but were not sculpture. And most scandalously from a modernist perspective, the three-dimensional objects and the pictorial representations were inextricably linked as parts of a whole and as descriptions of that whole, but they denied the spectator a unified artwork.

Owens's account of *Spiral Jetty* through the concept of allegory diverged somewhat with Rosalind Krauss's interpretation of the phenomenological significance of the work. In her book *Passages in Modern Sculpture,* Krauss discusses the jetty in terms of the way it physically disorients the spectator. Not only is the work situated in an isolated and surreal landscape on the north end of the Great Salt Lake, several miles away from the closest reference point, the Golden Spike monument, but in addition the shape of the work leads the viewer around in circles. The experience of *Spiral Jetty,* Krauss describes, is "one of continually being decentered within the great expanse of lake and sky."[22] Smithson conveys this sensation in his essay, listing the view in each direction from the end of the sculpture: "North—Mud, salt crystals, rocks, water; North by East—Mud, salt crystals, rocks, water; Northeast by North—Mud, salt crystals, rocks, water; Northeast by East—Mud, salt crystals, rocks, water."[23] No sense of direction can be discerned from the center of the work; every view looks exactly the same. In this way, *Spiral Jetty* envelops the spectator and renders it impossible to make the landscape coherent from any single perspective.

The rubric of disorientation that the sculpture elicits can also be attributed to the properties of the lake itself. As Ric Collier and Jim Edwards describe, the Great

Salt Lake epitomizes change and unpredictability. Like the Dead Sea, the lake is buoyant because of its high salinity. Because of its salt content, they note, it has been called "the Lake of Paradoxes . . . an ironic joke of nature—water that is itself more desert than a desert." The fluctuating water levels continually change the contours of the lake by hundreds of square miles across its surface area.[24] Among the lake's most distinctive features, however, is its changing color, which, depending on the levels of algae and brine, varies from red to blue to green.

In contrast to the changing lake, *Spiral Jetty* is built out of solid rock and earth. For Owens, the jetty is not just a pathway that leads us into a disoriented experience of the site; it can also be read as a textual inscription. In allegory, he qualifies, the image is like a pictogram, a hieroglyph, or any writing composed of concrete images.[25] *Spiral Jetty* synthesizes the significance of the site by affixing the emblem directly onto it. But the textualization, and correspondingly the allegorization, of the site does not end with the sculpture. Like the nonsite, Owens argues, the sculpture is "not a discrete work but one link in a chain of signifiers which summon and refer to one another in a dizzying spiral."[26] The layering of meaning from one signifier to the next, beginning with the sculpture and leading to the film and the essay, demonstrates the way allegory reads one text through another. Owens explains that allegory does not restore an original meaning that may have been lost; it adds another meaning supplanting an antecedent one.[27] The site is allegorized by the sculptural inscription that is applied to it, and in turn the sculpture is covered over by the texts that bring it into view. The textualized artwork masks the site, even as it tries to reveal it to the spectator:

> Unintelligible at close range, the spiral form of the *Jetty* is completely intuitable only from a distance, and that distance is most often achieved by imposing a *text* between viewer and work. Smithson thus accomplishes a radical dislocation of the notion of a point-of-view, which is no longer a function of physical location, but of the *mode* (photographic, cinematic, textual) of confrontation of the work of art. The work is henceforth defined by the position it occupies in an infinite chain extending from the site itself.[28]

The question arises, is a textual mode of confrontation antithetical to a phenomenological engagement with the site, or does it perhaps open the door to a more thorough expression of that physical experience? The correspondences between the actual *shape* of the texts (their behavior as material objects) and the disorienting experience of the sculpture should not be overlooked. Indeed, Smithson does not so much absent the site pure and simple as show how the chain of signifiers are all similarly marked by the loss of the site and how this loss actually orients them. Interestingly, Walter Benjamin invokes the whirlpool as a metaphor for the loss of origin in his discussion of the baroque *Trauerspiel* in *The Origin of German Tragic Drama*. For Benjamin, in recovering and accumulating fragments from history, the allegorical image conjoins the present to the past just as two currents of water spin into a single vortex with no center or source, no beginning or end. The term "origin," he says:

> is not intended to describe the process by which the existent came into being, but rather to describe that which emerges from the process of becoming and disappearance. Origin is an eddy in the stream of becoming, and in its current it swallows the material involved in the process of genesis. That which is original is never revealed in the naked and manifest existence of the factual; its rhythm is apparent only to a dual insight. On the one hand it needs to be recognized as a process of restoration and re-establishment, but on the other hand, and precisely because of this, as something perfect and incomplete.[29]

As *Spiral Jetty* layers text onto the Great Salt Lake, it presents the site in the rhythm of becoming and disappearance that Benjamin describes. The spectator cannot witness the presence of the site in all its magnitude and complexity; instead, the site is mediated by the artwork inscribed onto it. By marking the site, Smithson makes it visually available, but only through representations that incite its expenditure. The site is not merely absented in the process of textualization; the artist's concern with the respective material compositions of the site and the texts—the former fluid and dynamic, the latter hard and fragmentary—and with their impact on the spectator's "mode of confrontation" through the artwork is unmistakable.

## The Elemental as Volatile Subtext

Like the mirror displacements, *Spiral Jetty* requires a departure from the understanding of the artwork strictly as text. In his essay on the work, Smithson expanded his previous definition of the site and the nonsite as abstract terms and came to distinguish them instead through their contrasting materialities. This conceptualization of *Spiral Jetty* braids the site and the text together and circles them around points of disruption that correlate to both an expulsion of dynamic substance and the loss of discursive coherence. The all-encompassing fluidity of the site threatens logical sense altogether. In his description of his first visit to the site at Rozel Point, Smithson writes:

> As I looked out at the site, it reverberated out to the horizons only to suggest an immobile cyclone while flickering light made the entire landscape appear to quake. . . . From the gyrating space emerged the possibility of the *Spiral Jetty*. No ideas, no concepts, no systems, no structures, no abstractions could hold themselves in the actuality of that evidence. My dialectics of site and nonsite whirled into an indeterminate state, where solid and liquid lost themselves in each other. . . . No sense wondering about classifications and categories, there were none.[30]

In this dramatic account, the overwhelming magnitude and force of the site rebuffs any possibility of being articulated through language, thought, art object, or representation: no abstractions can withstand "the actuality of that evidence." The force of the site arrests all thought, even dialectical movement, and instead, the "immobile cyclone" collapses all concepts that differentiate one another. Nonsite coils into site, just as the rock of the sculpture winds into the lake. Though the site and the text are still, in a sense, dialectical opposites, Smithson complicates their polarity: "Both sides are present and absent at the same time. The land or ground of the Site is placed *in* the art (Nonsite) rather than the art placed *on* the ground. . . . Is the Site a reflection of the Nonsite (mirror) or is it the other way around? The rules of this network of signs are discovered as you go along uncertain trails both mental and physical."[31] The artist uses the tension between solidity and fluidity to recast the dialectical relationship between the nonsite and the site onto a shared space that does not assume a straightforward split between the site and its representation. Thus, *Spiral Jetty* mobilizes the site as a fluid tissue that surges up within the text's calcified substance.

Smithson continually returns to the theme of the whirlpool's empty center, which he uses to evoke the corresponding ideas that the site inhibits its own articulation as a text and that the cohesiveness of the texts is precarious. More subtly though, he inflects the image of the whirlpool into his essay, referring to various blind spots, voids, or holes that act as thresholds to a subterranean fluid. After the narrative about his searching for the site, constructing the jetty, walking over the sculpture, and viewing it from a helicopter, Smithson lists a "scale of centers" around which the artwork and his description of its production circumnavigate. Yet the items on his list are all examples of forms that, like a spiral, do not have centers at all but instead are centered on a void. Interestingly, the items are also always accompanied by descriptions of the artist's loss of orientation. It is in these descriptions that Smithson insists on an attentiveness to the earth as an unfathomable phenomenological event. Moreover, the various dislocations also give rise to an overflow of sensation.

Among the items on the list is an ion in a cyclotron, by which Smithson refers to the irregular structure of a salt crystal called a "screw dislocation." The second item is a nucleus, which he mentions as the unattainable core at the end of the sculpture. The artist's pursuit of this elusive nucleus causes him to "slip outside himself and dissolve into a unicellular beginning."[32] Next, Smithson mentions a dislocation point and a wooden stake in the mud, in reference to the process of mapping out the site by marking certain points where the jetty would be built. In the essay, though, he says the stake "leads to a meandering zone," and though the trucks attempt to fill in the area marked by the stakes with rock and earth, their wheels sink "into a quagmire of sticky gumbo mud."[33] The stake in the mud is thus a precarious center, set in a slurry foundation and then covered over with hard rock. The artist also lists the axis of the helicopter propeller, the point that lines up the two blades. He is quick to point out the origin of the word "helicopter": it comes, he says, "from the Greek *helix, helikos* meaning spiral."[34] The spiral has no central source; it revolves around emptiness. Smithson records yet another spiral shape, James Joyce's ear channel, with reference to Constantin Brancusi's sketch portrait of James Joyce as a spiral ear. Smithson then lists the sun, which may appear to be an enclosed entity. However, as the artist explains in the film, the sun is not "a single flaming star but millions upon millions of them." It is really, in fact, a "vast spiral nebula of innumerable suns." And finally, the last item on the scale of centers is the hole in a film reel, a vacancy around which the film revolves.

Smithson's "uncertain scale of centers" has a corollary in "an equally uncertain 'scale of edges.'" It is significant that the items on this list are malleable and elusive, hardly edges at all: particles, protoplasmic solutions, dizziness, ripples, flashes of light, sections, foot steps, pink water. The edges of the work overwhelm its centralized orientation; the work is surrounded by the uncontained movement of the site (particles, protoplasm, ripples, pink water) and the physical sensations (dizziness, flashes of light) that disrupt any assessment of the work as a whole. Even sections and footsteps, which seem at first to be concrete, prove to be markers of the disassembly of a stable division between the center and the periphery of the work. With respect to the sectioning of *Spiral Jetty* into measured lengths, the artist comments, "in the Spiral Jetty the surd takes over and leads one into a world that cannot be expressed by number or rationality." Sections are only an illusion, the limit of framing of the site that is always at the point of being dissolved. Likewise the footsteps mark a descent into a state of irrationality: "After a point, measurable steps . . . descend from logic to the 'surd state.'"[35] Where Smithson had previously established a dialectical fracture of center and periphery in his site/nonsites, here he sets them against one another by making the center a gateway to an unstable territory whose earthly foundation is perpetually unraveling.

As Smithson charts his experience of making the jetty in his essay, he exposes several gaps in his ability to describe the site, and at these junctures he can express only raw physical sensation. Most often, these lapses are described as blind spots, located at the point where the artist is incapable of seeing the site in fullness and clarity: "On the slopes of Rozel Point I closed my eyes, and the sun burned crimson through the lids"; "my sight was saturated by the color of red algae circulating in the heart of the lake, pumping in ruby currents"; "my eyes became combustion chambers churning orbs of blood blazing by the light of the sun"; "rays of glare hit my eyes with the frequency of a Geiger counter."[36] The artist's vision is affronted by the elemental potency of the location. He closes his eyes and the sun burns through his eyelids; his sight is saturated by the red color of the lake; the blood in his eyes is blazed with light. Smithson's lapses in sight are immediately flooded with the visceral fluids that permeate the site.

The artist cannot gather his perceptions of the Great Salt Lake into a reasonable description because its volatile substance overcomes any meaning he tries to affix to it. "Logical purity," he says, "suddenly finds itself in a bog.... The *alogos* undermines the *logos*."[37] Unable to sustain a correspondence between the site's viscosity and his representation of it, Smithson is led by the site to a primordial state of being: "The tail leads into an undifferentiated state of matter"; "following the spiral steps we return to our origins, back to some pulpy protoplasm, a floating eye adrift in an antediluvian ocean"; "I was slipping out of myself again, dissolving into a unicellular beginning."[38] Smithson's blind spots, which join his bodily fluids to the streaming elements of the site, merging his blood with the rays of light and salty red water, reenact the whirlpool's magnetic pull downward into an undifferentiated condition. The reader/viewer is led vicariously downward to an earthly origin, but this origin is the antithesis of a definitive point of differentiation; it is "pulpy protoplasm."

Smithson shows the lapses in his narrative description to be symptomatic of an amorphous condition encrypted within the facade of textual representation. Though he conceives of language as a "terrain of particles, each containing its own void," drawing a comparison between words and minerals, texts and hard geological sediment, the voids in his essay trigger a wellspring of elemental fluid. Confirming the essay's vulnerability to being pulled downward by the centripetal force of the site, Smithson writes, "The equation of my language remains unstable . . . an arrangement of variables spilling into surds. My equation is as clear as mud—a muddy spiral."[39] His essay, like the sculpture, is an inscription set in the unsteady foundation of the earth. Smithson's words are, absurdly, "clear as mud." Sight fills with blood; logic sinks into a bog; language is muddied. The artist combines the text with elemental force, using the essay itself to induce the sensorial overflow that stems from the boundlessness of the site. There is thus a primacy to the Great Salt Lake that cannot be denied because it is the nebulous underpinning of the text.

As Smithson explains, "The rationality of a grid on a map sinks into what it is supposed to define."[40]

## Film and the Surplus of Sensation

In a similar vein, Smithson evidences the fragility of the textual mode through sensorial disruptions in his film. The thirty-five-minute, 16 mm film splices together disjointed images alongside his documentation of the construction of the jetty (Figure 27). The film opens with a blinding shot of the sun, then proceeds to alternate between shots of the road to Rozel Point, shots of scattered pieces of paper—some of them topographic maps of the prehistoric world, some of them pages from history books—and footage of the Hall of the Late Dinosaurs at the American Museum of Natural History in New York, which is accompanied by the sound of

FIGURE 27. Robert Smithson, *Spiral Jetty,* film stills, 1970. Black-and-white silver gelatin prints, three panels, each 25¼ × 43½ feet. Copyright Estate of Robert Smithson. Licensed by VAGA, New York. Courtesy of James Cohan Gallery, New York. Collection of Museet for Samtiskunst, Norway.

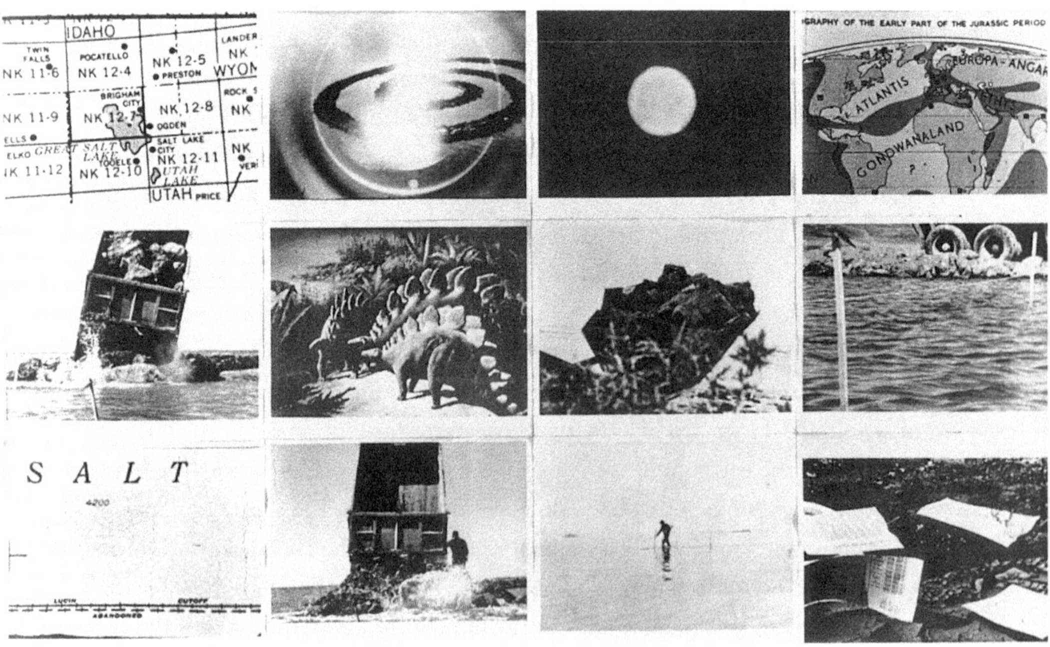

an echoing pendulum, as though the foray through prehistoric remains produces a reverberation of time whereby the dissonant echoes of the past can still be heard in the present. This is conducive to the film acting as "a map that would show the prehistoric world as coextensive with the world I existed in."[41] Next, the film initiates an arduous sequence of a dump truck backing into the lake, emptying heaps of rock and earth into it. Shots of heavy machinery, however, are interspersed with shots of the water, its surface rippling gently and reflecting sparkles of sunlight (Figure 28). Smithson thus revisits the intertwinement of earth and light that played a part in the design of his mirror displacements and his *Eight-Part Piece* in 1969.

Like the essay, the film recalls the prehistoric world by connecting it to both elementals and bodily fluids. Indeed, the film is imbued with surplus sensations of light, with the sound of moving water, and it impresses the viewer with the visceral fullness of the Great Salt Lake. Its receptivity to the site is also apparent in the shots

FIGURE 28. Robert Smithson, *Spiral Jetty,* film still, 1970. Estate of Robert Smithson. Licensed by VAGA, New York.

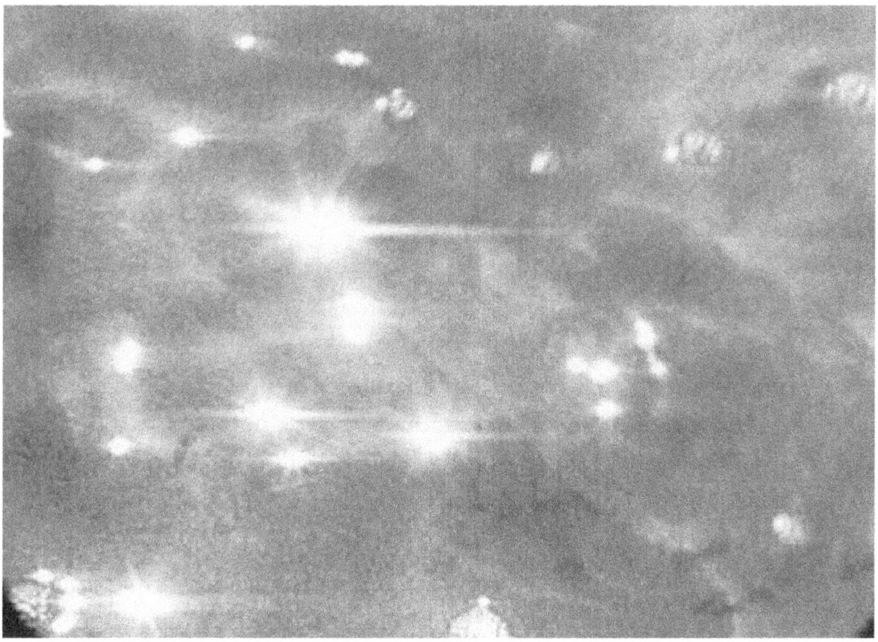

of the American Museum of Natural History, which were filmed through a red filter, summoning a physiological bond between the spectator, the primordial past, and the texture of the image. The red filter recalls the color of blood and of the lake. Between the essay and the film, Smithson evokes a shared corporeality with the site, a procedure that propels the viewer's orientation to the prehistoric past. He states, "Chemically speaking, our blood is analogous in composition to the primordial seas."[42]

Through this imagined journey back in time, the artist revives a sense of the site's immediacy. But he is also conscious of filming as a process of fossilizing this vital quality. He describes film as inert matter in which the life of a site has been ensnared. The film is "a bramble of stabilized fragments taken from things obscure and fluid, ingredients trapped in a succession of frames, a stream of viscosities both still and moving." And more strikingly, the film is made of "masses of impenetrable material. The sun, the spiral, the salt buried in lengths of footage."[43] The dense substance of the film is not to be confused with the "viscous" life of the Great Salt Lake that it depicts. But nor does the film mask the site entirely; rather, it pivots around the site attempting to take the viewer deeper into it as the camera circles around the jetty.

Just as the essay evokes the gravitational pull of the whirlpool, Smithson enacts a spiraling descent into the lake by having himself filmed running the course of the jetty in counterclockwise circles from the shore to the middle. He is filmed from a helicopter; as it loops around the sculpture, all sense of direction is lost; there is no horizon or vantage point to reinstate a centralized perspective. In fact, Smithson saw this disorientation as essential to the medium of film, stating, "A film is a spiral made up of frames."[44] The last sequence, shot from the sky looking down, follows Smithson's erratic gait. At this point, the filmstrip appears textured by the contrast between the solid rock of the sculpture and the rays of light reflected off the lake. The tension of the film mounts as the circling intensifies a sense of dizziness. The desired effect is a sense of impending collapse: "My movie would end in sunstroke."[45] The culmination of the film is hardly explosive; it would be more accurate to describe it as existential. Smithson runs up to the edge of the sculpture and looks down over it into the water. At this moment, the artist comes to the very limit of form—where the water laps at the edge of the sculpture. This confrontation brings the film to an end that is, as Smithson describes, a dissolution of the filmic image: "Between heat lightning and heat exhaustion, the spiral curled into vaporization."[46] This sense of exhaustion is confirmed as the film concludes with a shot of a studio littered with strewn film reels and a large photostat of the sculpture.

The film and the essay, as parts of a chain of signifiers, do not, then, as Owens seems to suggest, impose a text *between* the viewer and the site. Rather, the text stands as the horizon from which the site exceeds perceptual mastery. Though the allegorical emblem of the whirlpool divulges the artwork's loss of an origin—a loss of the primary experience of the site and of its original meaning—Smithson's gravitation to the various loci of this process of evacuation is significant. In bringing the loss of the site into the spectator's trajectory, he calls forth bodily sensations while acknowledging his inability to encapsulate the site as a textual representation. "Adrift amid scraps of film, one is unable to infuse into them any meaning, they seem worn-out, ossified views, degraded and pointless, yet they are powerful enough to hurl one into a lucid vertigo."[47] The film itself is ossified, unable in and of itself to stand in for the dynamic matter of the site. Yet it has one redeeming feature: it can bring on a lucid vertigo, or otherwise put, a perceptual disruption that is punctuated by sensorial surplus. Though the site cannot be figured, the residue of its dispersed vitality somehow touches the exhausted fragments of text.

In chapter 1, I discussed the influence of Merleau-Ponty's model of the chiasm in the analysis of body art. Merleau-Ponty's flesh ontology presumes that our knowledge of the world and of ourselves is informed by our precognitive bodily experience and that our perception is situated in an intercorporeal sense of being. That is to say, the body's flesh is instantiated in the "flesh of the world," and our perception emerges out of the contact of that flesh folded back on itself. Merleau-Ponty uses the image of infolded flesh to explain the gap between thought and perception, between mind and body. It is this gap that concerns me here, for as I have shown, Smithson evokes bodily conditions and sensations at precisely the lapses in textual representation and meaning.

Yet the important point that Irigaray raises about Merleau-Ponty's flesh ontology is equally pertinent to the bodily experience that Smithson develops in *Spiral Jetty*. Irigaray argues that Merleau-Ponty's flesh ontology relies on a metaphorics of fluidity that is distinctly feminine and maternal. The idea that one perceives by inhabiting the world and the other and that the seer enters into an intimate connection with the visible world in which "he" resides in an indeterminate state is, as Elizabeth Grosz points out, deeply suggestive of the intrauterine state of the child surrounded by amniotic fluid.[48] The gap between the mind and the body, the visible and the invisible, by which all knowledge of the world is amalgamated into a coherent whole, begins for Irigaray in this physical intertwinement. Grosz further explains that in the nocturnal state of the womb there is only tactile sensation and that this darkness makes vision possible.[49]

For Merleau-Ponty, the invisible world of tactility precedes and ultimately orients vision. He explains that "there is a strict ideality in experiences that are experiences of the flesh: the moments of the sonata, the fragments of the luminous field, adhere to one another with a cohesion without concept which is of the same type as the cohesion of the parts of my body, or the cohesion of my body with the world."[50] The perception of the world coheres without concept; it is a knowledge that is as harmonious as the coordination of body parts and of the body's movement in the world. It is not surprising then, that Smithson suggests the bodily experience of *Spiral Jetty* at precisely the places where sight fails. Yet he recognizes that these lapses are intertwined with a desire for coherence. He writes, "Eyesight is often slaughtered by the other senses, and when that happens it becomes necessary to seek out dispassionate abstractions."[51] Clearly, there is a correlation between being overwhelmed by bodily sensation, a consequent failure to see, and the attempt to clearly articulate this phenomenal engagement.

Irigaray makes another pertinent point about Merleau-Ponty's model of the chiasm: despite our attempts to abstract our tactile connection with the world, the gap between tactility and vision can be bridged. Tactility is never entirely obscured by vision; rather, it intercedes in the confrontation with color, which functions as a fluid. Color, she explains, "resuscitates in me all of that prior life, the preconceptual, preobjective, presubjective, this *ground* of the visible where seeing and seen are not yet distinguished. . . . Color bathes my gaze, which sees it, perceives it more or less well, changes in its visibility, but can never delimit it, create it, bend it to its decisions."[52] The color red bolsters Smithson's vibrant imagery, particularly in the frequent references to blood and to the sun that burned crimson through his lids, and in the use of the red filter through which he films the Hall of the Late Dinosaurs.

Moreover, the artist bridges his essay and film with his bodily experience of the site, coding the phenomenological encounter with surges of elementals. In drawing a parallel between the coursing liquids of the body, the saline water of the lake, and the blazing light of the sun, Smithson merges his body with the site. He also links this state to a "primordial sea" and an "antediluvian ocean," positioning the site as a geological womb (though one that is not necessarily anthropomorphized and feminized). The process of representation is thus enveloped in vital fluids that stream through the site and the artist's body and erupt into the texts.

From the cracks in the brittle materiality of the texts, the Great Salt Lake burgeons forth as an elemental fluid, arresting the capacity to "read" the text as a document of the site and instead suggesting the site through visual sensations that upset the coherence of representation. Smithson's references to an intercorporeal experience between his body and the site disclose a phenomenological connection to the site that overcomes the text's attempt to cover it. More than presenting the site in the allegorical rhythm of concealing and revealing, *Spiral Jetty* recovers the site through an excess of sensation at the point where representation fails.

## Entropy and the Expenditure of Time

It is not merely the case, then, that the site of *Spiral Jetty* is fragmented into texts; rather, the residual substance of the absent site also plays an integral role in activating the continual upheaval of meaning. Nevertheless, Owens's theory of the allegorical impulse is relevant to Smithson's notorious preoccupation with entropy. In Smithson's positioning of the site as a primordial past, he already identifies a temporal disjunction—the site is the prehistory of the artwork, and so *Spiral Jetty* becomes a "ruin in reverse."[53] But although Owens anticipates that the sited sculpture is abandoned to the Great Salt Lake and that its disappearance necessitates a textual mode of confrontation, in fact Smithson did not design the sculpture to be progressively absorbed by the site. To the contrary: his goal was to introduce a sense of duration to the artwork without dismantling it. While the concept of entropy that Smithson developed is certainly related to allegory's aesthetic of ruination, *Spiral Jetty* was not bound for a straightforward dematerialization. Contrary to what many assume, Smithson was concerned here not with the linear degeneration of matter, but rather with identifying a temporal circuit of progress and regress.

The sculpture persists at the site for precisely the same reason that the site persists in the texts: because the artwork positions the site as its primordial past, and it is perpetually guided to retrieve that lost origin as representation—a quest that it can never fulfill because of the site's uncontainable materiality. This turn back in time to coalesce history into a single image is also central to the paradigm of allegory and results in the solidification of matter and the accumulation of fragments. The point to be emphasized here is that in his vain attempt to retrieve the artwork's original unity with the site, Smithson insinuates the site's elemental quality. What deserves consideration, then, is how the artwork reveals its irreducible substance, as well as its unending drive to return to it, through the expenditure of time.

In Owens's reading of allegory through Benjamin, the ruin is the penultimate allegorical fragment; it stands for the irreversible process of history's decay and the progressive distancing from a point of origin as time passes.[54] The ruin signals the integration of history by the natural landscape; the fragments of human civilizations become absorbed by their setting. Indeed, for Benjamin, allegory "is the form in which man's subjection to nature is most obvious."[55] Owens associates the allegorical cult of the ruin with site-specific art, for at the time, many earth artists did embed their works in natural settings with the explicit goal of creating an ethos of prehistory. The kinship of site-specific sculptures to prehistoric monuments links them to the "petrified, primordial landscape" of history seen in allegorical ruins.

Implicit in Owens's analysis of *Spiral Jetty,* then, is his assumption that like many other site-specific works, it was intended to be ephemeral: "Site-specific works are impermanent, installed in particular locations for a limited duration, their impermanence providing the measure of their circumstantiality. Yet they are rarely dismantled but simply abandoned to nature. . . . In this, the site-specific work becomes an emblem of transience." Owens secures a relationship between the work's supposed impermanence and its dispersal into fragments of text. The textualized artwork is allegorical in that it attempts to fix into representation that which is transitory, and consequently it offers only an assembly of fragments that affirm their own contingency to one another.[56] By this logic, Smithson's works are the prime example of the allegorical tendency to fragment the art object by submitting it to the degrading forces of the earth. "When the Great Salt Lake rose and submerged the *Spiral Jetty*," Owens argues, "the salt deposits left on its surface became yet another link in the chain of crystalline forms which makes possible the description of the *Jetty* as a text."[57]

There is a certain ambiguity to this statement, however, for while it is certainly true that the lake submerges the jetty and then subsides, leaving it encrusted with salt crystals, by connecting the immersion of the sculpture and its textualization to the process of decay, Owens inadvertently implies that the sculpture is on a linear temporal course and is destined to be decomposed by the site. Indeed, the association of the earthwork with ruins perpetuated several subsequent interpretations underpinned by the expectation that the lake was destroying the jetty and thus rendering it entirely invisible. In an essay written in 1988, for example, Ann Reynolds writes, "Because of its location and physical fragility, few of us have actually experienced it in this way [in person]. Instead we see it neatly framed in a photographic image that is endlessly reproduced."[58] Similarly, in her more recent analysis of the film, Reynolds describes the intercutting between shots of the heavy machinery constructing the sculpture and shots of the lapping water of the lake. This rhythm, she argues, corresponds with the building of the jetty and the forces of its "slow, imperceptible but inevitable dissolution."[59]

Reynolds's characterization of *Spiral Jetty*'s "physical fragility" and the projection of its "inevitable dissolution" reiterates Owens's presumption that Smithson built the work with the intention of having the site reabsorb it, thereby securing its induction into text. This kind of analysis frames the lake's activity as a destructive force pitted against the art object—the splitting of the work into uprooted textual fragments is a function of the sculpture's disassembly. But the submergence of the jetty was only one part of its interaction with the site. Smithson states that he constructed the work to be "physical enough to be able to withstand all these climate changes, yet it's intimately involved with those climate changes and natural disturbances."[60]

The problem with modern art, according to Smithson, is that it was a closed system professing to be without time. He criticizes modernism's drive to transcend the material world: "Pure art tends to view abstraction as independent of nature, there's no accounting for change or the temporality of the mundane world. *Abstraction rules in a void, pretending to be free of time.*"[61] Not only was he well aware of modernism's denial of certain modes of temporality in favor of the instantaneous aesthetic experience (or "presentness," as Michael Fried describes it), but he also recognized that introducing a sense of duration to the artwork was concomitant with its textualization. He observes, "The strata of the Earth is a jumbled museum. Embedded in the sediment is a text that contains limits and boundaries which evade the rational order, and social structures which confine art. In order to read the rocks we must become conscious of geologic time, and of the layers of prehistoric material that is entombed in the Earth's crust."[62] His association of words and grammar with strata of rock deposits in the earth's crust affirms the materiality of language, but it also foregrounds a temporal awareness that redefined the textual artwork in terms of what he called "geologic time."

For Smithson, temporality has a paradoxical relationship to the artwork; it causes the object to fragment, yet it is the mechanism or "mental ground" by which it emerges as art. Like Benjamin, who claims that the authenticity of an art object rests on its capacity to endure through time and to stand as "historical testimony,"[63] Smithson suggests that it is only through the passage of time that an object becomes a work of art. He explains, "When a *thing* is seen through the consciousness of temporality, it is changed into something that is nothing. This all-engulfing sense provides the mental ground for the object, so that it ceases being a mere object and becomes art. The object gets to be less and less but exists as something clearer. Every object, if it is art, is charged with the rush of time."[64] Smithson's statement that the consciousness of temporality changes the object from something into nothing, however, is not as literal as it appears. He does not simply mean that time makes the object disappear; rather, he is saying that meaning is generated by the object over time; it is not inherent but accrues on the object as time passes. Thus, the object in itself is meaningless except as an index of the passage of time. This idea recalls the passage at the end of his essay on *Spiral Jetty* in which he describes the scraps of film as ossified remains that are degraded and pointless and that hold no meaning in and of themselves but instead hurl the viewer into a lucid vertigo. What makes an object art, for Smithson, is its suggestion of a flow of time. Time, however, does not lead to decomposition, nor does it rest within the object. Instead, it leaves the object in a state of exhausted equilibrium.

In this sense, Smithson engages the idea of the artwork as a ruin; the textualized art object is composed of inert matter and thus evokes the effects of progressive geological time. It might, however, be more accurate to say that the textual art object is a consequence and a symptom of temporal progression but is no longer subjected to time. This very idea is latent in Owens's essay when he writes that the earthwork is an emblem of transience; that is, it is an *emblem* of transience but is not itself transient. To what extent, then, can we say that Smithson's interest in entropy and his use of the earth implicated *Spiral Jetty* in a process of decay? To the artist's mind, entropy was indeed a process of disintegration, but it was also inherently finite. More accurately, it led to an irreversible state of fragmentation. Entropy exemplifies both fracture and stability; "it's a condition that's moving towards a gradual equilibrium. . . . You have a closed system which eventually deteriorates and starts to break apart and there's no way you can really piece it back together again."[65] These two tenets of entropy, fragmentation and equilibrium, were instrumental to Smithson's conception of *Spiral Jetty*. By lodging the sculpture in the earth, Smithson leads us to read the artwork not as an object in the process of decay but as an index of time having passed. The sculpture, and indeed the other texts, are all shaped by the outflow of time but are not undone by it.

The periodic reemergence of *Spiral Jetty* over the last thirty-five years poses a problem to claims about the relationship between the artwork's decay and its textualization. Almost as soon as it was built, the jetty disappeared into the lake for two months in the summer of 1971, but it reappeared covered with salt crystals. Since that time, as Suzaan Boettger has pointed out, the sculpture has had a relatively regular cycle of being immersed for most of the year and then rising up above or just under the water in the early fall.[66] But the sculpture has never decayed. In fact, the continuance of the jetty has inspired recent attempts to reconcile the differential between the concept of entropy and the work's refusal to be absorbed by the lake. Gary Shapiro notes that Smithson never wanted to let the sculpture disappear and that in 1972, shortly before the artist died, he expressed an interest in building it up above the water level if the lake did not recede.[67] Boettger argues further that the sculpture's submergence into the water is not a good example of entropy because the lake does not bring the sculpture to a simpler organization.[68] Moreover, she remarks that allowing the jetty to deteriorate would thwart Smithson's basic intention to facilitate the salt encrustation that would contrast it to the water. Rather than take the position that *Spiral Jetty* is unrelated to entropy, I would suggest that entropy need not be equated with progressive decay. Instead, entropy positions *Spiral Jetty* as a deposit at the endpoint of duration: an object through which time has already passed.

Jennifer Roberts argues that at the beginning of his career in the early sixties, Smithson critiqued the wave of performance art that was gaining popularity at the time, for precisely the reason that to dematerialize art was to engender textual by-products that he thought of as dead matter.[69] His criticism of happenings was akin to his rejection of action painting in the style of the abstract expressionists; if art was grounded in action and not in an object, in his opinion, it was doomed: "All modern schools of art, that are infused with action, ultimately 'despair and die.'" He concludes, "Action leads to dead matter while passion leads to spirit life."[70] Roberts connects the artist's vehement reaction to action-based practices to a personal crisis in the mid-sixties, during which he was tormented by the apparent opposition between the transcendent realm of spirituality and the transient, mundane world of matter. She explains, however, that Smithson emerged from this tumultuous period determined to reconcile these polarities by producing artworks that were bound to materiality, and were thus subject to temporality, and that yet transcended or overcame time.

Crystallography was an avenue into this compromise for Smithson, because in a crystal, the passage of time is marked as molecules amass and take shape. Otherwise put, the flow of time resulted in a hypermaterialization rather than a dematerialization. Further, as Roberts argues, the crystal demonstrates that time is not an empty container but rather is replete with matter, which it deposes in fully formed units, namely, the molecules that accumulate around a slip or imperfection on a surface.[71] Smithson was also attracted to the paradox that because a crystal accumulates around an irregularity on a surface (for example, salt crystallizes on the cracks of a rock face), it is held together and separated by a fracture. Roberts maintains that for Smithson, entropy, like the growth of a crystal, conditions matter to be simultaneously unified and fragmented. In the operations of both entropy and crystallization, time deposits matter in a static yet irredeemably divided state around a fissure or split that is never covered over.[72] Smithson states that the crystal is "the configuration of maximum wholeness [and] at the same time that of maximum division or entropy."[73]

Whether we understand the sculpture as the emblematization of the salt crystal or as a repository of the multitudes of crystals attached to it, the sculpture is a testament to the operation of entropy. The key point to be made, though, is that Smithson dislocates the sculpture from the perpetuity of the site's temporality because he associates entropy with sedimentation; the jetty is bound not to organic growth but rather to the layers of material accumulated after time has passed. In the object, temporality has always already vanished and left its mark. Smithson positions the artwork as having been shaped by temporal flux while no longer being imbricated in that flux. The artist thus identifies two temporal trajectories: "The Natural world is ruled by the temporal (dynamic history), whereas the crystalline world is ruled by the atemporal (non-dynamic time)."[74] The site, as part of the natural world, is continually shifting, but the artwork, Smithson shows us, is part of the crystalline world and is therefore atemporal. Because he prefigures the sculpture as crystalline, Smithson demonstrates that the lake is not an antagonistic force that destroys the work. The sculpture is a vestige, matter discarded by time. Smithson subtly ejects the art object outside the lake's ongoing process of rising and falling while acknowledging that activity as the work's premise, thus weaving together the lake and the artwork across their temporal disarticulation. The work thereby achieves maximum wholeness—the spiral shape that emblematizes the passage of time—but also maximum division: the artwork is split apart into texts with no possibility of a reintegration into the vital activity of natural time. More strongly, it points toward the site's temporality as a past duration, as time lost.

Yet it is not enough to say that the sculpture stands as a fait accompli, for as I have suggested, what is most interesting about the work is how it continues to behave with the site's continual changes without being undone by them. With each seasonal emergence, the lake seemingly reconstitutes the sculpture, even building it up with crystals. The opposing temporalities are thus evident in the sculpture's cycle of rising up thick with salt crystals when the lake recedes and then itself receding when the water level rises. In an interview with Gregoire Müller, Smithson discusses at length the transformations of the jetty when it appeared at the end of the summer of 1971 after two months of being submerged in the lake: "The *Jetty* was almost entirely surfaced and almost entirely encrusted with salt crystals. There were various types of salt crystal growth—sometimes the crystals take the form of a perfect square. Then at other times, there is a different kind of mineral that looks like wax dripping on the rocks."[75]

Even more significant is his identification of the sculpture's durable foundation, which stands in tension with natural activity: "The day after I visited the *Jetty* some huge thunderstorms came in and completely dissolved all the crystals and turned the *Jetty* back to naked rock. Its mass was intact because it's almost 80% solid rock, so that it held its shape. Yet at the same time it was affected by the contingencies of nature."[76] As Smithson describes it, the sculpture acts as a yardstick for passing weather systems, varying water levels, and fluctuating elements. It retains its shape though it is embedded in the site. There is an unusual correlation between the positioning of the site's activity as spent time and the consequent cycle of the sculpture's thickening and thinning. The variations on the sculpture's surface continually reformulate its connection to the lake. Given Smithson's correlation of entropy and crystallography, in which he conceived of entropy as leading to a stable condition at the end of temporal flow, the periodic changes to the surface of the sculpture, as well as the work's rise out of and fall back into the lake, point toward a complex interaction between the two realms of dynamic nature and the atemporal artwork.

## The *Spiral Jetty*'s Future Returns

Entropy, for Smithson, does not lead the artwork to fully merge with the site in a mass of homogenous matter. Because it aims to express the loss of time as the pretext of its own origination—an act of swallowing its material of genesis, to use Benjamin's terms—the artwork never degenerates into formlessness but rather is deposited by the lake in its entropic drive forward in time. The question is, what initiates that drive in the first place? The answer lies in the allegorical paradigm—it is the melancholic turn back and the work's vain quest to uncover its lost origin that galvanize the entropic move forward in the first place. The work's orientation toward the elusive lake causes it to expel time, and this consequently pushes the work into a state of entropic stability in an imagined future where it exists as crystallized sediment. Dynamic temporality and the atemporal state are bound to one another across a constitutive rupture that prevents the artwork from devolving back into the site.

It is worth revisiting Benjamin's metaphor of the whirlpool as a figure of allegory's loss of origin in relation to *Spiral Jetty*'s unfulfilled drive to retrieve its preformed condition in the lake. In connection with its desire to hold on to the past, Benjamin describes allegory as melancholic; it is, in a sense, the psychic lens by which history is perceived in ruins. The true vitality of the past is drained out of the historical fragment in the process of being appropriated by the allegorical image. He writes, "If melancholy causes life to flow out of it [the fragment from the past] and it remains behind dead, but eternally secure, then it is exposed to the allegorist, it is unconditionally in his power."[77] The allegorist's desire to cling to the past stimulates an expenditure of its vitality, yielding it to the present by stripping it of life. The philosopher Mick Smith further explains that the melancholic ego wants to hold on to the past by consuming it and fixing it to itself. Yet because the past is irretrievable in its entirety, the inevitable result is that the melancholic withdraws into tragic self-absorption centered on the loss of the past, which in turn causes the present to be envisaged as a realm of decay.[78] Similarly, *Spiral Jetty* situates the Great Salt Lake as a past that it seeks to retrieve. And precisely because its allegorical structure instigates this turn back toward its elusive origin in dynamic time, *Spiral Jetty* propels itself forward to the end of entropy, where it is hard sediment voided of the flow of time.

Smithson's formulation of *Spiral Jetty* as a set of ossified remains, fossils, or geological sediment might at first appear to be an instance of environmental melancholy, for he locates the Great Salt Lake in the prehistoric past. Yet by making the temporal rupture between the artwork and the lake explicit, the artwork slightly alters the melancholy of its allegorical paradigm. Mick Smith points out that allegory offers redemption of a kind because it opens the slightest of gaps between the subject's representation of the object of loss and the object itself. This critical difference is enough to jar the subject out of melancholy, in a revelation of the emptiness left by the lost object. The melancholic can thereby reconcile with the passing of time.[79] It is this potential to distinguish between the artificial image of the object of loss and the object of loss itself that resonates with *Spiral Jetty*.

The sculpture does not appropriate the site strictly in the manner of an allegorical image, for it exposes its own operation of absenting the site. The image of the whirlpool is par excellence the emblem of the loss of origin. In likening the whirlpool to the salt crystal, moreover, *Spiral Jetty* rearticulates the loss of origin as an expulsion of temporality—a loss that is the very condition of its structure and its emergence as art. This internalization of the loss of the temporalized site identifies a break from strict melancholy and a move toward revealing the irreducible elemental forces and temporal dynamism of the site, while not attempting to contain them. The persistence of the artwork exposes its disjunction from the site, and this is further materialized by the accumulation of salt crystals, which gauge time on its surface and underscore the enduring shape of the armature underneath. Though the sculpture accumulates salt over linear time, seemingly advancing into the future, the shape of the spiral reinforces its circling back, coiling in a counterclockwise direction as though back in time. This push forward and pull back is endlessly reenacted by the rising and falling water levels, as first the water recedes, revealing the sculpture covered in crystals in a fulfillment of the frozen state at the end of entropy, and then as the sculpture falls back into the lake as though back to its original state of continuity with the site.

What exists, then, is not a textual inscription of the site, which itself merely erodes. *Spiral Jetty* fails to represent the site but reveals an indexical connection to it in the friction between solid matter and amorphous fluid, crystalline atemporality and dynamic time, a drive into an entropic future and a return to the primordial past. The artwork presents the site by asserting the hard materiality of its limits against the uncontainable dimensions of the site (fluid, light, atmosphere, and temporality). In its retraction from representation, which appears as a drive to seek out its own preformed state, and in the reconfiguration of the artwork into a textual surface that yields the traces of that elemental condition, *Spiral Jetty* radicalizes the possibilities of confronting the earth without suffocating it in preconceived meaning. In this sense, the text is not simply discarded or formless matter; it is receptive to the site and interacts with it. It is this notion of the artwork as a surface of visibility for elementals that has continued in later generations of earth art.

THREE

# Ecotechnology and the Receptive Surface

*Spiral Jetty* does not merely use the earth as a medium of architectonic shaping; that is to say, it is not just a formed space in the land that can be occupied by the spectator. Rather, through textual modes of presenting the site, it reconfigures the dialectic between sites and nonsites (external nature and representation) as an intertwining of elementals. It thus enacts a confrontation between the impenetrable solidity of the earth and the dynamic temporality of water and light, drawing out this tension through textual modes of presentation. Through this overlap of elementals, *Spiral Jetty* demonstrates the earth's impenetrability and its resistance to the unification of form and meaning. Not only does the earth divide itself and thus prevent representation, but this fragmentation occurs in conjunction with an uprise of elemental fluid that induces moments of sensorial saturation. In this way, elementals both constitute and destabilize the textual media of the artwork, delivering sensibility while foreclosing the coherence of words, the visual unity of the image, the seamless continuity of film, and the linearity of time. In short, Smithson articulates the point at which representation fails and thereby stages his own retraction from a presumed immersion in the site. In so doing, he relocates the sensory encounter with elementals onto textual surfaces. What deserves consideration, then, are the questions of what it means to disclose the earth as elemental and how this demands a specifically withdrawn and receptive mode of confrontation.

## Elementals and Ecotechnology

To posit the earth as elemental is to insist on its irreducibility to the human world and to distinguish it from a bounded and intelligible thing. John Sallis outlines the main differences between things and elementals. First, he suggests, elementals are encompassing, by which he means that they are without bounds; they surround things, fill space, and even intersect with one another. The way the sky colors a valley in the dark atmosphere before a storm or the meeting of a choppy sea with a jagged cliff are examples of how, in their overlap, elementals shape and contour environments, while themselves remaining indefinite. Because they manifest as gigantic expanses without proportionality or form, Sallis argues, elementals such as sky, air, light, sea, and earth are opaque.[1] Like Heidegger's allegory of the stone, elementals are fundamentally withdrawn. To attempt to access the essential core of the stone only splits it into equally withdrawn pieces. Similarly, an elemental cannot be known through a penetrating touch or grasped as a tangible thing. Though they are not bound objects, elementals are nevertheless sensible. They present themselves in the perceptual field—they can be seen, touched, smelled, and tasted—but they inevitably engulf and exceed it. We respond to and interact with elementals, but they register through a different mode of contact. Neither image nor object, neither material nor immaterial, and existing in a state between surface and depth, elementals resist the perceptual intention to conceive of the earth environment as a set of things or as a closed system.

What is perhaps most significant about Sallis's elucidation of elementals is his claim that the indeterminacy of elementals complicates the philosophical distinction between sensibility and intelligibility. Indeed, this rupture is an imperative to challenge the distinction between the two and instead seek a living ground for thought.[2] How, then, is the conceptualization of the earth as elemental ethically relevant? The deconstruction of the division between sensibility and intelligibility opens the opportunity for a reconceptualization of the earth itself and of our position in relation to it. Certainly, the earth is a planet, a solitary entity, as well as a source from which all living things issue. To posit the earth itself as elemental, however, is to make an assertion about how we conceive it, or more precisely, how it resists our concepts. It is to suggest that the earth is both all-encompassing (that it surrounds and interpenetrates our world) and at the same time uncontainable, which is to say that it exists outside the human schema of production, consumption, or meaning.

Perhaps, though, something further than the distinction between thing and elemental, intelligibility and sensibility is demanded in the movement toward an ecological consciousness. For while considering the earth's elementality counters an instrumental view of it, the most pressing environmental issues in the public consciousness seem to relate not only to the reaping of the earth's resources (in the mining of oil for example) but also, more importantly, to the concomitant pollution of elementals. Thus, whereas at the end of the twentieth century, anxieties about the excessive production of nonbiodegradable waste ran high (the widely disseminated footage of heaps of diapers being tipped into landfills by dump trucks figured largely at this time), at the beginning of the twenty-first, the most central issues have been the contamination of air because of greenhouse-gas emissions, the changing atmosphere because of global warming, and massive oil spills and other toxic dumping in bodies of water. It seems that elementals themselves can in fact be probed and tainted by industry.

In his essay "The Question Concerning Technology," Heidegger describes the subjugation of the earth as an unconcealment by which it is harnessed as a "standing reserve" of vital energies. Modern technology, he argues, sets upon the earth, unlocking, exposing, and unrelentingly stockpiling it. The earth is mined for ore (such as uranium), the air for nitrogen, the soil for mineral deposits, and water for electricity. He writes, "Everywhere everything is ordered to stand by, to be immediately at hand, indeed to stand there just so that it may be on call for a further ordering." When nature is unlocked and stored as standing reserve, it "no longer stands over against us as object."[3] What is lost for Heidegger, it seems, is not so much the "thingness" of the earth as the quality of remove that elementals present in their ability to stand over and against us. In a similar vein, Jean-Luc Nancy describes the predicament of *ecotechnology.* He suggests that "natural life" (human, animal, vegetal, and viral) and the discourses that frame nature are inseparable from a set of technological conditions that are produced for us and by us.[4] That is to say, natural life is not autoproduced or automaintained; it is always already produced by the technologies that manage it, and always for human purposes. Thus, there is no nature that is not thought *through* ecotechnology, through a reductive biological model, through conservation, resource management, sustainability, or environmental crisis, or in short, through a human-oriented framework. Nature is constituted by technological processes of denaturalization.

For both Heidegger and Nancy, however, there is a saving power in the questioning of technology. Technology unconceals the earth in order to instrumentalize it, yet Heidegger suggests that it enables a "coming to presence of truth." Thus, ecotechnology exposes the earth as resource, but it also brings forth the idea of nature, or the "truth" of the elemental earth. These two facets, the unconcealment of nature through apparatuses of ecotechnology and the revealing of the elemental earth, "draw past each other like the paths of two stars in the course of the heavens. But precisely this, their passing by, is the hidden side of their nearness."[5] That is to say, the truth of nature brushes against the machinations of ecotechnology; the unconcealment of the earth as standing reserve happens in tandem with the revealing of it as elemental. The trenchant questioning of ecotechnological apparatuses, then, opens a window of opportunity to understand how the earth exists on its own terms. Thus, the turn to the elemental is not a move "back to nature"; instead, as Sallis suggests, it is "a turn to that in nature which exceeds nature, toward that which, itself of nature, is nonetheless beyond the things of nature to such an extent as to constitute the encompassing elements within which, coming to pass, things show themselves."[6]

For Heidegger, art holds the potential to question technology and possesses the saving power to reveal truth. In ancient Greece, he notes, the fine arts were also called *techne.* However, "the arts were not derived from the artistic. Art works were not enjoyed aesthetically. Art was not a sector of cultural activity. . . . Why did art bear the modest name *techne*? Because it was a revealing brought forth and hither, and therefore belonged within *poiesis.*"[7] In its conjoining of *techne* and *poiesis,* art is the agent of the questioning of technology and is thus the locus of the coming to presence of truth. "Because the essence of technology is nothing technological, essential reflection upon technology and decisive confrontation with it must happen in a realm that is, on the one hand, akin to the essence of technology and, on the other, fundamentally different from it. Such a realm is art."[8]

Interestingly, in his shift from demonstrating how modern technology is an all-pervasive "Enframement" that reduces nature to a standing reserve, to his definition of art as *poiesis,* as that which presences the truth of technology, Heidegger mobilizes a certain mode of being in relation to the earth. He writes, "The same poet from whom we heard the words, *But where danger is, grows the saving power also,* says to us, . . . *poetically dwells man upon this earth.*"[9] Thus, Heidegger considers the poetic instrument of art as a particular way of dwelling on earth that is distinct from the "setting upon" nature of technological enframement. Heidegger affirms this contrast when he describes technology as an "irresistible ordering," as opposed to the "restraint of the saving power" of art.[10] It is particularly noticeable that he describes *poiesis* both as restraint and as a means of revealing truth. It is as though withdrawal from technology is the very mechanism that lets art question it and reveal its underlying truth. This is not to suggest, all too optimistically, that art can step outside enframement; rather, it is to suggest that art can step back from within it, as a way to face it. Significantly then, the movement of retraction that initiates a revealing of technology corresponds to a poetic dwelling *on* (or perhaps *with*) the earth, as opposed to a dwelling *within* the earth. Art occupies an intermediary zone between the opacity of the elemental and the impulse to occupy and order. Or perhaps more aptly, it enables that intermediary zone, and reveals that opacity.

That contemporary artists facilitate a sense of the elemental earth, therefore, does not simply mean that they create the artwork from nature or aspire to forge a circuitry between natural activity and embodied experience. Rather, they use the artwork to articulate an involution in, and a turn to face, the earth in order to extricate the spectator from the presumed continuity between the body and "nature."

Many contemporary artists problematize the perception of elementals by, on the one hand, fabricating immersive situations for the spectator but, on the other, presenting natural phenomena through the assertion of seemingly opaque surfaces. As artist James Turrell writes, "My interest in the perception of light is in giving it *thingness.* It exists just as a physical object has presence. I make *thingness* of perception by putting limits on it in a formal manner."[11] In keeping with John Sallis's argument that the philosophical turn toward the elemental earth involves a deconstruction of the distinction between the sensible and the intelligible, it is important to note that Turrell's statement involves not making elementals into bound things but rather giving them thingness, or presence. As the artist frequently describes, his artworks often generate the desire to touch light but frustrate that desire since light cannot be delivered as an object. To present the elemental, then, is to bring the spectator into contact with it at the limits of perception and to keep it at that limit, where sensibility arises and then dissipates.

It is also worth remarking, however, that in order to forge this noninvasive contact, Turrell insists that making thingness involves the construction of a formal limit. By this, he means not that he is attempting to contain light as a formal thing but rather that he designs a threshold to it. The difference is important, for in their indeterminacy and depth, elementals defy objective form. They do, however, as Sallis points out, disclose one another in their concurrence.[12] The sea, he argues, is an elemental opposite to the earth, for while the earth's elemental quality is its support of all things (from which all other support is somehow borrowed), the sea essentially does not provide support. However, it divides and articulates the earth's surface, and thus, in their mutually contrasting qualities, earth and sea reveal one another. Similarly, he suggests that the sky, in its seemingly unlimited height and expanse, formulates a horizon in its overlap with the earth, against and through which all things that issue from the earth "shine forth."[13] The formal limit that Turrell so succinctly describes, then, is a device by which to draw attention to, or even reconstruct, the overlap of elementals. It is the means by which to disclose rather than enclose them.

It is this assertion of a limit that corresponds to the ethical gesture of retraction. That is to say, by presenting the elemental as a surface, contemporary artists open contact with the earth's alterity. This may seem at first a counterintuitive approach to earth art. Certainly, the three artists that I am about to consider, James Turrell, Chris Drury, and Olafur Eliasson, are known for the way their artworks surround spectators—be it in an ambient chamber, an earthen structure, or an installation situation—and confront them with elementals such as light (natural, artificial, colored, or reflected), water, and sky. However, in each case, elementals appear at a point of division, such as a quasi-solid plane of color or a wall of reflected light—partitions that resist a penetrating look or touch and thereby expose the limits of the perceptual field. Their artworks thus undertake a gravitation into the elemental and a withdrawal from within it. Otherwise put, the artworks surround the viewer but also demarcate a surface of presentation for elementals, thus demanding the viewer's retraction in order to demarcate a surface of visibility for the elemental.

The potential of the elemental to destabilize the insularity of human thinking has long been the subject of Irigaray's writing, particularly in her critiques of phenomenology and ethics. Indeed, for Irigaray all intersubjective relations are situated within elemental phenomena such as light, water, and air. Her work invites us, however, to consider what part elementals play in developing an ethical stance toward the earth itself. If elementals afford a sense of alterity, is it possible that they could also evoke an ethical mode of contact with the earth? Perhaps the most pertinent issue that Irigaray's ethics raise is the way in which elementals both call attention to and disrupt embodied perception. Specifically, her work challenges the presumed reversibility of the senses of vision and touch and, more strongly, posits a different *mode* of sensation.

The critical necessity of acknowledging the excess of the other and of the world underpins Irigaray's critique of Merleau-Ponty's ontology of the flesh. Irigaray argues that Merleau-Ponty never delineates a recognizable distinction between oneself and the flesh of the world, so that the phenomenological subject exists in a state of primordial indeterminacy akin to intrauterine nesting. He therefore does not identify a point of birth and separation from the visible world. Perception occurs in a "fog" or "mist" of the seer's intentions, and the external world becomes a landscape of the maternal body to which the subject has unencumbered tactile access. Since the subject is in this incorporated state, she or he never really sees the world and others in it. Correspondingly, the subject is never seen through the eyes of the other and is thus never privy to a truly reciprocal exchange. Irigaray remarks, "According to Merleau-Ponty, energy plays itself out in the backward-and-forward motion of a loom. But weaving the visible and my look in this way, I could just as well say that I close them off from myself. The texture becomes increasingly tight, taking me into it, sheltering me there but imprisoning me as well." Irigaray maintains that if there is no recognition of the necessary process of differentiation, then a model of perception based on solipsism results. The subject "never emerges from an osmosis that allows him to say to the other . . . 'What sort of event do we represent for each other when together?' . . . The phenomenology of the flesh that Merleau-Ponty attempts is without question(s)."[14] All sensation becomes translated into "Sameness" and merely fulfills one's perceptual expectations, so that no true understanding of difference can register. Without a fundamental separation from the world, the subject does not enter it but is always absorbed in a totalizing physical perception of it from within.

Above all, Irigaray insists that in order to truly open oneself to the other and the world, the subject must create distance and space by receding from that other and that world. Though one is attracted to difference and driven to explore it, the only way to support this otherness and forge a path of communicability and intimacy is via the subject's separation and gathering back. Otherness is thereby protected by the growth of distance and time that the withdrawal of the subject generates:

> The beloved [the other] is sheltered in the silence of the heart, in the mystery of thinking, in the restraint of the gesture, its inward gathering, and a self-touching guaranteeing a possible safeguarding of the other and of the world. . . . In order to be able to welcome the other, a certain fullness must be restored, which escapes the control of a will. Time is indispensable for such a reconsti-

tution which will permit the memory of oneself, of the other, of their difference and of their approach.[15]

Irigaray thereby calls for a retracted mode of being that leads to an opening of the senses. By insisting on an involution from within the precognitive state of immersion and on a recognition that the subject is delineated from the other, Irigaray suggests that the partition of difference prevents the covering of the other's expression and opens "a screen of resting before and after seeing, a reserve for new landscapes, new lights, a punctuation in which the eyes reconstitute for themselves the frame, the screen, the horizon of vision."[16] Moreover, she reintroduces the elemental as the medium of alterity, "the object of wonder or attraction" that remains unable "to delimit, impose, identify . . . the atmosphere, the sky, the sea, the sun."[17] As we shall see, this "screen of resting" that delivers a sense of alterity materializes in the various surfaces of visibility on which the elemental appears in contemporary art.

Contemporary art produces a retracted mode of perception and a radicalization of the senses, thus conceiving of an ethical relationship to the earth through the aesthetics of the elemental. The sensorial experience of artworks such as those offered by Turrell, Drury, and Eliasson, moreover, correspond in many ways to the aesthetic of the sublime. That is to say, they involve both a recognition of the earth's excess and an opening of the senses at the limits of intelligible form. Whereas traditionally, and particularly since Kant's "Analytic of the Sublime," the sublime was considered to be an experience (both painful and pleasurable) resulting from the meeting of the limits of the imagination and the limitlessness of reason, certain aspects of the sublime are revived in the discourse of alterity that Irigaray proposes. Particularly in her elaboration of the other in elemental terms, as an object of wonder that remains impossible to grasp, Irigaray's philosophy brings the sublime to bear on the encounter with the other's excess. Further, her insistence on the sensorial and elemental dimensions of the other as sublime relates to the overturning of the distinction between sensibility and intelligibility.

In Nancy's work, the sublime is the dramatic overflow of sense that takes place at the limit of form, the point at which thinking breaks free of representation. As he describes, the sublime is the sensation of the fading of the sensible. He writes,

"Stretched to the limit, the limit (the contour of the figure) is stretched to the breaking point, as one says, and it in fact does break, dividing itself in the instant between two borders, the border of the figure and its unlimited unbordering. Sublime presentation is the feeling of this striving at the instant of rupture, the imagination still for an instant sensible to itself although no longer itself, in extreme tension and distension ('overflowing' or 'abyss')."[18] If art is to be considered in terms of how it forges a contact with the alterity of the earth, then it is important to consider its relationship to the sublime, for, as Nancy argues, what is at stake in the sublime is the *end* of art, in that it enacts the suspension of art at the point at which art gives way to something else (to thought, to truth, to philosophy, or, in Kant's terms, to the supersensible).

As we have seen with Robert Smithson, early earthworks involved not simply an expansion of the space of experience but rather the radicalization of art by opening its boundaries to the infinite horizon of the earth and other elementals. Thus, the artwork releases itself from the insularity of its confines and opens the potential for a consideration of its disavowed elemental basis. Nancy suggests that in the sublime, art becomes something else at this point of release—though, to be precise, it does not become a "thing" at all; it becomes the freedom of thinking unbound from representation. For Irigaray, the limitlessness of thought is precisely the territory of the other's alterity as it overflows the limits of one's visible world. More strongly, the elemental is the condition for the freedom of thinking that allows a sense of the other. I am suggesting that contemporary art deploys the sublime to yield a sense of the earth's excess at the limit of representational form. In opening a threshold between the artwork and the earth, between the sensible and the supersensible, between oneself and the elemental, the sublime recovers a place for aesthetics in art and for art in aesthetics.

## Roden Crater: Thresholds to the Elemental

The work of American artist James Turrell occupies a curious middle ground between early earthworks and more recent installation art. Turrell's famed multimillion-dollar project *Roden Crater*, conceived in 1975 and begun in 1979, has sealed his association with earthwork artists such as Smithson, Michael Heizer, and Walter De Maria. This connection is due partly to the scale of the project and partly to its location in the Painted Desert near Flagstaff, Arizona. With the aid of several donors, including the Dia Foundation for the Arts and a grant from the Guggenheim Foundation, Turrell purchased an inactive volcano that stands at an elevation of 5,415 feet and has a bowl 114 feet deep and 1,100 feet wide, making it perhaps the largest earthwork to date. Yet long before he started *Roden Crater,* Turrell had established a slightly different aesthetic concern with the perception of light. In the sixties, he produced many works that are perhaps best described as ambient spaces: he constructed rooms in such a way as to control their light sources, framing and directing exterior light or cutting it off and then illuminating the room artificially through colored filters. *Roden Crater* can therefore be considered both an environment built into the earth and an ecotechnology that mediates spectacles of light and natural phenomena.

In addition to clearing out the bowl of the volcano and smoothing it into an even elliptical shape, Turrell initiated the construction of several viewing chambers at the crater's base, at the fumarole, at the lip of the bowl, and at its center, thus leading the visitor up and around the crater through a program of vantage points. Unlike earthworks such as Serra's *Shift* or Heizer's *Double Negative,* which blur the lines between sculptural object and architectonic shape, *Roden Crater* behaves as an observatory that directs the spectator toward transient natural activity and celestial phenomena. The subtle distinction is that between an artwork that is formulated through the peripatetic experience (in the case of Serra's and Heizer's works) and an artwork that mediates, and stands as the threshold to, elemental events. To elaborate further, Turrell's practice problematizes the commonly held view that the aim of earthworks is to elicit active and intentional gestures of seeing and interpreting, for his installations and light chambers often require one to stand still, sit, or lie down in a particular place in order to witness a play of light, sound, or atmosphere. This is not to say that the viewer is no longer an active, intentional, embodied being; rather, the artwork disrupts that movement and intention in order to fully open the senses to the elemental (a point to which I shall return).

While for some artists one of the central tenets of earth art is that the spectator must be immersed in the artwork in order to perceive it, Turrell creates a somewhat different scenario with *Roden Crater.* Though the artwork is still essentially a

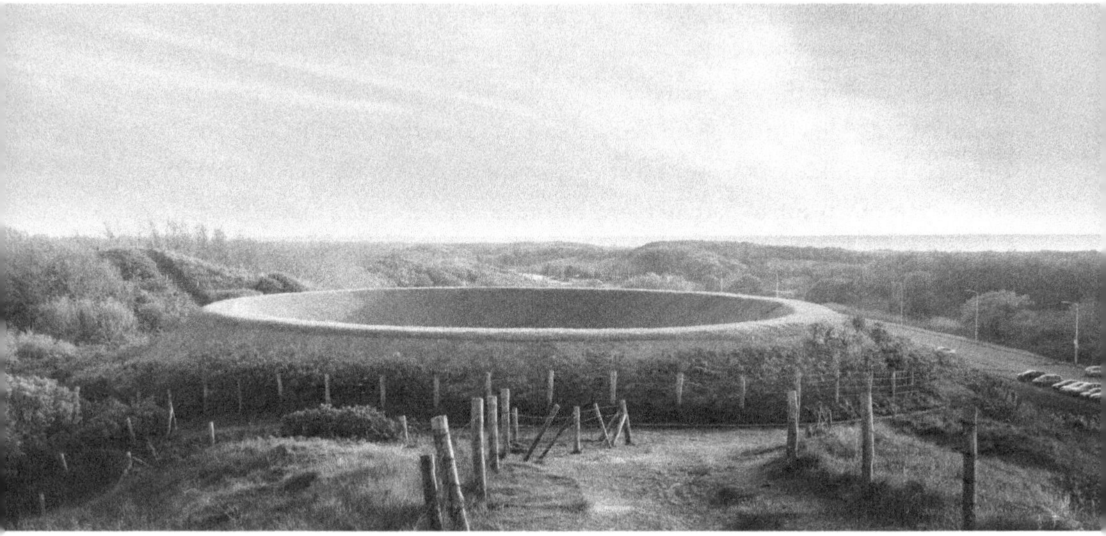

FIGURE 29. James Turrell, *The Celestial Vault in Kijkduin* (The Hague, Netherlands), 1996 (restored 2008). Simulated crater, 30 × 40 × 5 meters. Photograph by Gerrit Schreurs Fotografie. Courtesy of Stroom den Hague.

situation rather than an object (or more precisely, a series of situations), the idea is not to lead the spectator *into* the earth. Quite the opposite: the work has a decidedly skyward orientation. As Turrell states, "I wanted to advance from the floor of the desert up into the sky. I did not want to go up a mountain and down into a hole."[19] He therefore makes a comparison between *Roden Crater* and stupas, the domelike structures found in South and Southeast Asia and associated with Buddhism, which are used as both shrines and pilgrimage sites. A stupa is usually not entered; rather, it is circumambulated, and some, such as Borobudur in Indonesia (ninth century CE), guide the pilgrim up stairways to the top of the structure, signifying an ascent to a greater level of enlightenment in Buddhist cosmology. Similarly, *Roden Crater* takes the viewer through a number of chambers, starting with four at the esplanade of the volcano (one at each of the cardinal directions), then up to the fumarole, which has seven viewing spaces, and finally up a staircase to the tip of the crater bowl. The crater itself is thus not the object of attention; it is a pathway that affords an experience of the desert and sky as one spirals around and

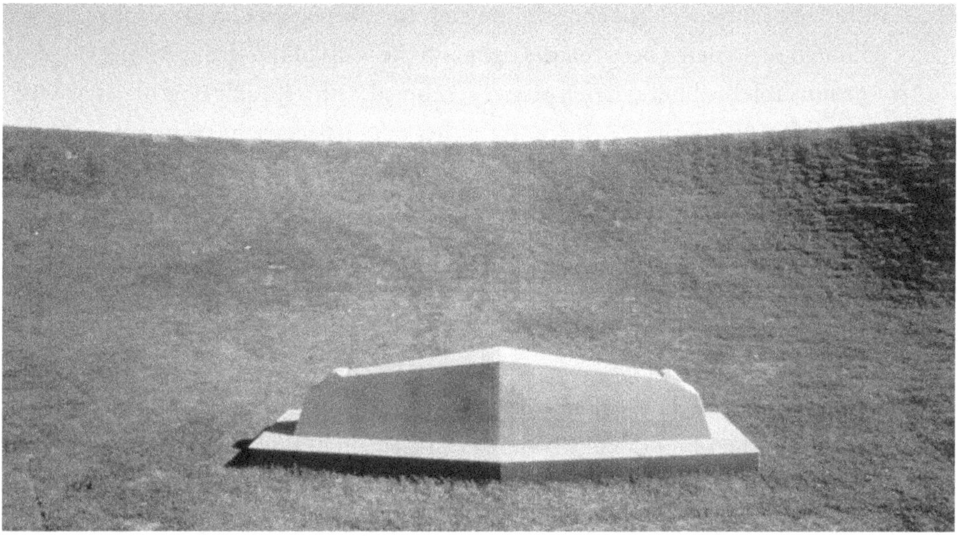

FIGURE 30. James Turrell, *The Celestial Vault in Kijkduin,* central stone slab (The Hague, Netherlands), 1996 (restored 2008). Photograph by Jannes Linders. Courtesy of Stroom den Hague.

up, climbing through portals and passageways, in the tunnels and various pockets of light encrypted in its base and sides. The process of ascent and the propulsion of sight toward the sky replaces a sense of phenomenological entry into the earth. The crater bowl is the final vantage point of the artwork and stands as the apotheosis of what the preceding viewing chambers reveal: the exteriorization of the sky and the earth that occurs at the point of their conjunction.

One might say that each chamber is a microcosm of the overlap and withdrawal of these elementals from one another. The spaces are apertures in the earth that deliver a sense of the sky. At this intermediary zone between elementals, light becomes almost palpable as it pours into the chambers. In part, Turrell designed the chambers to observe rare phenomena such as the green flash that occurs at the margin of the sun's disc just before dawn and just before dusk. The green flash is a result of the scattering of the sun's rays when, under certain weather conditions, the atmosphere is thick with moisture and dust particles absorb red and orange light, scatter blue and violet light, and leave the color green.[20] More than framing these unusual occurrences, though, the viewing chambers create an atmospheric space through the synergy between the light and the walls of the chamber. The spaces at the fumarole are built out of a plaster combined with a specific type of desert sand, chosen because of the way it absorbs rather than reflects light.[21] This allows for an effect of light hanging as though it were a textured and evenly dispersed color that clings to the air. There are two ways to understand this effect: the chamber renders light substantial (or gives it thingness, to use Turrell's term), and the light calls attention to the walls of the chamber, making the materiality and texture of the volcano apparent through the thickening of atmosphere.

In this way, the visitor is immersed in light at the meeting of earth and sky. The sense of being enclosed in an earthen space that is permeated by light, however, changes at the tip of the bowl when both elementals pull back from the eye into their respective closed fields. Turrell explains that when one passes through the tunnel in the fumarole to the crater bowl, the sky opens up and appears to be convex, while the ground below looks concave, seeming to hollow out and bow upward. The effect of celestial vaulting suspends the visitor between the two curvatures; however, there is no definitive suture at the edges of the earth and sky. Despite the previous sense of being enfolded in ambient light in the viewing chambers, at the bowl's interstitial zone, earth and sky repel one another and in so doing disrupt the viewer's "natural" orientation.

This undoing of orientation is in fact integrated into the structure of the bowl. Significantly, Turrell designed four thick beds of granite to be built in the center of the crater bowl to prompt the viewer to lie down for a better view of the dome of the sky. Indeed, this specific positioning of the viewer has been repeated at several other venues that replicate the bowl of the crater, such as *The Celestial Vault in Kijkduin,* in the Netherlands, built in 1996 and renovated in 2008 (Figure 29). In the dunes of The Hague, Turrell constructed a downsized and more accessible elliptical crater bowl. To enter the simulated crater, visitors climb a stairway and pass through a six-foot-long concrete passageway that opens out to the grassy field. As at *Roden Crater,* the curvature of the bowl precipitates a sense of the upward bow of the sky, an experience that is heightened when the visitor lies down on the large stone slab that sits in the middle of the bowl (Figure 30). Through this disorientation, the boundlessness of the sky stretches the visual field to its furthest reaches.

The eye cannot grasp a landscape but rather is suspended between the sky that balloons upward and the land that bottoms out. Vision overflows as the elementals draw back from one another and prevent the grasp of the eye.

The circumambulation around *Roden Crater* and the orientation toward ascendance thus lays out a sequence of encounters that reveal natural phenomena in their temporality, depth, fullness, and impenetrability, eventually culminating in a presentation of the unlimitedness of both earth and sky. In this way, *Roden Crater* leads one through a filling and priming of the senses in situations that are oriented toward the depth and color of the sky. At the crater bowl, the parameters of the viewing chambers are lifted and brought to the brink of overflow. Craig Adcock describes the experience: "At night, inside the reshaped Crater Bowl, this immensity will be a velvet black vault of space populated with thousands of stars. From the upper rim, on a starry moonless night, we will be able to look into what is probably the maximum amount of space visually comprehensible. . . . We will be able to observe the maximum number of stars visible to the naked eye."[22] This emphasis on the absolute limits of vision ("the maximum amount of space" and "the maximum number of stars") cues us to the way in which the aesthetic of the sublime accompanies the experience of elementals. As Nancy explains, sublime presentation occurs in an instant that is divided into the feeling of striving at the boundaries of the imagination and an unlimited unbordering and overflow of sense. It is thus experienced as both an extreme tension and distension.[23] Likewise at *Roden Crater*, the viewer is overwhelmed by the feeling of reaching the limits of vision and at the same time by an extreme filling of the eye with the limitless depth of the sky. Again, there is a difference between the phenomenological experience of a thing and the undoing of the visual field in the face of elementals.

By locating the visitor at the very site where elementals meet, overlap, and draw back from one another, Turrell constructs an apparatus of perception that yields the fullness of elementals in their resistance to defined form. Turrell describes his viewing chambers as "apertures," by which we can understand that the artwork not only opens to the sky but also, more strongly, enables an opening of the perceptual field. The artist states, "An experience is not framed so much as a situation is made in which experience can be created. I use the word aperture because it describes an opening that has a purposeful relationship of inside and outside."[24] In other words,

Turrell's goal is to register a sense of the external world differently, not through the assurance of a tactile grasp of light but through the creation of the conditions in which sensation abounds. But these conditions are predicated on a distinct positioning of the body and on a delimitation of the visual field. When the artist says he aims at a "purposeful" relationship of inside and outside, he is describing not a scenario in which the interiorized subject projects her or his intentions outward in order to take hold of sense, but rather a situation in which the subject's intentions are geared toward withholding action and receiving sense at the point of contact between her- or himself and the world.

## Horizontality and Animality in Turrell's *Skyspaces*

Though *Roden Crater* is not yet open to the public, over the past three decades Turrell has constructed many *Skyspaces* that one could think of as adjuncts to the larger project or as microcosmic reproductions of the crater itself. Each *Skyspace* reconstructs the basic situation of the viewing chambers at *Roden Crater*: the visitor enters an enclosed area with an aperture to the sky. Turrell's 2003 project *Light Reign,* at the Henry Art Gallery in Seattle, Washington, is a freestanding elliptical structure with an aperture of the same shape centered in the ceiling. A bench where spectators can sit and look up at the aperture lines the base of an interior wall. The walls of this lower area are built of wood panels, behind which a ring of soft ambient light is emitted, providing a soft contrast to the white surface of the upper chamber and ceiling. Like the chambers embedded in *Roden Crater, Light Reign* can be thought of in terms of the tension between being enclosed in light and looking upward into the simultaneous depth and opacity of the sky. Though the aperture of the installation directs vision upward, at the same time, the curvature of the ceiling and the deep vaulted recess of the aperture give the impression that the color of the sky is a palpable surface that protrudes into (or we might say, looks back at) the chamber. The *Skyspaces* thereby sustain a dialectic between the two trajectories of looking up into the depth of the sky and withdrawing the look as it is rebuffed.

Most noticeable about Turrell's *Skyspaces,* however, is that they demand a rearrangement of bodily orientation and in this way challenge one's mode of visual confrontation. The first thing one observes upon entering a *Skyspace* is that other visitors are either lying down on the benches or sitting with their heads craned upward. Leo Steinberg suggests that stylistic cycles are definable by their built-in idea of the spectator.[25] He argues that in modernism, the concept of pictorial flatness is primarily a function of how the orientation of the image is directed at the spectator's experience, or more precisely, how the pictorial surface tilts into the space of the viewer's imagination. A "natural" perspective, he notes, is one that is oriented toward the viewer's upright, vertical position. Beginning in the Renaissance, a picture would affirm this vertical position of the spectator and would be experienced from a normal, erect posture. Even Jackson Pollock, who executed his drip paintings by pouring paint on a canvas that lay on the ground, would tack the painting up on the wall before it was finished in order to become acquainted with the painting in its upright state.[26] Steinberg posits that a drip painting might be read as a thicket, for this vertical orientation fundamentally recalls a state of nature. Renaissance and abstract expressionist paintings alike acknowledge the same gravitational force.

Steinberg hypothesizes that one of the most significant shifts in the history of modernism occurred in the 1950s, when artworks began to internalize a horizontal, as opposed to a vertical, orientation.[27] Though a painting by Robert Rauschenberg or Jean Dubuffet usually hangs vertically on the wall (Steinberg singles out these two artists in particular), it nevertheless tilts the spectator's psychic address so that she or he is located perpendicular to the image, looking down at it from above. Steinberg's theory of the "flatbed picture plane," a term he borrows from the flatbed printing press, stresses that the horizontal orientation of the painting references the labor of art-making, in contrast to the vertical orientation that was a requisite of the illusion of space and depth in Renaissance perspective. More than this, however, the horizontal orientation marks a new "psychic address," or "mode of imaginative confrontation," which Steinberg summarizes as expressing a shift from nature to culture. By this, he means that whereas a vertically oriented perspective inherently references the upright human posture—a presumably natural position by which the world is seen—horizontality references the domain of work and of those activities that are associated with culture. Horizontality implicates hard surfaces on which the work of art takes place: the studio floor, tabletops, or the workbench. Equally significant is the idea that horizontality is tied to language and the transmission of information: newspapers, charts, maps, or "any receptor surface on which . . . information may be received, printed, impressed."[28] Significantly, in its attentiveness to the coextensiveness of the picture plane with surfaces on which language appears, Steinberg anticipates Craig Owens's claim that the textualization of art is linked to an allegorical impulse.

Though Steinberg associates horizontality with a paradigm shift in art from nature to culture, it might be more accurate to suggest that the correspondence between art and work—one of Steinberg's central preoccupations in this essay—challenges the naturalization of art-making or interpretation. That is to say, horizontality calls into question the artist's position of visual mastery. The artist's goal is not to reproduce or express the world from her or his given perspective but rather to reveal the work involved in coming to grips with (or one might say, finding a ground from which to see) the world. This is achieved not through the assertion of one's assumed bodily stance—and the implicit repetition of this stance in the perspective of the artwork—but by reorienting vision to the register of receptor surfaces. It is important to make this distinction here, because Steinberg's astute observation does not imply the evacuation of "nature" from art in the sense of reiterating a tired binary between the natural realm and the cultural world. Rather, he sees a call for a different way of being and of becoming oriented in one's environment. "Nature" for Steinberg is not the ecological environment as a particular topic of representation but rather one's assumed bodily orientation. His prognosis of a shift toward culture in art involves the overturn of that orientation and is nothing short of the radicalization of art's mode of confrontation with the external world.

This shift is especially pertinent to Turrell's *Skyspaces* for a number of reasons. Though the installations do not locate the spectator looking down at a work (or textual) surface, they do function on a horizontal plane, since the visitor must either lie down on the bench or tilt the head far back. At some *Skyspaces,* such as *Tending (Blue)* at the Nasher Sculpture Center in Dallas, Texas, built in 2003, the walls behind the bench are sloped so that one can lean back. From this perspective, the aperture presents the sky as a surface, and equally the visitor becomes a receptive surface impressed on by the overhanging sky. The physical reorientation toward a horizontal position differs from that of Steinberg's flatbed picture plane in that spectatorship takes place from below looking up. However, this position coincides with the perceived densification and surfacing of the sky into a plane of color. That is to say, the sky becomes voluminous, while at the same time it forms a surface across the enclosure. In *Light Reign,* for example, the elliptical shape of the aperture creates the appearance that a curving screen of color is bending toward the viewer. Turrell explains, "I can make this bowing up and toward you, or I can make it go away from you. That's the skin, sense of surface, or 'glassing up,' that I want to work with."[29] The reorientation of the spectator and the surfacing of the sky work in tandem, and for this reason Turrell says of his practice in general, "First, I am dealing with no object. Perception is the object. Secondly, I am dealing with no image, because I want to avoid associative, symbolic thought. Thirdly, I am dealing with no focus or particular place to look. With no object, no image, no focus, what are you looking at? You are looking at you looking."[30]

The close reassessment of how one perceives, however, does not take place in a vacuous space; it occurs through elementals. Turrell is quick to distinguish himself from other earth artists in that his practice does not mark or change the land; it is specifically concerned with the act of perception. Or more precisely, he considers perception as an act, and further, one that is directed *toward* elemental phenomena. He points out, "I did not make a mark on the surface of the earth. I wanted to employ sunlight, moonlight, and starlight to empower a work of art. Instead of competing with the sunset, I wanted to use it, *to take it in* [my emphasis]. . . . I formed an interior space to be sensitive to that which occurred in the space outside—a sensing space."[31] Interestingly, Turrell identifies his practice as one that, unlike the outwardly expressive act of marking land, provides a space for natural phenomena to enter and become visible. That is to say, the interior spaces are receptive to the external world; they literally receive light as a volume and in so doing engender sensitivity to it. Also, we can note that while Turrell insists that *perception* is the object of his practice in general, when he describes his installations and the effect, he defaults to the notion of a "*sensing* space." That is to say that sensing in the *Skyspace* is a different mode of confrontation than the perception of intelligible things. Further, I would posit that sensation is enabled by the distinctly recessive orientation that the space mediates.

Evidently, horizontality invigorates the viewer's receptivity to sense in Turrell's

*Skyspaces.* But what exactly are the implications of horizontality? And how do the *Skyspaces* relate to Turrell's *Ganzfeld* works from the late sixties and to his more recent colored light installations that are viewed from an upright position? It appears that even in the *Ganzfeld* pieces and installations, Turrell complicates the penetrating intention of vision through a precise localization of the body, so that the visitor is often suspended in place and thereby gleans sense because her or his movement is impeded. The horizontal position of the spectator in the *Skyspaces* and *Roden Crater* therefore appears to be an extension of this original goal of immobilizing the viewer.

For *Danaë, Blue* at the Mattress Factory museum in Pittsburgh, Pennsylvania, Turrell creates a central conflict between what the eye perceives as an opaque plane of color and the body's movement through space. For this he made a large recess inside a wall and illuminated the space from above, thus producing a seemingly impenetrable screen. However, if one approaches the wall or inserts a hand in the recess, the screen of light gives way and one feels nothing. There is "a tension from the state of desiring touch or from knowing there is something there to touch but not having done it. . . . The feeling comes with the eyes and the eyes have a feeling as important as physical touch. . . . Here the tension cannot be satisfied by touch and so it is sustained. The eyes do the touching."[32] Turrell thus challenges the communicability between touch and sight, and in so doing he produces a different kind of tactile eye, one that is attuned to the limits, density, and surface of light even though these cannot be relayed through the hand.

The vertical installations thereby suspend the body's movement through space and correspondingly disrupt the "penetration of vision."[33] The *Skyspaces,* however, halt vision by holding the body back, or more accurately, by situating it in a position of supplication—the spectator lies down or leans back and looks up. Whereas in the vertical *Ganzfeld* works the body's progression forward in space causes the dispersal of the plane of color so that one must stand in place and suspend vision in order for the eye to "feel" the color, in the *Skyspaces* physical access to the aperture is impossible because it is situated in the ceiling. The viewer is quite literally grounded in order to see the sky. At the *Kielder Skyspace* (2000) at Cat Cairn near Kielder Village in Northumberland, in fact, the space is actually buried, and one must enter it through a tunnel. In this way, the horizontality of the body is related to its entombment in the ground. Nevertheless, the orientation is still skyward. By drawing the viewer's eye up to the aperture and yet encasing the body in the ground lying down, the *Skyspaces* yield a visual plenitude but immobilize the viewer and thereby prevent a tangible grasp of the sky.

We might consider the alteration of perception at stake in Turrell's work through Giorgio Agamben's account of Heidegger's notion of animality.[34] Agamben explains that for Heidegger, only humans are capable of world-forming. The animal, by contrast, is poor in world, which is to say that it exists in a state of encirclement or captivation in its environment; it is neither being nor nonbeing. Further, the animal is open to its surroundings, but its world remains opaque to it. That is to say, the animal cannot forge a relation with its world and cannot draw out the earth to form it into a ground of thought and meaning. Heidegger gives the example of a worker bee that is simply "given over" to the sun and to the period of its own flight without being able to grasp them as such.[35] The bee is so entirely driven that it is captivated in its behavior, without being able to reflect on or recognize it. He describes the animal's predicament, of being both wholly open to its environment and at the same time in a state of nonreflection, as a way of surrounding itself in a "disinhibiting ring." As Agamben writes, "The animal is *open* to a *closedness* . . . totally delivered over to something that obstinately refuses itself."[36]

Agamben argues, however, that Heidegger conceives the animal's poverty in world as a mode that, in its openness, yields to the abundance of the environment. Heidegger writes that animal life "is a domain which possesses a wealth of being-open of which the human world may know nothing at all."[37] Agamben suggests that the human distinguishes itself from the animal only in that human *Dasein* is "an animal that has *awakened from* its own captivation *to* its own captivation."[38] Agamben argues for a reclamation of the state of animal openness that permits an ejection from the human world, in much the way art, for Heidegger, creates a space of withdrawal within technological enframement. Through the suspension of animality, the human subject "opens a 'free and empty' zone in which life is captured and a-bandoned in a zone of exception."[39]

What is at stake in Agamben's reading of Heidegger is his argument for a human's appropriation of her or his own animality, not to master and govern it by means of technology but rather to abandon oneself to it in order to negotiate a space outside of being, knowledge, technology, or discourse. Animality holds the potential of a denaturalization of the human's relationship to the environment (and in particular to the earth) through a stripping of one's preexisting perceptual mode. Agamben underscores that the perceptual denial of the animal's condition readies a space for the human to be awakened to her or his own animality. For example, he cites the importance of boredom in Heidegger's elucidation of the process of becoming attuned to *Dasein.* Boredom is emptiness, being-held-in-suspense, a condition of being open to a closedness: "In being left empty by profound boredom something vibrates like an echo of that 'essential disruption' that arises in the animal from its being exposed and taken in an 'other' that is, however, never revealed to it as such. For this reason the man who becomes bored finds himself in the 'closest proximity'—even if it is only apparent—to animal captivation."[40] Interestingly, though Agamben's appropriation of animality implies an extrication from the larger perceptual field that defines the human world, animality nevertheless has the promise of delivering an intensified and irrefutable presentness that remains undefinable. Agamben posits that "insofar as the animal knows neither being nor nonbeings, neither open nor closed, it is outside of being; it is outside in an exteriority more external than any open, and inside in an intimacy more internal than any closedness. To let the animal be would then mean to let it be *outside of being.* . . . It is an existing, real thing that has gone beyond the difference between being and beings."[41]

In connection with Agamben's insistence on the importance of withdrawing from the totalizing perception of the human world into a state of suspended animality, we might reconsider Turrell's *Skyspaces* as precisely this kind of undoing of perceptual expectations in order to elicit an abandonment to the animal's radical exteriority and profound intimacy. From this perspective, the spectator's horizontality corresponds to the overturn of "natural" verticality (which we might associate with the entry into a state of world-forming) to a physical posture of abandonment. The human world is delayed; the environment is not divided into graspable things and instead is reconceived in terms of elementals that close against the senses. It is this closedness, or "disconcealment," of the environment that makes the sky appear through the aperture as opaque, or, in Turrell's terms, as a *skin.* Indeed, the aperture itself literalizes the notion of an opening to closedness that Agamben describes. Where Merleau-Ponty situates the subject as interpenetrated within the world-flesh, here Turrell reconfigures the viewer's position to one of both intimacy (inside an earthen chamber) and exteriority (the surfacing of world-flesh into elemental skin).

It may be argued that Turrell is less concerned with an ecological position than with "pure light" and elementals. However, it is certain that even his gallery installations are preoccupied with a retracted mode of perception that can be read in relation to *Roden Crater* and his *Skyspaces* and can thus be understood in terms of the ethical impetus of earth art. What I have identified as the process of "unworlding" perception and eliciting the abandonment of the viewer to elementals is played out in Turrell's *Perceptual Cells,* a set of built structures set in the gallery. Two in particular can be read as coextensive: *Soft Cell* (1992) and *Gasworks* (1993). In *Soft Cell,* the visitor enters a closetlike enclosure that is covered in black anechoic foam and is completely dark and soundproof. Turrell explains that when one remains inside one of his dark spaces, the difference between having one's eyes open and closed starts to narrow. Without a confirmed sense of closed interiority or remove from the external surroundings, the viewer experiences a hiatus between the mind and the environment—like a state of insomnia between sleep and wakefulness, or in Heidegger's terms, between being and nonbeing. Only after ten or fifteen minutes of this sensory deprivation can the viewer begin to distinguish a barely perceptible beam of light projected on the wall ahead. *Gasworks* institutes a similar condition; however, the disorientation of the viewer is caused by an abundance of color rather than by absolute darkness. Significantly, for this piece the visitor must *lie down* on a bed that slides into a spherical chamber twelve feet in diameter (the shape of a gas tank) that is illuminated with colored light. Surrounded in this way, the visitor loses the capacity to perceive depth.

The *Perceptual Cells* are immersive situations that undo the preexisting perceptual apparatus by closing off the spectator's surroundings and establishing sensorial deprivation or overload. More than this, they confound a hard-and-fast distinction between depth and surface, interiority and exteriority, a thing and an elemental medium, intelligibility and sensibility. They thereby summarize the destabilization and reorientation of the viewing subject that is required for the ethical encounter Turrell attempts in *Roden Crater* and the *Skyspaces.*

What is at stake in Turrell's oeuvre, then, is a retracted mode of perception, which opens the spectator to the closedness of the earth. Sensation occurs at this opening to the elemental. In this way, it is not surprising that Turrell refers to the planes of color in his works as "skins," for skin seals off the subject and culls sense, not merely in its brush against other surfaces but also in its ability to feel nebulous qualities of the surrounding environment such as warmth, cold, humidity, dryness, movement, and so forth. In short, skin is receptive to external nature without binding it into a fixed set of things. Turrell designs the aperture with this receptivity in mind, mobilizing it as a skinlike surface that receives and makes visible the manifestation of the elemental. Thus, while his works enact the withdrawal of the viewer (into the earth, into chambers, or into specially designed cells), often from a position of horizontal abandonment, a critical aspect of the artworks is also the surfaces on which elementals appear, or perhaps better put, the surfacing of the elemental. If, as Irigaray suggests, the withdrawal of the subject creates a space that shelters otherness, then the surface of appearance mediates between that space and sensation.

## Chris Drury's Camera Obscuras and the Receptive Image

The use of prephotographic techniques in contemporary earth art, such as the camera obscura, translates this surface of appearance more directly into a pictorial surface. The camera obscura is an optical device, ranging in size from a portable black box to a freestanding chamber, in which light passes through a hole and projects an upside-down image of the surrounding space onto a surface inside. Through the use of lenses, the image can be turned right side up or projected onto drawing paper (or some other "work surface"). In the mid-nineties, the British artist Chris Drury incorporated the camera obscura into his site-specific structures. In the early eighties, before he started using this technology, Drury executed a series of shelters, which he built most often in remote or wild environments. Fabricated out of branches, sticks, turf, grass, or whatever materials were available, Drury wove his shelters into the site. The artist conceived the shelters, however, not only as spaces of human dwelling but also, more conceptually, as means of opening a space for nature to dwell within the imagination. The shelter creates an inner sanctuary that frames a view of the exterior landscape. Drury says of these two contrasting

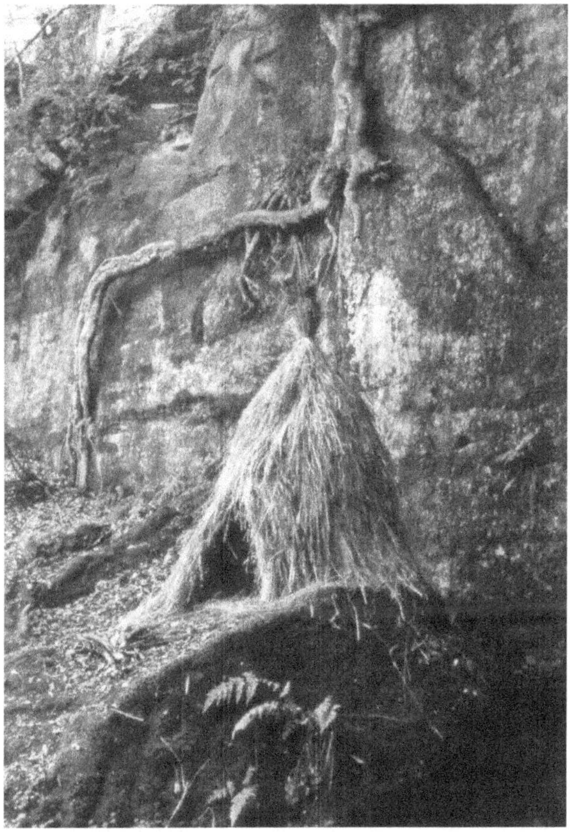

FIGURE 31. Chris Drury, *Shelter for the Forest Deer*, 1987. Sheffield Forest. Heather branches, grass. Courtesy of the artist.

perspectives, "I like the way that a shelter has an interior and an exterior. . . . I like the way this interior space draws you inside yourself, enclosing, protecting, just as mountains pull you outside yourself, pushing mind and body beyond their usual confines."[42] The artist thus describes two diverging trajectories: a drawing in of the spectator prompted by the physical enclosure and a pull from outside one's boundaries, which stretches the limits of what one can see. Like a reversible carapace, the shelter thus navigates a dialogue between interiority and exteriority, intertwining the visitor and external nature.

Much like Richard Long's marks on the land on his performance walks, Drury's shelters exist as an index of presence at the site. These shelters, he says, "may be tucked round the corner from houses or villages. . . . To those who discover the structures, they are like mushrooms that have sprung up overnight; in time they will rot back into the earth."[43] By the late eighties, Drury was demonstrating a subtle shift in his understanding of the shelter as a trace of human presence, considering it instead as a space offered *to* the site and correspondingly as an invitation for nature to dwell within the introspective space that the shelter cultivates. In *Shelter for the Forest Deer* (Figure 31) and similar projects such as *Shelter for the Trees* and *Shelter for the Northern Glaciers,* the artist built a place for natural phenomena, events, and other creatures, as the titles suggest. Though the shelters, like Turrell's chambers, function as apertures to the landscape, the act of offering a shelter inverts its function as a device for looking at nature and becomes an apparatus for drawing nature in. The shelter therefore doubles as a place for humans to be surrounded in, but not overrun by, the infinite expanse of the landscape and as a place for nature to thrive within the interior space of the subject, sheltered from a totalizing knowledge of it.

The artwork's way of enveloping and creating space for the subject in the elemental and for elemental phenomena in the subject materializes a tension inherent in the chiasmatic relation. Irigaray describes this tension as a rhythm in which one advances toward the other in desire and returns to oneself in wonder. She writes, "In the chiasmus . . . a presence unfolds that I could not anticipate through a logos already existing for me, nor in the absolute. . . . From the other irradiates a truth which we can receive without its source being visible. . . . [That meaning] remains a mystery for us but we can indirectly perceive something of it. . . . It says nothing in a way, pronounces no word but makes clear the limits of a horizon, of a site of thinking, of existing, of Being."[44] At the heart of Irigaray's project is another way of seeing and perceiving the other: not just as darkness and invisibility, but over distance and through difference; from across a breathing space that opens up the dense musculature of Merleau-Ponty's flesh ontology. The ethical feeling for the other, in Irigaray's words, "delivers them from the opacity of the night while still arranging nothing—only the unfolding of another manner of looking at the real. . . . It keeps alive the astonishment, the questioning, the movement of thinking."[45]

This opening to a way of seeing the earth without arranging it into a preconceived image is at stake in Drury's works of the mid-nineties, in which the artist refigures the shelter as a camera obscura. Drury transposed the alternating movement

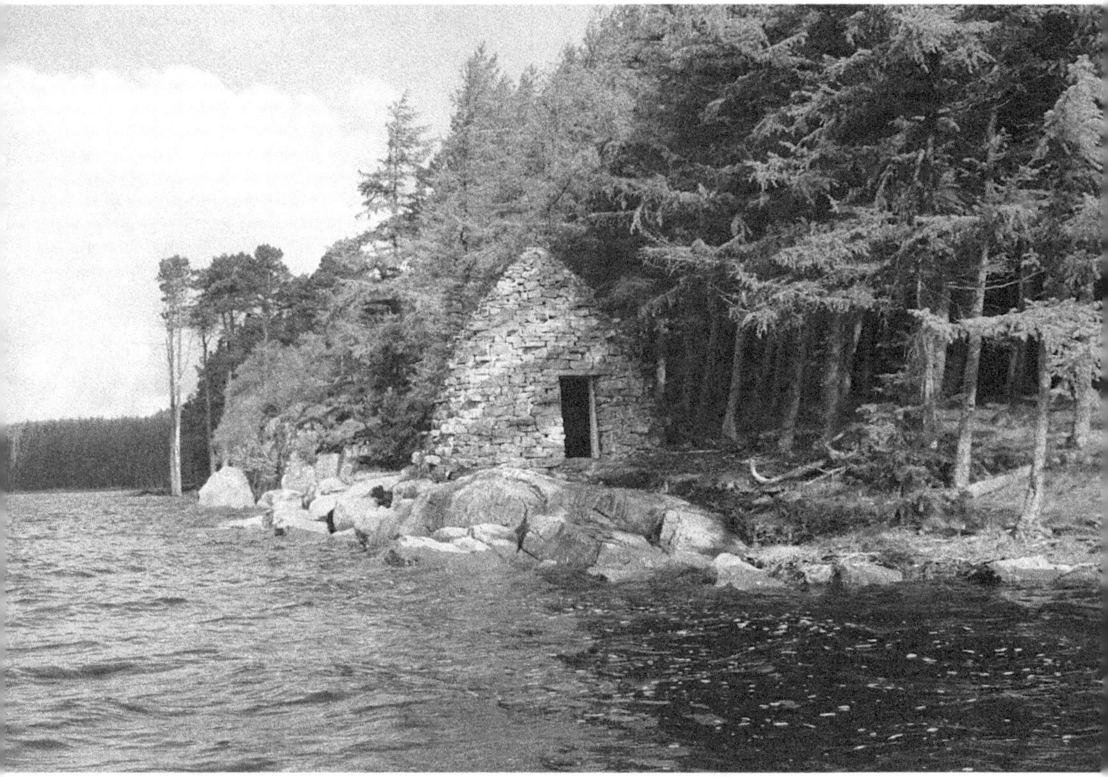

FIGURE 32. Chris Drury, *Wave Chamber,* 1996. Kielder Reservoir, Northumberland. Dry stone and mirror with lens in steel periscope. Courtesy of the artist.

between interior and exterior into an interplay between a two-dimensional image of the outside environment and the enclosed space of the shelter in which the image is viewed. By situating the visitor in a dark earthen space within a structure of rock, wood, dirt, and branches, the chamber produces an intensified awareness of being enclosed in the site. But in addition to this immersive situation, Drury adds a pictorial dimension by placing a periscope lens at the top of the structure and projecting a reflected image of either the sky, water, or the surrounding vegetation onto the ground. In *Wave Chamber* (Figure 32) for example, Drury built the camera obscura along the rocky shoreline of the Kielder Reservoir in Northumberland and focused the periscope entirely on the water. A reflection, replete with movement,

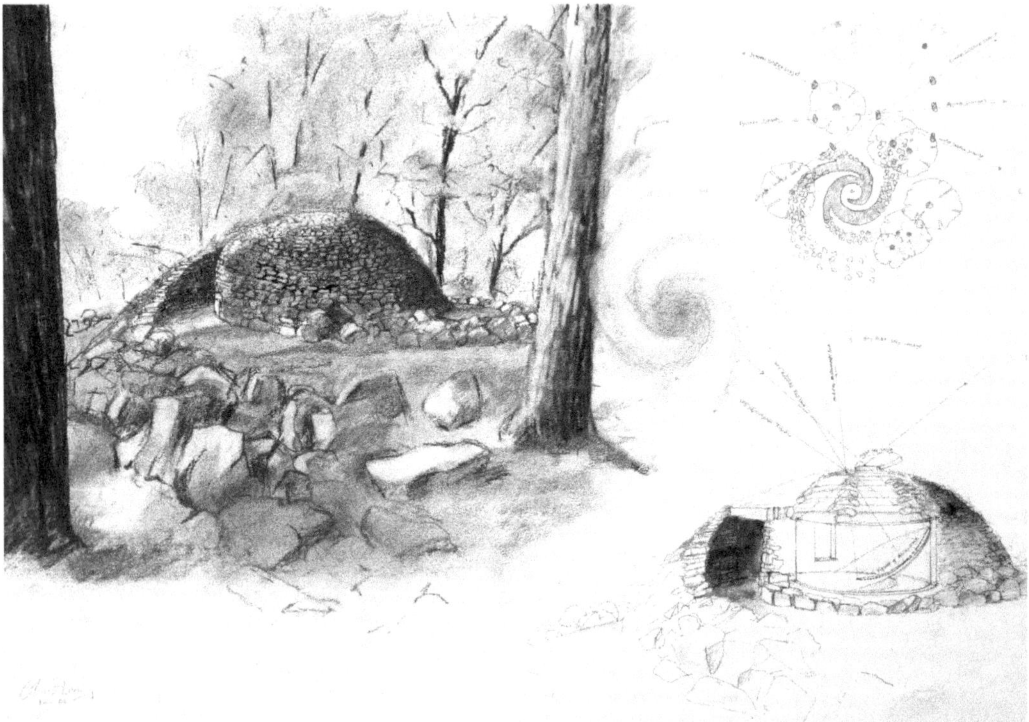

color, and texture, moves across the floor with a vaporous quality. Drury remarks of the *Wave Chamber,* "I really didn't know if it would work until the point when we put the door on and the inside went dark. At that moment the afternoon sun was hitting the water just where the mirror was angled. Inside it was as if a thousand silver coins were dancing across the floor. As the sun moved away, this changed to ghostly ripples, giving you the feeling of standing on liquid."[46] The camera obscura thereby disintegrates and reconstitutes the site within the chamber in the tenuous form of echoes and reflections.

In another camera obscura work, the *Star Chamber* at Dyer Observatory at Vanderbilt University, Drury designed the chamber as a kind of vortex that siphons off a pocket of darkness at the end of a spiraling passage (Figure 33). The exterior is built out of two hundred tons of limestone and provides a durable shell around the interior chamber. The roof is an octagonal dome made of oak logs that surround

*opposite*
FIGURE 33. Chris Drury, *Star Chamber,* diagram, 2006. Dyer Observatory, Vanderbilt University. Courtesy of the artist.

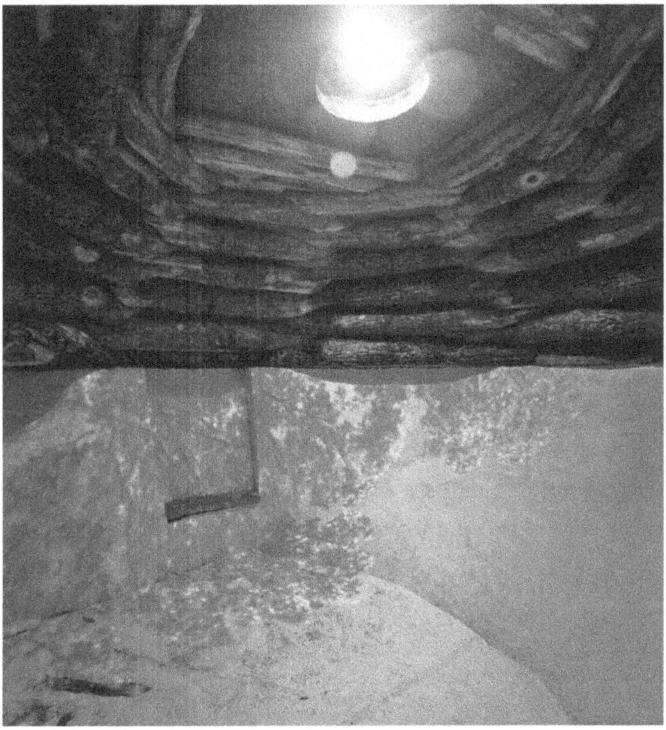

FIGURE 34. Chris Drury, *Star Chamber,* interior, 2006. Courtesy of the artist.

a metal plate and an aperture that is opened at night. During the day, a lens from the lid of the dome projects images of the surrounding trees and sky onto the dish-shaped plaster floor (Figure 34). In addition, Drury embedded an analema shape made out of glass in the plaster. The vertical figure eight traces out the path of the sun as the earth orbits around it over the course of the year. Acting as a calendar, the glass analema tracks the earth's elliptical rotations as it reflects the changing position of the sunlight, marking equinoxes when light hits the cross of the analema and the summer and winter solstices when it strikes the top and bottom. Like Agamben's animal that is open to the closedness of its environment, Drury's camera obscuras show how an opening to external nature is predicated on the limitation and concentration of the perceptual field. The camera obscuras curb the penetrating eye by closing off a view of the landscape as one enters the chamber. Instead of an open vista, the observatory instead provides a surface on which a visual spectacle of natural phenomena appears through the periscope image. Because the visitor experiences the site as weightless, in transient currents of light and sound, elemental presence resists the transition from sensation to intelligible image.

Jonathan Crary has argued that from the sixteenth century onward, the camera obscura was implicated in a metaphysic of interiority, whereby the body of the observer is rendered ambiguous and vision decorporealized.[47] However, Drury elaborates his chambers out of an entirely different framework, by which the chamber is not the premise for mind–body dualism but the condition for the perception of the encompassing quality of earth and the fluid movement of other elementals such as light and water. Vision is not delivered from the body to a coherent abstraction, as Crary suggests of the camera obscura. Though the inner chamber ostensibly detaches the visitor from the surrounding site, this is not to suggest that bodily perception has been nullified or that the artist is striving for a disembodied perspective. Instead, the wave chamber saturates the senses with an abundance of natural phenomena in flux. Drury thus complicates a vertical pictorial mode of confrontation by providing an image that not only is on the ground but also changes unpredictably in rhythm and intensity. The image denies the closure of the perceptual intention that characterizes Merleau-Ponty's description of the eye as a quasi hand that "envelops" and "palpates" its object of attention.[48]

Drury's camera obscuras are not apparatuses that discipline vision into seeing the environment as coherent and stable. They neither enforce the primacy of vision in a disembodied subject nor mechanize external nature. And though they are located in particular sites and attune the visitor to those particular places, what is of interest in the shelters and camera obscuras is not the places in which they are located but the way they cultivate the viewer's receptivity to the natural phenomena there. The central question is thus no longer about the artificiality of human technology and the "naturalness" of the site, a binary that is as inadequate for the trajectory of earth art as that between the virtual and the actual. Rather, more as in Nancy's notion of ecotechnology, the camera obscura functions as an apparatus that defines nature through the denaturalization of the technological apparatus. Here, though, the camera obscura produces a sense of natural phenomena while challenging visual mastery through the dispersed and transient image reflection. Drury's work shows that the ethical question is how the artwork as "biomachine"—where the natural is relayed through the technological—challenges the ideological underpinnings of the enframement of the earth as a standing reserve through the relocation of perception to a receptive surface.

## Olafur Eliasson and the Periphery of Vision

The work of Olafur Eliasson is pertinent in this regard, both because he constructs installations that mediate an experience of natural phenomena and because his works question the spectator's perceptual mode. What is perhaps most often remarked upon about Eliasson's works is that they expose their own technological (constructed or artificial) qualities, though they are often centered on elemental activity such as rainbows, waterfalls, vegetal growth, and the movement and color of light. The goal is therefore not to recover nature in a disenchanted modern environment but rather to show how technology might be redirected toward the destabilization of habitual ways of perceiving natural events and can be the basis of a sensitive interaction with the earth. The givenness of nature is therefore no longer assumed, and concomitantly, the notion of nature as the foundation of an environment becomes uncertain. Again, the idea of the "site" of art gives way to the more mobile idea of an encounter with elementals, which is not to say that elementals are merely the medium through which the artwork takes place but that they are that to which and against which perception is directed.

For *The mediated motion,* for example, Eliasson transformed the exhibition spaces on three floors of the Kunsthaus Bregenz in Austria. Leading the visitor along a constructed pathway through each room and up the flights of stairs that conjoined them, the artist created a prescribed set of conditions through which to confront elementals, specifically water, earth, and air (in the form of fog). The installation thus confined and directed the spectator's movement, or more precisely, posited the elemental as an obstacle to this movement. In their presentation of each elemental, the rooms of *The mediated motion* had an accompanying set of physical constraints that became more evident in the progression through the exhibition. It began with a flight of stairs from the lobby of the Kunsthaus Bregenz to a room where the floor was covered by a shallow pool of water coated by a layer of duckweed (Figure

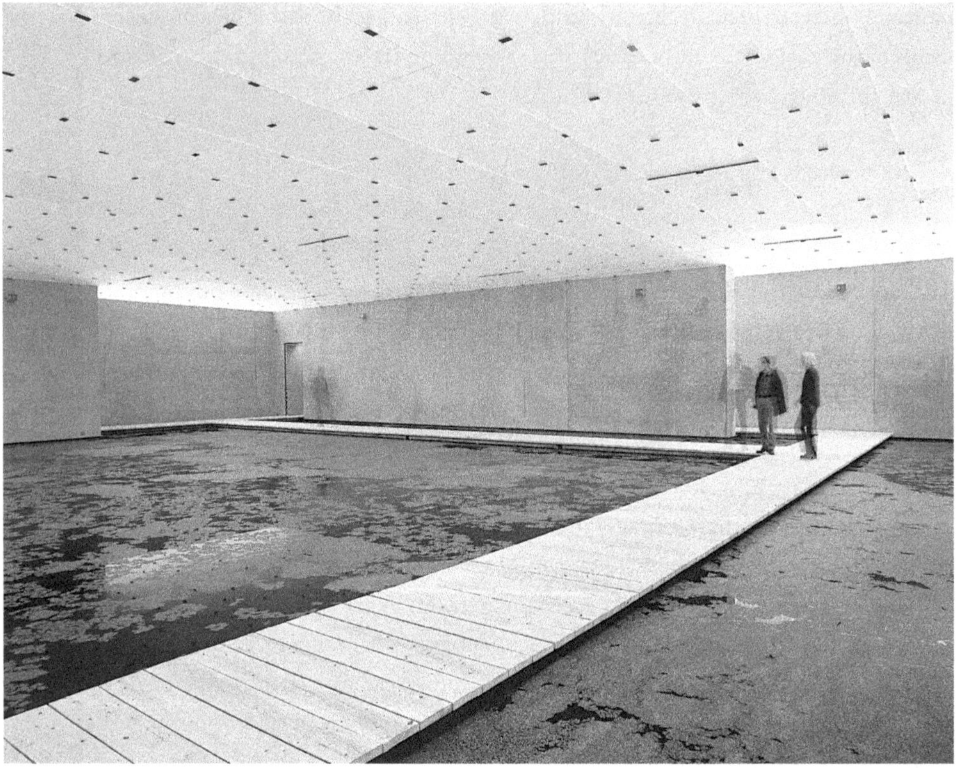

FIGURE 35. Olafur Eliasson, *The mediated motion,* 2001. Water, wood, compressed soil, fog machine, metal, foil, *Lemna minor,* and *Lentinula edodes.* Kunsthaus Bregenz, Austria. Courtesy of the artist; neugerriemschneider, Berlin; and Tanya Bonakdar Gallery, New York.

35). Over the course of the exhibition, the duckweed followed its short life cycle, changing under the natural light (provided by skylights) from dark green to yellow. Though carefully planned by the artist, this aspect of spontaneous growth and the unusual sight of an entire floor covered in water nevertheless had a disarming effect, with its connotations of flood and spreading growth and of the possibility that other forms of life might emerge in the water. This was tempered, however, by the straight wooden footbridge that ran up one side and then across the room, dividing the pool into geometric sections.

The path led up a steep and narrow flight of stairs to the next room, whose floor

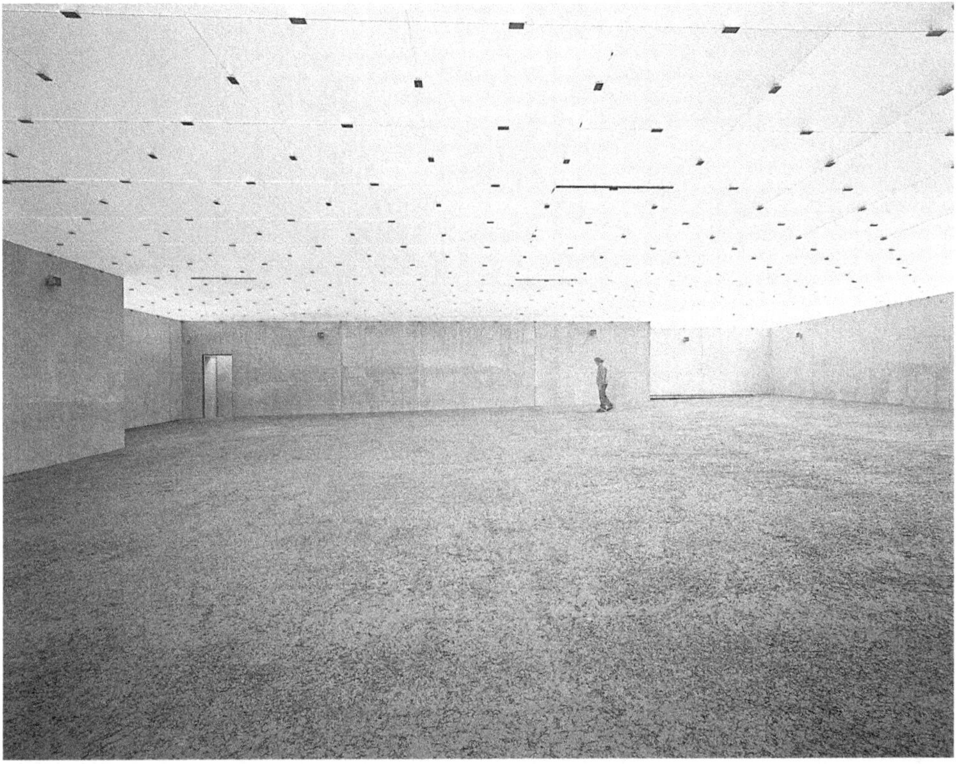

FIGURE 36. Olafur Eliasson, *The mediated motion,* 2001. Kunsthaus Bregenz, Austria. Courtesy of the artist; neugerriemschneider, Berlin; and Tanya Bonakdar Gallery, New York.

was completely covered with a compressed claylike substance made of excavated soil and crushed brick (Figure 36). Before putting down the layer of earth, Eliasson built the floor of the room with a 1.5-meter diagonal slope so that it was higher at the entrance and descended almost imperceptibly toward the other side of the room.[49] The visitor had to step off the wooden pathway onto the textured substance and cross the slanting floor. In addition to having an uncertain surface that emitted a strong earthy smell, the angled floor gave the illusion that the walls were tipping slightly, as though bolstered only by the precarious foundation of the soil ground. The production of a quasi earth—an indoor topography—disrupted the

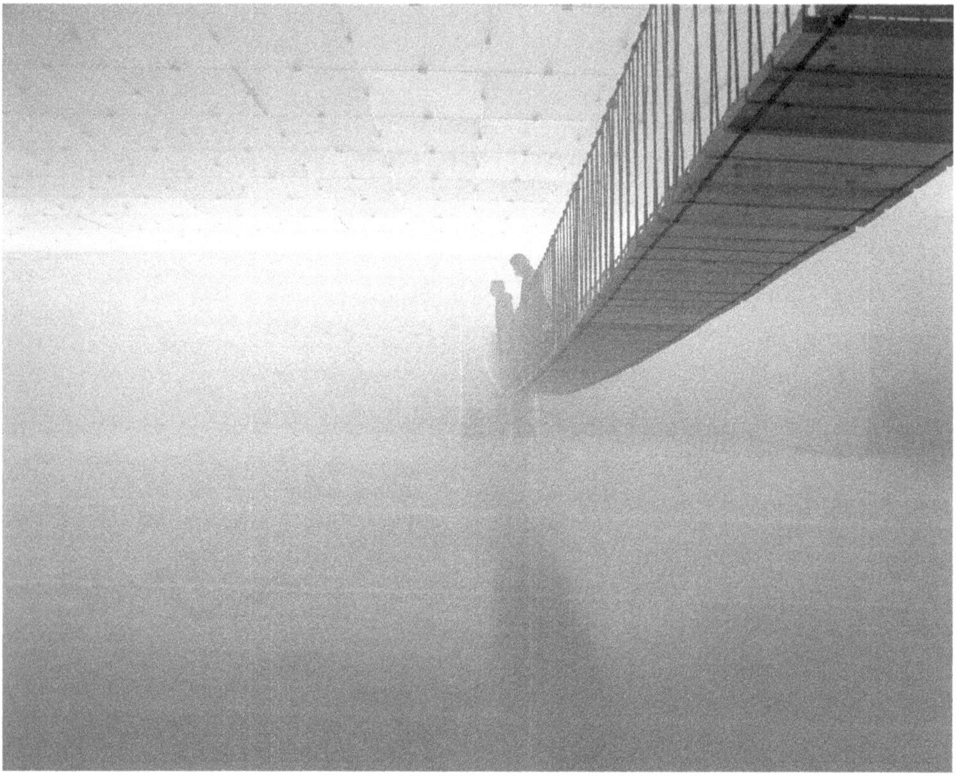

FIGURE 37. Olafur Eliasson, *The mediated motion,* 2001. Kunsthaus Bregenz, Austria. Courtesy of the artist; neugerriemschneider, Berlin; and Tanya Bonakdar Gallery, New York.

expectation of an organized space, thereby interrogating the distinction between interior and exterior space.

Finally, after another flight of stairs, the installation led to a room filled with artificial fog that was pumped through slits along the floor every forty minutes (Figure 37). When first pumped in, the fog was cool and gathered at the floor of the room, but gradually it warmed, lifted, and was eventually sucked out from the ceiling. Most disconcerting, though, was the challenge to the visitor to cross the room on a wooden suspension bridge that was entirely cloaked in the thick accumulation of mist, so that one could neither clearly ascertain the distance to the ground below nor see the other end of the bridge. From a fluid ground, to a reconstructed earth, and finally to an environment entirely obscured, Eliasson set the uncanny appearance of elementals indoors against the expectation of a predictably ordered space. Eliasson shows that, when left unanchored in the exhibition space, elementals are fundamentally impossible to localize and, precisely because of this, pose a challenge to orientation.

The issue, then, is not as simple as the placement of elementals in indoor environments. The problem at hand is that elementals straddle the line between natural and artificial. That is, while the fog is real air and moisture, it is a controlled rather than naturally occurring phenomenon. To summarize this point, Eliasson concluded the exhibition on the main floor of the building in a room containing a row of thirty logs of varying thickness, each of which served as a nutrient-rich base for a proliferation of shiitake mushrooms that grew out of the bark. Growing the mushrooms was a labor-intensive project that involved importing a costly mushroom culture from Japan, preparing the logs by storing them for six months before implanting them with the culture, and after leaving them under water for twenty-four hours, watering them in the shade every day and then sealing them under plastic foil at night. The room thus punctuates the intermingling of the natural with the technological and, in the case of this specific part of *The mediated motion,* the conflation of a functioning ecosystem with the economics of agriculture.

Yet it is not enough to merely posit the artwork as an ecotechnology, for the elementals here are not delivered up for easy visual consumption. Though they are in a certain respect mediated through an apparatus constructed for spectatorship, at the same time, in their unexpected appearance indoors, they are excessive and disruptive. Through this sensorial unassimilability, the artwork gains a foothold by which to question ecotechnology and the way in which it produces and delivers natural phenomena. Though an indoor exhibition may not seem a likely place for a sublime experience as it is traditionally understood, what is important to note is how the elementals, though included in the installation by design, reconfigure the limits of the space and in so doing upset the possibilities for orienting oneself in that space. One is confronted with the necessity of stabilizing one's position in relation to the ungraspable boundaries of water, earth, and air.

Jonathan Crary cautions against interpreting Eliasson's works as sublime. He argues that in its contemporary usage, the sublime characterizes those experiences in which there has been a loss of individual agency, a regression into a pre-Oedipal disorganization, and a breakdown of one's ability to control language or representation.[50] Eliasson's works, he posits, create a set of conditions from which distinctly nonsublime events occur, namely, communication, interpersonal exchange, and new provisional forms of understanding one's place in the environment. But are these conditions and interactions without the wonder of the sublime? Or are they, as Irigaray suggests, encounters that bring us to the limits of our horizon of being? We might think of Smithson's imagined regression into a state of intercorporeality with the Great Salt Lake, at which point language and thought are lost, as an example of the sublime, as Crary describes it. However, as I have argued, Smithson shifted into the retracted mode of text, which has been extracted from the site, by way of which he offers the artwork as a receptive medium *after* the point of differentiation and the fall into language and representation. It is this move, rather than the phenomenological state that precedes it, that is in fact closer to the sublime situation as Nancy would have it. Nancy mobilizes the sublime as an offering of form, suggesting that the sublime experience takes place at its limit:

> The sublime offering is the limit of presentation, and it takes place on and all along this limit, along the contour of form. The thing offered can be a thing of nature, and this is ordinarily according to Kant, the occasion of the feeling of the sublime. But since this thing, as a thing of liberty, is not merely offered but also offers itself, offers liberty . . . then this thing will be instead a thing of art (moreover, nature itself is always grasped here as a work of art, a work of supreme liberty).[51]

Here, the consideration of the sublime as an offering of the limit of form ensures a distinction between the presentation of nature as art and art representing nature through mimetic depiction. Smithson's *Spiral Jetty,* for instance, does not "represent" the site, but rather offers text as a medium against which the site's fluidity and temporality can manifest itself.

Eliasson's work, like that of Smithson, Turrell, and Drury, does not represent nature so much as it presents nature *as* a threshold to the elemental and *as* the surface

FIGURE 38. Olafur Eliasson, *Beauty,* 1993. Spotlight, water, nozzles, wood, hose, pump. Courtesy of the artist; neugerriemschneider, Berlin; and Tanya Bonakdar Gallery, New York.

against which contact and sense occur. There is no doubt that the artwork mediates the elemental; Eliasson's project has never been to present an idealized, untouched nature. But though his works like *The mediated motion* are ecotechnologies in that they constitute the idea of nature through a process of denaturalization, they also possess what Heidegger terms the "saving power" of art. That is, they render the apparatus of technological enframement transparent, and in so doing, they create the possibility for a "poetic dwelling on earth," which, as I have been arguing, is connected to a withdrawn mode of perception. Indeed, Eliasson's works are primarily focused on the subjective experience and are directed toward undoing habitual modes of perception when confronted with the ineffability of elemental presence. By revealing their own status as ecotechnologies, Eliasson's works pit the desire for a perceptual grasp against the excess of the elemental, cinching them together but pushing them apart in the contact that the exhibition forges.

In *Beauty* (Figure 38), sensation of the elemental occurs by way of a distinctly intangible surface, namely, a rainbow inside a darkened room. First executing the work in a warehouse in Copenhagen but since re-creating it in other venues, Eliasson fabricated *Beauty* by placing a perforated hose pipe on the ceiling, close to the interior wall. By releasing tiny drops of water from the hose and illuminating the mist from above with a spotlight, the artist generated a compelling, multihued screen. The visual fullness of the work, elaborated further by the increased humidity in the room and the gentle sound of the mist hitting the ground, however, depends on the limitation of the viewer's mobility. Once the viewer has found the privileged location for the rainbow to come into view, any movement could cause it to disappear. Or, in Eliasson's words, "since the rainbow is obviously dependent on the angle between the water, the light, and your eye, if the light doesn't go onto your eyes, there is no rainbow."[52] The extreme contingency between the viewer and the screen of mist, as in Turrell's *Skyspaces* and *Perceptual Cells,* restricts one to the point of immobility if one is to see the water and light *as* an array of color. There is thus a heightened awareness of the inaccessibility of the rainbow, for one cannot move toward it. Moreover, the confinement of the viewer, which is the precondition for the eye's receptivity to the light, brings about an awareness of the limits of subjective experience.

To discuss a work entitled *Beauty* in terms of the sublime would seem to be inviting contradiction. However, the fact that Eliasson hinges the rainbow along the very specific parameters of the visual field and at the same time locates the rainbow away from any tangible purchase implicates it in an exteriorization of the viewing subject and a revelation of the inscrutability of the elemental. Nancy reads the aesthetic categories of the beautiful and the sublime in relation to one another. He argues, "The sublime represents . . . nothing less than that without which the beautiful could not be the beautiful. . . . It does not merely add itself to the beautiful but transforms or transfigures the beautiful."[53] The presentation of the rainbow is predicated on holding the spectator back from the surface where the spotlight passes through the water. Further, the beauty of the artwork is activated and wholly dependent on an external influence, the introduction of the viewer's perceptual field as a limit. The rainbow itself does not exist without the spectator. If, as Nancy suggests, form and contour are the domain of the beautiful, whereas the unlimitation that occurs at the limit of form is the concern of the sublime, then we cannot consider the rainbow as a "beautiful thing." Instead, Eliasson locates beauty squarely at a predetermined point at which the spectator must stand, and the screen of illuminated mist that is the elemental basis of the rainbow cannot be approached or touched, for this movement causes the object of beauty to transform or fall out of sight.

It is perhaps through this revision of the sublime as the unbordering of the supersensible at the limits of representational form that we might understand the artworks. Moreover, what is at stake is the pointed surfacing of the limits of the ecotechnologies by which one encounters the elemental, including one's own body, the perceptual field, and the artwork as receptor surface. This occurs concurrently with the realization of the sensorial excesses of the elemental, for though the elemental appears within the parameters of the artwork, it is not delivered in any conclusive form. *Beauty* imparts a fulfillment and overflowing of sense, generating the openness of Agamben's animal, but in its revealing of its own "artificial" or technological mediation, it insists on orienting spectatorship to the resistance of the elemental.

*Beauty* exposes the limits of the perceptual field in order to relay the elemental. In this respect, Eliasson's work is, as Crary suggests, a kind of communicative interface. But we cannot assume that this communicability is unencumbered or that the artwork makes elementals accessible. It is precisely because of their unfixability that the artwork produces the need for communication; the need to consider the elemental, and by extension, the earth at large; and the need to mediate it as abundant sense. As Irigaray argues, ethical contact acknowledges the other's presentation without arranging it. The other, for Irigaray, appears at the horizon of one's perceptual being and is the excess that sparks the movement of the mind characteristic of the sublime experience. Thus, to understand Eliasson's works in terms of the new forms of interpersonal exchange they inspire does not necessarily take them outside the realm of the sublime. In fact, it is to recognize that the alterity of external nature, because it is sublime, triggers the desire to make contact through language, motion, and touch (and equally, the conscious drawing back from all of these). These interactions and this contact do not necessarily arrange nature for us. Crary posits that for Eliasson, transcendence is driven back into the actual world and made to serve an immanent function in terms of embodied reality.[54] But this does not strip immanent reality of sublimity; quite the opposite: Eliasson uncovers its sublime dimension and in doing so responds to an ethical and ecologically charged imperative.

If the problem with Merleau-Ponty's phenomenology for Irigaray is that it denies the importance of striving to communicate with the other and simply assimilates all phenomena into a solipsistic legibility, then what is required of the ethical subject is both a self-gathering and an offering of one's own "horizon of being" to the other. This horizon thereby becomes the locus of reception of sense of that other and of the world as other. Eliasson acknowledges this attentiveness to the external boundaries of experience by propelling attention to the periphery of the perceptual field. In *Your spiral view,* exhibited at the Fondation Bayeler in Basel in 2002 (Figure 39), Eliasson built a twenty-six-foot-long tunnel out of steel, lining the interior with triangular shards of mirror angled in such a way as to create the effect of reflections spiraling around the interior surface of the tunnel. Significantly, one end of the tunnel was pointed toward a window that looked out on a tranquil green space with a pond, and the view from the window was reflected in the mirrors. A variation of previous works, such as *Your circumspection disclosed* (1999) or *Well for Villa Medici* (1998), *Your spiral view* is a reconfiguration of the eye itself. On the one hand, it inclines sight toward a framed view of the park outside like a telescope. More subtly, though, it absorbs and disperses that view into fragments on the interior surface. Vision does not take place *in* the eye or *in* the mind; rather, it occurs at the edges of the visual field delineated by the tunnel.

In the same way that Drury's camera obscuras reflect the elemental as a spectral image on a surface inside a viewing chamber, Eliasson repudiates the interiority of spectatorship and in effect distributes the image to the fringes of the visitor's surrounding space. Interestingly, the interior surface doubles as an orb that encircles

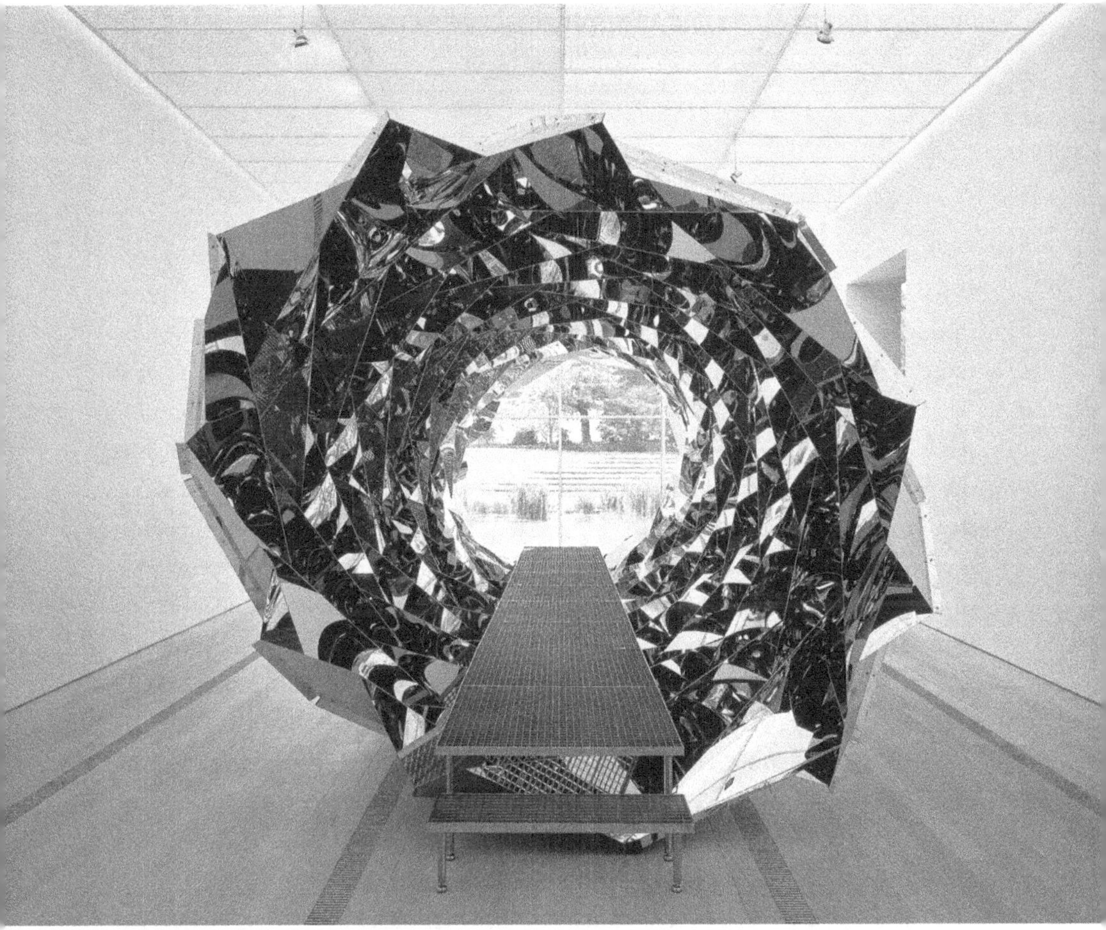

FIGURE 39. Olafur Eliasson, *Your spiral view,* 2002. Stainless steel mirrors. Fondation Bayeler, Basel. Boros Collection, Berlin. Courtesy of the artist and neugerriemschneider, Berlin.

the body, for the spectator is led by a ramp directly into the tunnel and is therefore not merely supposed to look through it or at it but be reflected inside it as well, which consequently pushes attention to the outer aspects of the viewer's own body. That is to say, the limits of the perceptual field converge with the armature of the artwork. Furthermore, the reflected body combines with the reflections of the landscape outside, so that the tunnel both reflects images and becomes a surface on which the spectator's exchange with the world outside comes into visibility, an exchange that is predicated on the subject's attentiveness to her or his externality.

## Earth Art as Sublime Interface

"What do you think happens when people occupy and move in these spaces? What do they see? Do they see themselves—sensing their own presence, activated through their surroundings? Or do they forget themselves (and their bodies) because of the non-reflecting surroundings?"[55] Eliasson's provocative questions demonstrate that an environment can either desensitize the viewer to the surrounding space or it can make present the constitutive relation between them by reflecting the viewer back to her- or himself as intertwined with the environment. However, there are two important points to be made about Eliasson's practice and that of other contemporary earth artists such as Turrell and Drury. First, the self-presencing of the visitor does not occur without a destabilization of the mode of confrontation. In each case, this occurs through the relocation of the interaction between the subject and the environment to a surface that elicits the retraction of the subject and is receptive to a manifestation of elemental phenomena. Second, the artworks do not merely direct one toward an "environment" in the abstract; they direct perception toward the sensation of elementals. Elementals, as opposed to an ideal of nature, a "natural thing," or a "thing" in general, illuminate, color, add shape and texture to, and upset the solipsistic worldview that instrumentalizes the earth.

In making the subject present to her- or himself, the artworks also evidence their own basis in an ecotechnological enframement that mediates the elemental. This revealing of the apparatus, however, is tantamount to a questioning of that enframement. The mechanism at play is seemingly contradictory: it inspires at once a self-gathering and an opening to the closedness of the elemental. The artwork as receptive surface (be it a *Skyspace,* the image of a camera obscura, or a reflective mirror at the periphery of vision) permits a manifestation of the elemental in its sublime alterity, yielding a sensorial plenitude that touches and unborders the limits that uphold bodily orientation.

The deployment of elementals opens up a different conceptualization of the earth as mobile, overlapping material conditions rather than as a located place or a closed system. Contemporary artists have thereby cultivated an attentiveness to this irreducibility, gearing artworks toward a communicative interface with the earth and its manifestation in elementals. Whereas Smithson positioned the textual artwork as a way of recovering the elemental qualities of the Great Salt Lake by opening representational media to the excess of sense, Turrell, Drury, and Eliasson further develop the notion of the artwork as a receptive surface by positioning visitors in immersive situations (viewing chambers, cells, or installations), a move that primes the senses but subsequently turns them out from the immersive state, arresting them at the limit beyond which the body cannot move, the hand cannot grasp, the eye cannot penetrate. The confrontation with the elemental thus occurs, to return to Irigaray's words, at "a screen of resting before and after seeing, a reserve for new landscapes." Eliasson's *Your spiral view* introduces a new dimension to earth art, moreover, in mobilizing the receptive surface as the locus of the intertwining of the exteriorized body and external nature. The suggestion is that the mechanism of the artwork, to enact a recession of the subject and to assert a differentiating membrane against which the elemental presents itself, can be activated on the body itself. It is therefore this topic—the body as a receptive surface—that the next chapter addresses.

FOUR

# The Body as Limit

The artworks I discussed in chapter 3 take two complementary approaches to making the earth visible: first, they confront the viewer with elemental phenomena, and second, in troubling the viewer's mode of encounter, they posit the earth as a sensorial excess, thus foregrounding the limits of the perceptual field. By providing a surface of visibility for elementals, be it the aperture of a *Skyspace,* the reflection from a camera obscura, or the dispersed images, colors, and atmospheric conditions in an installation, Turrell, Drury, and Eliasson mobilize an ethical contact with natural activity. Significantly, the ethical encounter here is founded on technologies of receptivity that mediate elementals while precluding or overturning the stability of representation. So while the artworks are designed to reveal natural activity, this process does not facilitate unencumbered visual or tactile access, as one might expect. Instead, sensation occurs at the threshold to the elemental, beyond which the viewer cannot grasp.

Similarly, in this chapter I examine the alignment of aesthetic and ethical strategies in projects that deploy various media to redefine the terms of perception so that it is predicated on an ethical act of receiving sensation. Whereas in chapter 3 I focused on environments that present the viewer with a surface of visibility for the presentation of elementals, here that surface is the human body itself. That is to say, in order to foreground the performance of perception as receptivity to the earth, artists use the body as the locus of the ethical relationship to the earth. This is not to suggest the emergence of a humanized nature or an idealized "natural" human body. To the contrary: in these artworks the human body is distorted and rendered alien by natural activity, and nature is equally disconcerting in its appearance on human body parts. Though it informs the sensorial experience of the work, elemental presence is a cue to the limits of bodily perception. Indeed, as in the previous chapters, not only does the artwork interrogate the ontological status of the body, but it also posits a particular phenomenological stance before the earth. The intertwining of natural activity and the human body is taken as a given; the precise role of the artwork is to suggest how our perceptual apparatus can orient us toward the alterity of the earth while being interconnected with it. The artworks position touching, seeing, and in one case even tasting natural activity as a detection of bodily limits and as the reception of sense, not in spite of but because of those limits.

## Facing the Earth

The artists considered in this chapter elaborate an ethics of ecology, not only by expressing moments of physical engagement with natural forces but also by making the character of that encounter the subject matter of the artwork. The artworks are not the sedimented objects of a dialectical collision between base materiality and discursive meaning; they enact a mode of perception that is the condition for and the result of the emergence of the earth as an aesthetic and ethical subject. The ethical relationship with the earth is founded on a contact that permits the sensation of its unboundedness and a withdrawal from the drive to coalesce it into representation.

To mobilize the contiguity of the body and the earth, the works I examine here operate in an expanded field of practice that includes body art, process art, and installation, from the earth–body sculptures of the Cuban American artist Ana Mendieta to the photograms of the British artist Susan Derges and the "bio-sculptures" of the American artist Jackie Brookner. Despite the different media, what links the artists together is the way in which they utilize a tension between three-dimensional space and two-dimensional surface in order to forge the ethical relation to the earth. As I have suggested in the previous chapters, the entanglement of tactility and vision are key to the ethical paradigm of earth art. These senses are each provoked, suspended, and reestablished through one another, as a means of eliciting a "facing" of the earth. Often, tactility is a cue to a shared materiality or interpenetration of the body and nature on which the artwork is founded. However, in the assertion of a two-dimensional surface, elemental phenomena become visible and enact the differentiation of the body and the earth. Thus, the intertwinement of the viewer and the earth is relayed through the friction between surfaces. The sensations of elementals escape both the assured materiality that would fulfill a tactile grasp and the organization of the visual field. The artwork functions as an intermediary between immersion in and abstraction of the earth. Though the body is located in a network of natural activity, then, the artworks instigate an involution or turn against the earth in order to gain a perspective of it as other.

The ethical relation is thus at the heart of the breakdown of medium. The discrete categories of "the pictorial image," usually associated with vision, and "sculpture," usually associated with tactility, are not accurate to describe the aesthetic object of earth art practice. Instead, the body–earth relation that appears at the interstices between image and object, stasis and temporality (or "natural time," in Smithson's words), representation and excess incites the disordering of sense. Thus, the textures, atmospheres, and visual arrays of the elemental both forge the ethical relation and constitute what I term the "face" of the earth.

I have been arguing that the elemental resists intelligibility but nevertheless manifests in surpluses of sensation. The earth is thus a kind of excess of representation that arises within the artwork. Interestingly, John Sallis suggests that the earth reveals itself within natural things ("things of the earth"), like a countenance that is inseparable from a face: "It is the visage of something that withholds itself precisely in offering its physiognomy, of something that displays its secret strength but in such a way as to keep it secret in the very display."[1] In a similar vein, contemporary artists situate the body as emergent from the earth (as among the "things of the earth"), while at the same time demonstrating the earth's resistance to intelligibility, whereby it cannot be stabilized within the body. As the site of the artwork, the body does not offer up the earth to an invasive perception. Instead, to use Sallis's analogy of an opaque visage, the human body is the surface on and through which the countenance of the earth comes into view. The body thus becomes exteriorized and positioned as the receptive surface of the earth's manifestation, or its face.

The manifestation of the face is also what distinguishes the earth from brute matter. Though the artists immerse themselves in an elemental substance, be it sand, soil, or water, they do so in order to identify a turning point at which the earth's material becomes an "other" presence. The mechanism of the artwork is the artist's assertion of the body against the elemental, as a means of evidencing the earth's "closedness" from intelligibility. The visual phenomena that I am calling the earth's face are fundamentally resistant to the bodily forms on which they are disclosed. Because the body is the locus of the emergence of the face, artists evoke the sensation of natural presence, but they do not deliver it as a totalized perception. Through the interplay between the immersion of the body in the depths of elemental substance and the friction of encountering that substance as surface, artists pose the question of how nature is sensed via the withdrawal from perceptual expectations and representation.

Though the initial principles of phenomenological encounter developed by Merleau-Ponty suggest that perception stems from intercorporeal engagement with the world-flesh, contemporary artists deal more explicitly with the inability to subsume the earth into representational form. Their approach of receiving sensation diverges from Merleau-Ponty's phenomenology, in which the subject reaches for, intends toward, and penetrates the other or the object of sensation. Irigaray counters Merleau-Ponty's rhetoric with her own model of vision, which is governed by a tactile logic, whereby we see and explore one another through contact with the other's surface. Irigaray's tactile vision is heavily influenced by Levinas's ethics of alterity, and particularly his scenario of the face-to-face. Levinas describes the face-to-face encounter as a relation by which a subject is formed in response to the other and is born of a fundamental awareness of the other's difference. The irreducibility of the other in this encounter is the origin of ethical acknowledgment.

In her exposition of tactile vision, Irigaray rewrites the face-to-face scenario with a view to accounting for sexual difference. Her strongest critique of Levinas is that his notion of the ethical relation takes place between male subjects and that he thus restricts his own notion of alterity and thereby forecloses it. Irigaray advances the Levinasian paradigm, however, by insisting on the fundamental inconceivability of the other, so that the other exceeds any category of subjectivity that has been affixed to it. It is this argument that opens the opportunity to eco-phenomenologists to consider nonhumans and other natural phenomena ethically, without anthropomorphizing them.

Additionally, Irigaray maintains that the ethical relation takes place through physical contact. The other, for Irigaray, is not penetrated, sculpted, or grasped in the mode of Merleau-Ponty, but rather is felt at the divisions that mark alterity. Similarly, Alphonso Lingis develops Levinas's face-to-face scenario by elaborating its physicality and its inextricability from the elemental. The elemental courses through humans and characterizes our encounters with others. It reveals the earth to us and reveals us to one another, but it also encompasses an opacity or withdrawal from total exposure. Lingis's rewriting of the face-to-face, much like Irigaray's, is founded on a tactile contact with alterity, whereby the face manifests not as identifiable features but in the character of physical sensations that pass between oneself and another. Most pertinent to earth art is that this transaction of physical sensations is always located within and through elemental substance.

What draws Levinas, Irigaray, and Lingis together is the mode of contact with the other: alterity permeates the senses but is entirely unrepresentable. As Levinas puts it:

> The way in which the other presents himself, exceeding *the idea of the other in me,* we here name face. This *mode* does not consist in figuring as a theme under my gaze, in spreading itself forth as a set of qualities forming an image. The face of the Other at each moment destroys and overflows the plastic image it leaves me.... It does not manifest itself by these qualities.... It *expresses itself.*[2]

When artists perform the reception of sensation on the human body, then, the body exteriorizes itself in order to provide a surface for the earth's self-expression. Because the earth is visible but nevertheless withholds itself, sensation is not taken but rather is effected by the revealing of the face. The artwork demonstrates that we sense the earth and are physically marked by this contact, but the earth nevertheless cannot be subsumed.

## Ana Mendieta: Performing the Body's Receptivity

Ana Mendieta, a Cuban-born artist exiled to the United States in her youth, is best known for her *Silueta Series,* which took place from 1973 to 1980. In a practice that the artist called "earth–body sculpture," Mendieta executed a sequence of performances in which she impressed her bodily form into the land. Usually, she staged and photographed the process of the *silueta*'s disassembly as it was washed away, burned, melted, or otherwise reintegrated into the land by elemental forces. The act of imprinting, in Mendieta's practice, encompasses both spatial and pictorial elements, not only because she photographed her sculpted form but also because she performed the body as constituted by elementals and applied it as a surface against them. The imprint, then, signals the interpenetration of the body and the earth, and it is the agent by which Mendieta performs their differentiation as a reciprocal marking of surfaces and as an act that delivers an abundance of sensation.

What is particular to Mendieta's practice is the way the *siluetas* enact the body receiving natural fluxes and asserting its exteriority against them. The *siluetas* are simultaneously concave and convex, a voluminous impression that fills with elementals and a flat surface that pushes this natural activity into visibility. Indeed, both the depth and the opacity of the artwork are necessary to galvanize the contiguity between the body and elementals. More strongly, the *siluetas* demonstrate the emergence of the earth in conjunction with the retraction of the body. This appearance on the locus of the withdrawn body corresponds to a statement about the body's capacity to receive sensation. Not coincidentally, Mendieta mobilizes the body through the definitive figure of touch: the imprint. The indexical properties of the imprint—its status as a physical marking of the land—coincide with its metaphoric connotations, as a figure of the sense of touch. In this way, the imprint provides a ground for the manifestation of volatile natural excesses that the body cannot contain but that nevertheless surround, enter, and exit it.

The body, in Mendieta's artworks, thus acts as both an overflowing receptacle and a surface that registers the point at which sensation abounds beyond the body's capacity to organize and interpret it. That is to say, the imprint demarcates a gesture of receiving and thereby opens itself to its own disassembly as natural activity distorts the shape of the body and overtakes the parameters of the *silueta.* Mendieta thus shows that while the earth is available to the senses, it is not bound to the limits of the body's field of perception. The series is thus oriented to the question of how an artwork can express a direct contact with the earth without either resorting to the notion that the earth is a stable foundation or reducing the sensorial experience to one of primordial immersion. The *silueta* stands as a figure of the body's shared materiality with the earth as well as a figure of its turn against the earth from within.

Peggy Phelan explains that in performance art, spectatorship is like consumption, for performance launches presence into visibility, and the spectator must try to take everything in before that presence disappears.[3] A performance can be documented, but because the bodily presence of the performer is irretrievable, any attempt to preserve the performance alters its meaning and rewrites it. For that reason, Phelan categorizes performance as nonreproductive and explains that performance deploys the body metonymically as opposed to metaphorically.[4] Metaphor, she notes, is reproductive; it works by erasing dissimilarity and negating difference. Metonymy, by contrast, is additive and associative; it secures a relation of contiguity and displacement. Phelan argues that in performance the body is metonymic of presence, so that despite its apparent availability, when the body is performed it disappears and becomes something else—dance, movement, sound, "art." That addition of meaning to the body, that which makes it art and not just presence, is the object of the spectator's gaze.

Mendieta's *siluetas* speak directly to the metonymic structure of the performed body. Indeed, the imprint is the ultimate figure of the supplementation of bodily presence, for it suggests presence as a trace. As Georges Didi-Huberman notes, however, the imprint mortifies its referent, tying together its moment of origin (when the body leaves its mark) with the perpetual loss of that moment.[5] An imprint is thus formed by the absenting of presence. In performing her body as imprint, Mendieta draws attention to the loss of presence that the performance initiates and thematizes that loss by figuring it as a trace. In this way, the indexical characteristics of the imprint and the supplementation of the body by its trace elaborate the metonymic structure of performance. Moreover, as Amelia Jones has argued, Mendieta echoes the loss that the *silueta* exemplifies by photographing it. The photograph is thus a double lack; the *silueta* is a proof of presence while at the same time deferring that presence, and the photograph supplements the *silueta,* initiating an infinite chain of supplementary mediations.[6]

But the question remains, what appears as a result of this absenting of the body? What is most obvious, but what often remains unacknowledged in interpretations of Mendieta's work, is that the body is supplemented by elementals that appear coextensively with the disappearance of the body and the distortion of the *silueta* over the course of the performance. As in Smithson's site/nonsite works, Long's carefully worn paths marking lines in the ground, or Fulton's text installations, Mendieta's contact with the site is only available in evidence that points as much to her absence as to her presence at the site. Moreover, the performances emphasize not just the body's absence but, more precisely, its process of dissolution. Paradoxically, natural activity galvanizes the trace of the body's presence to the earth by underscoring its disappearance. Body and earth reveal and undo one another in the liminal zone of the *silueta.*

Anne Raine argues that Mendieta's *siluetas* produce both pleasure and anxiety, remarking that the artist's bodily figure acts as an uncanny double that prompts in the spectator a palpable intimacy between body and earth.[7] Yet because a *silueta* is sculpted out of inert matter such as ice, flowers, stones, or sand, it closes off the possibility of identifying with it, of entering into it or replacing it with ourselves and experiencing the land intimately. By filling the human form with nonhuman materiality, Mendieta "insists on the unimaginable situation of human body and non-human landscape literally occupying the same space."[8] Mendieta characterizes this relation between the body and the earth as a kind of tactile pressure rather than an immersion in the earth or a "return to nature" as has sometimes been suggested. Mendieta presents the body as simultaneously filled out and consumed

FIGURE 40. Ana Mendieta, *Untitled (Silueta Series, Iowa)*, 1977. Copyright The Estate of Ana Mendieta Collection. Courtesy of Galerie Lelong, New York.

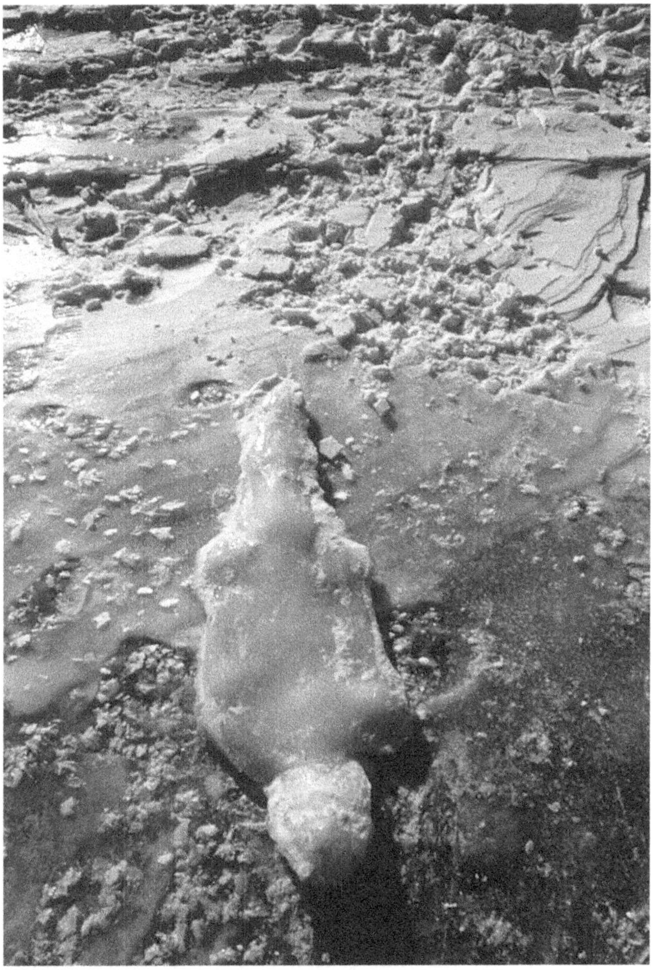

by the earth. She achieves this in a play between the three-dimensionality of the *silueta*—using it either as an object already filled with organic material or as a space that is filled up over the course of the performance—and its two-dimensionality, as a surface on which temporally charged elementals become visible. Mendieta shows that the body is replete with elementals but that sensation occurs in the delineation of a membrane that separates the body out from them.

In one *silueta* executed in Iowa in 1977, Mendieta formed a full and rounded bodily shape out of ice (Figure 40). The core feature of the artwork is the figure's impenetrability. One cannot distinguish the limbs of the body; indeed, the figure is so tightly bound and abstracted by the ice that it is not even identifiable as feminine. These alienating features, however, do not prevent a sense of tactile plenitude. Quite the opposite: the milky white surface invites an exploration of the figure's smooth texture and rounded shape. As Mieke Bal argues, in her attentiveness to the figure's surface, Mendieta imposes an irremediable exteriority on the subject and in fact posits the exteriority of the subject to herself as an indispensable critical perspective.[9]

The uncanny oscillation between the human form and the site is the means by which Mendieta creates a space of possibility for the body and the earth to coexist without evoking their conflation. The constitution of the body through the earth occurs through their mutual alienation, not through their commonality, a position that is also fundamental to the aesthetic sensibility that Mendieta advances. Though many of her performances feature the malleability of the *silueta* as it is overtaken by natural events, it is impossible to ignore Mendieta's insistence on the sculptural qualities by which the *silueta* comes into friction with the changing surface of the land. One presumes that the ice *silueta* will gradually melt way, but it is photographed as protruding, solid, and shapely against the erratic breaks of the snow banks that surround it. Though it is certain that the *silueta* is made from and will disappear back into the site, within the context of the performance the *silueta* stands apart through an ambivalent shifting between the bodily form and earthly matter.

Like Smithson's *Spiral Jetty,* Mendieta's performances suggest the body's return to a state of undifferentiation from the land. Yet in the same way that Smithson turns back from the edge of the jetty—a turn away from primordial immersion at the limit of form—Mendieta denies the return of the body to the earth. Instead, she elaborates the sensorial experience through the exploration of bodily and earthly surfaces, which challenges the equation of nature with primordial formlessness. Part of the appeal of the *silueta,* as Raine notes, is that the spectator imagines the pleasures to which the figures refer, namely, "the imagined experience of nestling in the curve of the silhouette and feeling the landscape along the surface of the skin."[10] The friction between the body and the land by which the *silueta* evokes

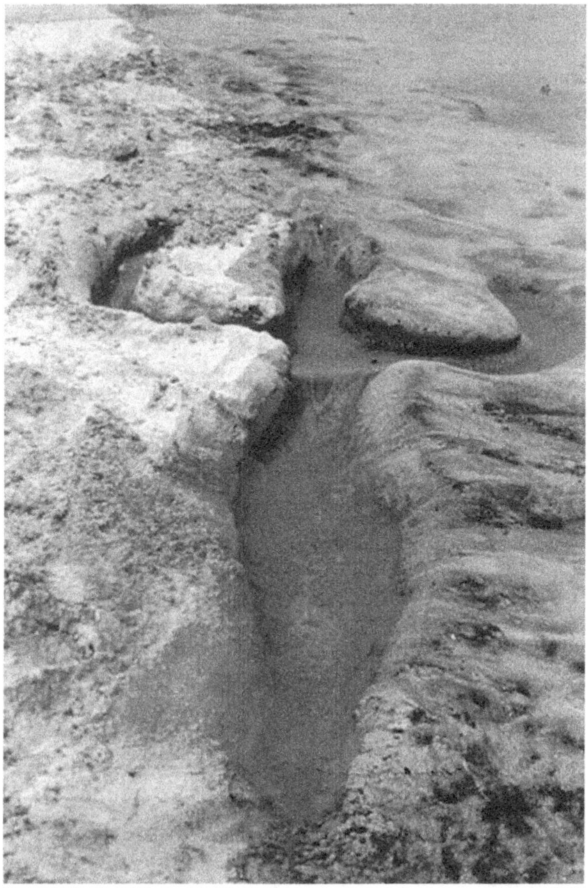

FIGURE 41. Ana Mendieta, *Untitled (Silueta Series, Oaxaca, Mexico)*, 1976. Copyright The Estate of Ana Mendieta Collection. Courtesy of Galerie Lelong, New York.

tactile sensation conflicts with the amorphous state into which it is devolving. Yet Mendieta nevertheless puts material continuity and physical differentiation into conversation. Provoking the overflow and temporality of the *silueta*'s materiality (ice that melts, sand that falls apart, soil that becomes overgrown), Mendieta hinges sensation on the earth's excessiveness, which the viewer detects at the confines of the performed body.

In a performance executed in Oaxaca, Mexico, in 1976, Mendieta uses the *silueta* as a vessel by which to harness an inflow of water (Figure 41). The *silueta* was impressed deeply into the sand on a beach, situated close enough to the water to interact with the waves as the tide rolled in. To animate the contact between the *silueta* and the water, Mendieta lined the imprint with red pigment. As the tide advanced, the water filled the imprint and mingled with the color. Gradually, the water rounded out the bodily form as it carried the pigment back into the ocean. Though the performed body fills with water, Mendieta inverts the suggestion of its continuity by highlighting its differentiation through a brightly colored two-dimensional surface. The red pigment, which mixes with the water, galvanizes the movement of the tide *across* the *silueta*. Whereas Smithson deploys the color red in *Spiral Jetty* to evoke amniotic fluid, thereby conveying his return to an amorphous condition, Mendieta uses the red pigment to track the trajectory of the water, marking its entry into and exit from the body as a play of color against the *silueta*'s recessed surface. Upon contact with the water, the *silueta* undulates, at once curving inward to hold the water and flattening out against it, thus making both water and the shape of the body visible. Mendieta corroborates the provoked sensations of being surrounded and filled by the influx of water by picturing the water's movement against the *silueta*'s surface as an array of red.

The notion of sensing nature from within and viewing it against a surface is encompassed by the photographic medium as well as by the performance. Though some of her *siluetas* are recorded in a single color slide, Mendieta photographed this particular intervention in Oaxaca in a series of 35 mm slides. Each slide documents the performance in a moment of fixity, but these intervals must also be read together as a set. Mendieta instigates the water's appearance both within and on the imprint by setting the photograph's instantaneity and two-dimensionality against the temporality and volume of the water. Rather than presenting the distortion of the *silueta* as a progression from sculpted object to indistinguishable matter on an uninterrupted film reel, the artist uses photography to highlight surface resistance as a chief feature of the *silueta*.

The sequence of still slides has the effect of montage, revealing the convergence and divergence of body and site through the deformation of the *silueta* from one frame to the next. Yve-Alain Bois argues that the key element of montage in film is not just the production of meaning through a discontinuity between shots; rather, and more precisely, discontinuity is transferred to the next fragment and is understood to come from within it. The effect of montage, as Bois quotes Sergei Eisen-

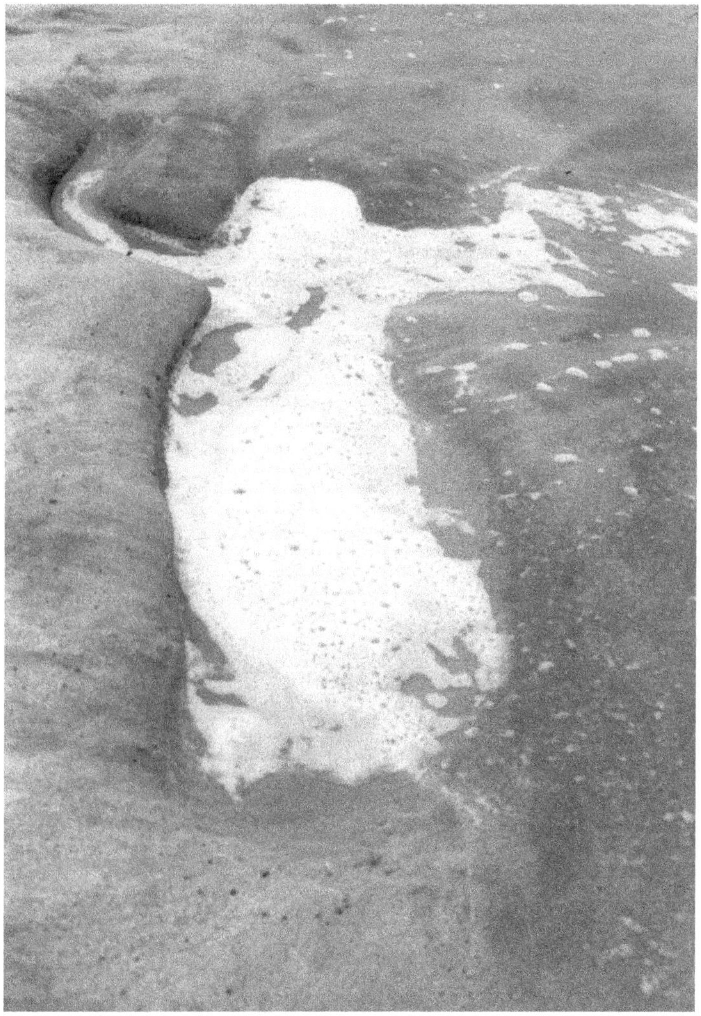

FIGURE 42. Ana Mendieta, *Untitled (Silueta Series, Oaxaca, Mexico),* 1976. Copyright The Estate of Ana Mendieta Collection. Courtesy of Galerie Lelong, New York.

stein, "is constructed on the capacity of our eye to continue by inertia a movement it has been given. The collision of this 'suggested' path of movement with another path substituted for it also produces the effect of a jolt."[11] Similarly, more than interrupting the path of movement, the photographed performance rebuffs a sense of identification with the *silueta* because of the ambiguity in its status as either empty vessel or exterior surface. In the push and pull of the tide, the water appears to both enter into and wash across it. Though the photograph cannot show the gradual encroachment of the water or its rhythmic withdrawals, from one slide to the next the influx of water appears to enter the *silueta* from the right-hand side of the frame. Over the sequence of slides, the *silueta* melts back into the direction from which the water comes (from left to right), its right side stretching to the point of being indistinguishable from the beach. Using the discontinuity of a photographic montage, Mendieta constructs an interrelation of natural activity and the shifting boundaries of the body's exterior. She connects the changes in the delineation of the *silueta* to the dynamic movement of the water and makes the trajectory of the water's movement visible using the pigment. There are thus two interrelated discontinuities. First, though the water enters from right to left, this is actually implied by the images of the *silueta* stretching out from left to right. Second, as the *silueta* flattens out, the volume and movement of the water is rendered as a play of color against the surface of the imprint.

The final photograph in the sequence of slides is not an image of the beach after the *silueta* has completely dissolved but rather an image of the imprint that is defined by only a curved ridge in the sand (Figure 42). The diluted pigment swells with the water over the remains of the imprint. The ridge of sand that pushes against the surging tide summarizes the body–earth relation that Mendieta advances. The ridge maintains the shape of the body but foregrounds the pressure of the water. It stands in as a boundary that discloses the body and the site as mutually defined through their contact. The tide laps against the curve of the *silueta,* as much impressed by the shape of the body as the imprint appears to have been shaped by the water. It recalls Merleau-Ponty's vivid description of the intercorporeal relation in *The Visible and the Invisible*: "It is as though our vision were formed in the heart of the visible, or as though there were between it and us an intimacy as close as between the sea and the strand."[12] This is a very significant "or" however—one that reveals a dormant ambiguity at play between the subject and the visible world in Merleau-Ponty's work. *Either* the subject is *in* the heart of the visible, *or* there is an intimacy as close as that *between* sea and strand. Irigaray draws out this uncertainty, arguing that the image risks the disappearance of the seer and the visible into one another and that in order to acknowledge the other, this conflation should be allayed. Equally, it seems that Mendieta emphasizes the latter condition, the one of intimate differentiation, for the performance insists on revealing a boundary between the body and the earth and the evoked sensation of friction that this generates.

As visually rich as the performance is, there is also a strong tactile foundation to it. However, that tactility is not one of a being at grips with the world but rather one that reveals how natural activity escapes vision. Irigaray remarks that color acts as a kind of dynamic elemental; it is a reminder of one's own archaic fluid that binds one to the world-flesh—it is the *ground* of the visible. It is also what recuperates a sense of touch and of the excess of the world within vision. She writes, "Color bathes my gaze, which sees it . . . but can never delimit it, create it, bend it to its decisions. Color constitutes a given that escapes the subjective realm."[13]

Through the synergy of color with water as the tide breaks the outline of the silueta, Mendieta shows how this excess upsets perceptual solipsism and phenomenological closure. Further, the ephemeral qualities of the water register as tactile sense—pressure, ebbing and flowing water—precisely because of a differentiating membrane between the subject and the world, here figured as the ridge of sand. One might think of the ridge as corresponding to a receptive mode of touch.

Irigaray explains the ethical potential of a tactile logic, which she distinguishes from Merleau-Ponty's model of the reversibility of the senses. Merleau-Ponty posits the experience of one hand touching the other to explain how tactility is always reciprocal (to touch is always also to be touched). From this statement he extends the claim that to see is always also to be seen. And furthermore, the sense of touch relays vision and vice versa. Irigaray counters, however, that in this scenario a certain privilege belongs to the hand that actively touches, sees, and embodies the world, and correspondingly to the active subject as opposed to the seemingly passive other. Indeed, in his analogy, one hand covers the other and even "takes hold" of it; the subject's tactile vision envelopes, penetrates, and palpates the visible world. In this paradigm, she argues, "We never catch sight of each other. . . . Movement is such that it would take extraordinary luck for two seers to catch sight of each other."[14] The other, and we might also say the otherness of the earth, are closed off in the tight weave of an all-encompassing grip.

As an alternative model that insists on the distinction between touch and sight, and correspondingly between oneself and the other, Irigaray evokes the image of two hands pressed together at the palms. The point here is not that there is a similarity of the one to the other (Irigaray is adamant about this) but rather that in the relation of simultaneous feeling–felt there is a passage between interior and exterior, between the tangible and the visible, between oneself and the other. This contact doubles the touching of lips, "silently applied to one another." The intimate touch of the lips allows for openness; one never closes over the other. As she describes them, they "remain always on the edge of speech, gathering at the edge without sealing it." Most interestingly, Irigaray employs this metaphor to describe the possibilities of seeing the other. This gesture, she continues, "could also be performed with the gaze: the eyes could meet in a sort of silence of vision, a screen of resting before and after seeing, a reserve for new landscapes, new lights, a punctuation in which the eyes reconstitute for themselves the frame, the screen, the horizon of vision."[15]

The ridge of sand that concludes Mendieta's performance not only encompasses a reciprocal touch between the body and the earth but also recapitulates a way of seeing the earth by receiving its "gaze." Clearly, for Mendieta, the idea is not that the earth has a literal gaze; rather, her performances show the appearance of the elemental as a gesture of meeting with the body in order to form a "new landscape" or "horizon of vision" founded on that contact. Though the *silueta* is filled and stretched by the water, the final slide that depicts the division between the two reiterates the thematic of ethical receptivity through a differentiating touch. Another way to put this is that Mendieta performs the contingency of the body and the earth and pictures it as a relation of mutual feeling–felt.

This understanding of the artwork as founded on a sensorial encounter implies that the earth is not just the material of the artwork, or even its catalyst, but an unfathomable presence engaged in a kind of quasi-intersubjective exchange with the artist. Though this argument risks anthropomorphizing elementals and reiterating the solipsistic phenomenology that Irigaray critiques, in fact there is a more subtle point to be made. The artwork entails a facing of the earth as a radical other, not as a human subject. In performing the contingency of the body and the earth, Mendieta neither anthropomorphizes the earth nor naturalizes the body. To the contrary: through their contact the body becomes alien and points toward the impenetrability of the elemental substance that fills it out and reshapes it.

Levinas formulates his understanding of the interaction between others through his notion of the elemental, which he understands as a realm of support through which we communicate and receive sensation. It would be useful to suggest further, though, that in earth art, elementals evoke sensation, but the earth itself is ultimately mobilized as a phenomenon of alterity. Mendieta realizes an elemental bond to the earth (the water that flows into the *silueta*) but also confronts the spectator with a progressive alienation from the human form as the *silueta* distorts. The destabilization of the body, then, allows it to become a receptive surface that reveals an earthly face.

Lingis explains the relationship between the elemental and the face, saying, "We do not relate to the light, the earth, the air and the warmth only with our individual sensibility and sensuality. We communicate to one another the light our eyes know, the ground that sustains our postures, and the air and the warmth with which we speak."[16] He suggests further that Levinas's face-to-face encounter takes place within the elemental, the medium through which texture, contour, and boundaries are sensed. In this scenario the other's face encompasses an appeal, a need, or an intrusion that must be heeded. This imperative is not only for recognition in an abstract sense, but for contact—to be physically received and reciprocated. This is why, as Lingis explains, the other's face manifests not necessarily as a look but also as a gesture, a pressure on the hand, or a shiver of the skin. Facing appears on a surface of exposure; he writes, "The skin . . . supports the signs of an alien intention and alien moods."[17] The elemental is crucial here, for there is no facing that is not understood through sensible qualities. The elemental yields the face, and itself surfaces in the gesture of facing.

But does the elemental only surface other beings and other things? Can the elemental yield the earth as a face, as an unnamable alterity, and as an ethical imperative? Can we receive the elemental as a means of giving the earth a voice without anthropomorphizing it, or to use Irigaray and Levinas's vocabulary, without subsuming it into sameness? I am arguing that this is precisely what artists attempt in creating works that are bound up in the elemental but that also yield sensation through gestures that simultaneously offer the body and infer the withdrawal of the subject's perceptual expectations.

Mendieta stages a facing of the earth in another *silueta* work executed in Oaxaca,

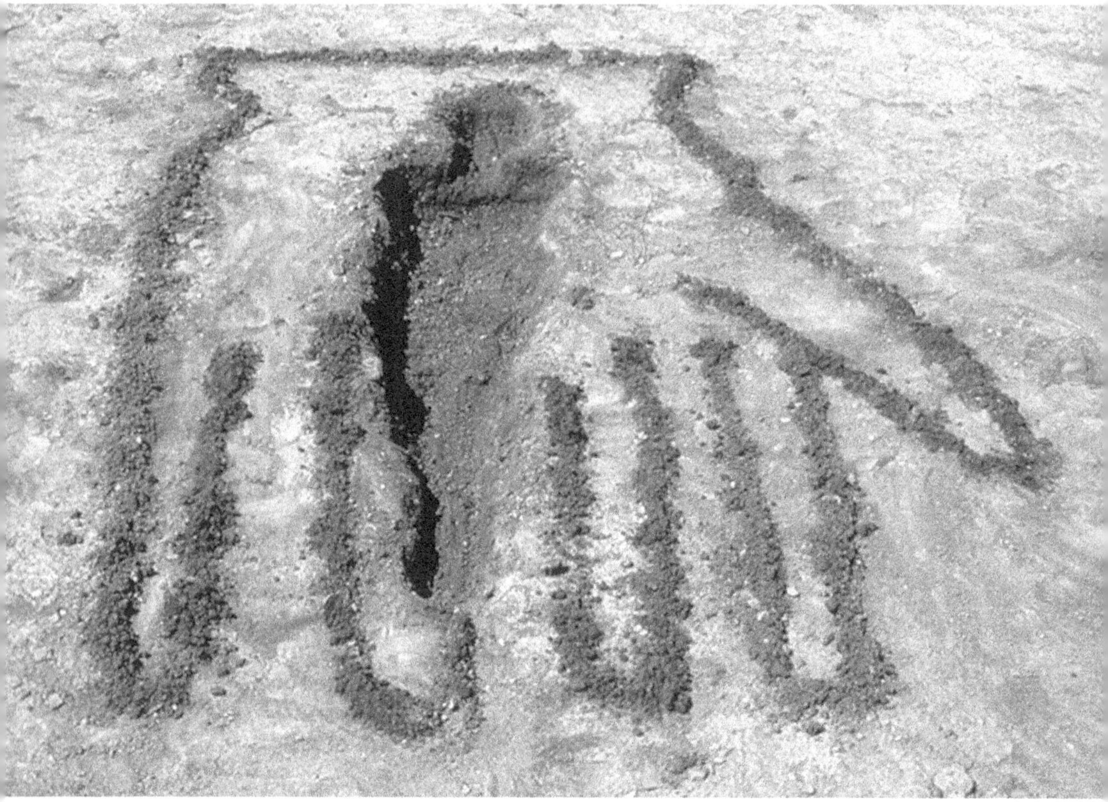

FIGURE 43. Ana Mendieta, *Incantation a Olokun-Yemayá,* 1977. Copyright The Estate of Ana Mendieta Collection. Courtesy of Galerie Lelong, New York.

Mexico in 1977. *Incantation a Olokun-Yemayá* (Figure 43) situates the imprint of the body inside the outline of a giant hand. The focus of this work is not the dissolving imprint—it wasn't photographed in a sequence as a temporal performance. The key is the division between the body and the earth's surface and the figuration of that contact as an act of touching and being touched. Mendieta created the hand by piling sand along the outline. The hand is not pushed into the land from above, as though in an aggrandized emblem of the artist's touch; rather, it gives the illusion that the edges of the hand are pushing out from underneath the land. The hand is thus set in tension with the bodily form pressed into it. The sense of pressure is further emphasized by the fact that the head of the *silueta* is set in the opposite direction of the fingers. The hand does not frame the imprinted body; the body is situated across it, the top opposite the tip of the finger into which it is laid. Moreover, the hand does not close around the *silueta*; it remains open and flat against the imprint, thus not absorbing it. Lingis writes that the elemental gives rise to sense, and is itself sensed, not by an intentional direction of the viewing eye and the grasping hand aiming at objectives but by a movement of involution.[18] Mendieta pictures this encounter as an exertion of pressure, akin to the tactile relation of the two hands pressed together that Irigaray proposes.

Mendieta's address to the earth is no return to nature as maternal body or descent into primordial fluidity. Rather, it is a turn against the earth, an imprint that is positioned against a reciprocal touch—the human body against the earth's hand. If we read *Incantation* in tandem with other performances in the *Silueta Series,* it is clear that the artist not only attempts to create a space for the earth to receive her body but also, through her withdrawal, provides a surface against which the elemental can appear—the *silueta* fills with water, combusts, or is blown apart—and illuminate the face of the earth.

## Susan Derges: The Photogram as Receptive Body

The photograms of the British artist Susan Derges similarly deploy the elemental as a means of giving the earth a face, but in this case, as in Drury's camera obscuras, it appears as a spectral image. In a series of photograms from 1998, Derges documented the changes to the River Taw in Britain. The photogram is derived from the calotype, a technology that produces images without the use of an optical apparatus, an invention that preceded the photographic camera, developed by William Henry Fox Talbot in the mid-nineteenth century. Likewise, Derges does not use cameras or lenses to generate an image; instead, the photogram is made by directly exposing Ilfochrome paper to a light source. Unlike standard photographic paper, Ilfochrome is a positive paper used to print transparencies and not negatives. It has three emulsion layers, each sensitized to one of the three primary colors so that each layer records different color information of the image. During development, in a process called dye destruction, unnecessary portions of the color dye are bleached out.[19]

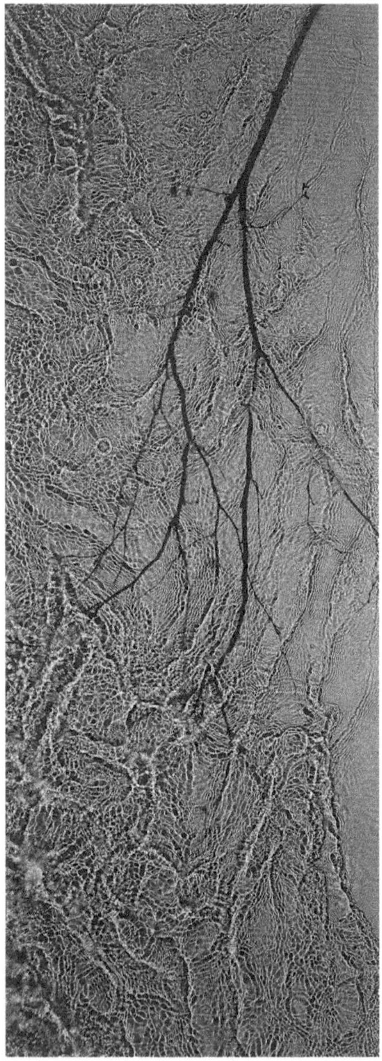

To create the necessary contrast between reflected light and dark background, Derges works at night. She submerges a sheet of the sensitized paper in the river and at the right moment affixes the image by exposing it to a flash of light. At that point, the paper absorbs the patterns of the water's movement. In *Camera Lucida,* Roland Barthes argues that the photograph is an ineluctable testament to what has been. This is perhaps even more strongly the case with the photogram, for it is produced by the immediate contact between the surface of the paper and the water whose patterns it absorbs. The pressure of one surface against another is secured through the chemical reaction stimulated by the flashlight. When the light exposes the water, the photogram is impressed with the shapes of the river's swirling vortices, ripples, or gentle ebbs and shadows. The primacy of a literal contact with nature has been central to this alternative photographic technique since its invention. Talbot's earliest works emphasized the principle that the technique allowed nature to render itself as art, hence the title of his series from the mid-1840s, *The Pencil of Nature.* The calotype captured minute details, achieved by coating drawing paper first with a salt solution and then with a solution of silver nitrate before placing a natural object, such as a leaf or an insect, on the paper and exposing it to light. The technology was thus located in the nineteenth century between the goals of precise scientific

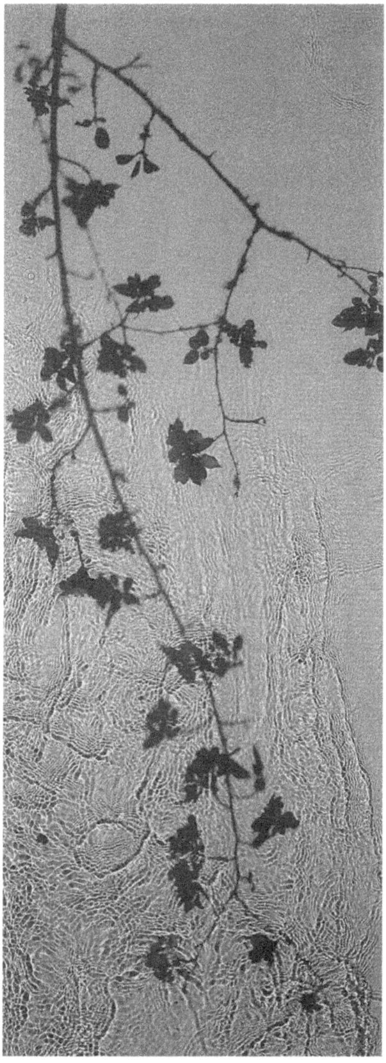

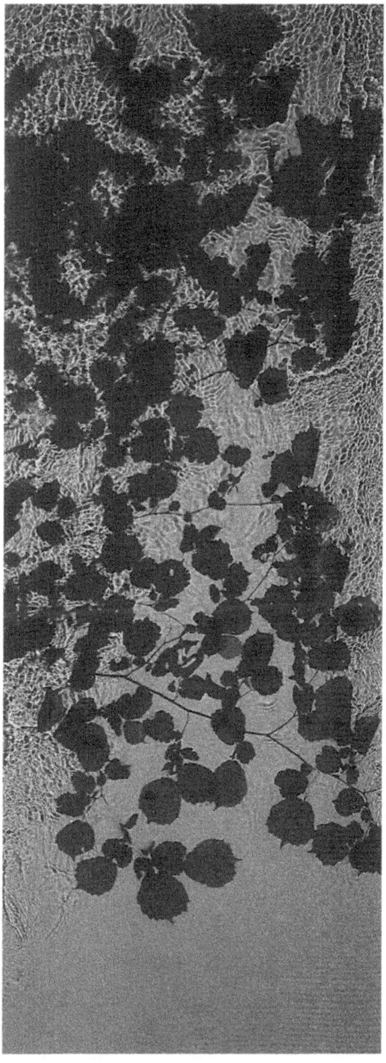

*opposite* FIGURE 44. Susan Derges, *River Taw (Birch), 12 January 1998,* 1998. Photogram on Ilfochrome paper, 66 × 24 inches. Copyright Susan Derges. Courtesy of Fraenkel Gallery, San Francisco.

*above left* FIGURE 45. Susan Derges, *River Taw (Crab Apple), 13 May 1998,* 1998. Photogram on Ilfochrome paper, 66 × 24 inches. Copyright Susan Derges. Courtesy of Fraenkel Gallery, San Francisco.

*above right* FIGURE 46. Susan Derges, *River Taw (Hazel), 16 June 1998,* 1998. Photogram on Ilfochrome paper, 66 × 24 inches. Copyright Susan Derges. Courtesy of Fraenkel Gallery, San Francisco.

illustration and the aesthetic of the picturesque, with its affinity for the asymmetry and irregular details of natural specimens.

Derges, however, alters the medium by attempting to capture the elemental fluxes that surround the stable components of the natural environment. Thus, the central object in a piece from her *River Taw* series is often the silhouette of a tree branch that hangs over the water. Yet the branch and leaves are always seen from underneath the water, as though through a lens of fluid movement and the atmospheric light caused by seasonal changes. If we compare *River Taw (Birch), 12 January 1998* (Figure 44), *River Taw (Crab Apple), 13 May 1998* (Figure 45), and *River Taw (Hazel), 16 June 1998* (Figure 46), we see obvious differences not only in the species of tree but also in the degree of coverage over the river. As curator Charlotte Cotton points out, the deep hues of the prints from the summer months express the cooling shade of the foliage while the lighter hues of the winter prints show the water's exposure to ambient light. The variation in color from one photogram to the next can be attributed to the water's sensitivity to subtle changes in external forces.[20] The vigor of the water gives the image shape and texture, and in its interaction with the leaves and tree branches, the River Taw appears in a synergy of light, movement, color, and atmosphere.

The tree branch is used, then, as a technical device to provide exposure or protection. But more than this, its shadow creates a tension on the surface of the water. When activated by the flash of light of the photogram, the tree branch assembles the River Taw into a visage. Like Mendieta in her performances, Derges pictures the face of the river through a scenario of reciprocal touch. In many of the photograms, the branches carry an uncanny resemblance to skeletal fingers. In others, the leaves or branches are less anthropomorphic, but they nevertheless evoke the sense that the river has come forward into a particular physical stance in relation to the spectator. The silhouettes thus become a definitive presence that comes forward against the swells of the river. This presence eerily mirrors the spectator's position in relation to the photogram. Indeed, the human scale of the photogram (at sixty-six inches long and twenty-four inches wide) emphasizes the corporeal dimension of the confrontation between the River Taw and the viewer.

There is a commonality with Mendieta's performances in the way that Derges positions the viewer in the water, as though immersed in the river, and at the same time rebuffs that entry with the image itself, which stands as a trace of the friction between the water and the pictorial surface, which also stands, I would suggest, for the surface of the body. Placing the Ilfochrome paper under the water, the artist locates the spectator lying horizontally and looking upward at the canopy of leaves that hangs over the river's surface. This horizontal position, as I suggested in chapter 3, simultaneously asserts a stance of disorientation from the vertical perspective and elicits an opening of the senses. Horizontality also requires a level of withdrawal from the unlimitedness of the elemental—in this case, the perspective of the river from underneath exposes a tension between the depth of the water and the surface of the image. Whereas in Turrell's work the reorientation of the viewer to a horizontal position opens the spectator to the plenitude of sensation at the limits of perception, in Derges's work there resonates the textual connotations of Steinberg's notion of the flatbed picture plane, with its suggestion of "hard surfaces such as tabletops, studio floors, charts, bulletin boards—any receptor surface on which objects are scattered, on which data is entered, *on which information may be received, printed, impressed* [my emphasis]."[21] Here, though, rather than looking down at the receptor surface, the spectator takes the stance of the receptor surface, lying down on the horizontal plane with the image floating above. Particularly in works such as *River Taw (Hazel)*, in which the leaves touch the water and flatten out against it, the tension at play on the surface of the river corroborates the suggestion that the viewer is also touched and marked. The horizontal perspective emphasizes the application of the image onto the surface of the photogram, as a transaction involving the receiving, printing, or impressing of information. Not only is the image analogous to the body, then, but its perspective initiates a passage between the provoked sense of bodily contact and the visual spectacle, as though the image of light and shadows are affixed to the photogram as pressure would register on the body. The technique of the photogram, which relies on a horizontal orientation, reroutes vision through tactility. Like skin, the photogram is a receptive medium; it absorbs the image but its receptivity is predicated on its assertion of surface.

The photogram thereby raises two crucial aspects of facing: first, the sensation of the face is mediated through the elemental, and second, the face surfaces *against* that medium. The branch is illuminated by the hues of reflected light and the pushing and pulling streams of water that move against its shadow. Equally, the tree branch interrupts the possible sense of a homogenous elemental plenum into which the spectator could dissolve and instead draws attention to the water as a specific river. Its face appears in the overlap of elementals: in its exposure to the sky, its relationship to changing light, and against the vegetation that grows against its banks. These conditions disclose the river but do not figure it as such. Rather, they mark the photogram as a trace on a surface that parallels the limit of the viewer's body.

The photogram is thus the inverse of what Edward Casey calls body-mapping. Body-mapping in art, he explains, emerged with abstract expressionism, when artists used their bodies as a means of indexing on the canvas a visceral sense of the place that is the subject of the painting. The circumambient landscape is retraced in bodily motions, and these same motions leave traces on the canvas, not representing the landscape's precise contours but reimplacing the bodily perception of them on the pictorial surface.[22] Willem de Kooning's abstract landscapes, for example, seem to spread the body out over the landscape, committing it to the canvas by its very motions, so that the canvas becomes the trace of the meeting of the body and the surface of the earth. Body-mapping marks the body's perception as it moves; however, it does not necessarily evidence elemental movements. In the very formulation of the landscape as body-map, elemental shifts are blocked out in order to give intelligibility and precedence to the subjective bodily experience. Derges's photograms, on the other hand, attempt to uncover these elemental flows. The photogram, and by extension the body of the spectator, is marked by the river, instead of by the artist's tracing of her movement onto the site. Indeed, it is important to point out that Derges's practice cultivates an awareness of the river's transformation over time. Each photogram acts as an entry in a yearlong diary of the river. The series does not represent the river in motion; its temporality is not to be confused with a sense of duration. Rather, the image reveals the river's changes in telling instants, from one image to the next. As the stark branch in January gives way to delicate blooms in May, to fuller branches in June, and to isolated leaves tossing in the wind in November, and as the hues convey both seasonal changes and diurnal shifts in atmosphere, Derges documents the River Taw as a sequence of elemental events.

The artworks present the river in moments at which the process of image-making stimulates the river to rise up, make contact, and become visible momentarily.

Inherently contradictory, for the still image is created by ephemeral conditions, the photogram reveals the river's resistance to transparency as, in John Sallis's words, a face that is continually threatened because its coming forth is always a coming to pass.[23] The countenance that the water brings to light, and that appears as a consequence of the division that the photogram inserts within the water, is both present and unintelligible, impenetrable but still fragile in its exposure. The visage of the river is thus closed off to the invasive movement of seeing as grasping, in the mode of Merleau-Ponty's phenomenology, or of perceiving as marking, in Casey's example of the landscape as body-map. Instead, the River Taw pushes against the surface of the photogram, coming forward through the spectral appearances of the branches. Derges's photograms therefore propose an aesthetic encounter similar to Irigaray's scenario in which the other withholds from one's own self-same perception and "irradiates a truth which we can receive without its source being visible . . . [and] remains a mystery for us but we can indirectly perceive something of it."[24]

## The Ethics of Receiving: Jackie Brookner's Gift

Mendieta's earth–body sculptures and Derges's photograms entail a facing of the earth, not by way of an exchange of gazes nor by "taking hold" but by stimulating its appearance on the surface of the elemental. The sculptures of the American artist Jackie Brookner likewise revolve around strategies that initiate the earth's manifestation on bodily surfaces. Like those of Mendieta and Derges, Brookner's works evoke the bodily sensations of natural processes; however, they cultivate an approach to sensibility through reciprocity: gestures that glean sense through the offering of the body. That is, Brookner locates her artworks in a circuitry of exchange, in which they elicit natural events and thematize the receiving of sensation within and against the elemental.

The question of how art can literally "articulate" natural processes is the subject of *Prima Lingua* (Figures 47 and 48). Like many of Brookner's works, *Prima Lingua* is a biosculpture, an object engineered to function as a water filtration

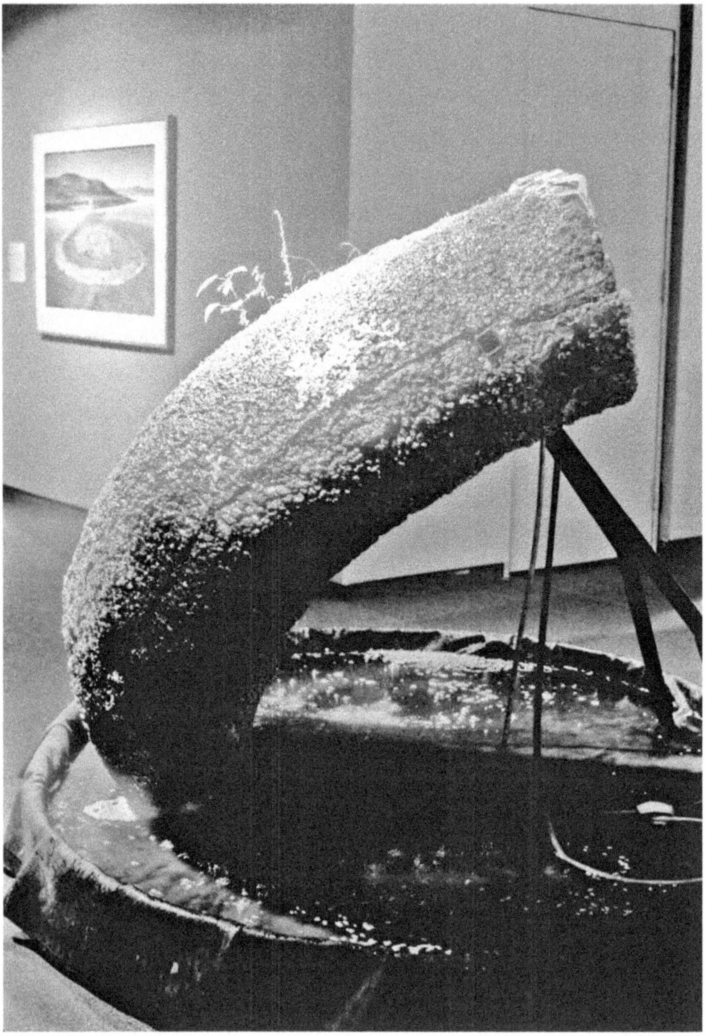

FIGURE 47. Jackie Brookner, *Prima Lingua,* 1996–present. Concrete, volcanic rock, mosses, ferns, wetland plants, fish, steel, 64 × 101 × 80 inches; shown here in 1996. Copyright Jackie Brookner.

*opposite*
FIGURE 48. Jackie Brookner, *Prima Lingua,* shown here in 2001, with mosses and ferns grown in. Copyright Jackie Brookner.

system. Brookner's biosculptures are made of stone, rock, or concrete, materials on which mosses, liverworts, ferns, and snails can grow and proliferate. The artist explains that the sculpture is a biogeochemical filter: as water flows over it, plants, bacteria, and other organisms transform pollutants into sustaining nutrients, demonstrating how in a healthy ecosystem waste can be transformed and reintegrated.[25]

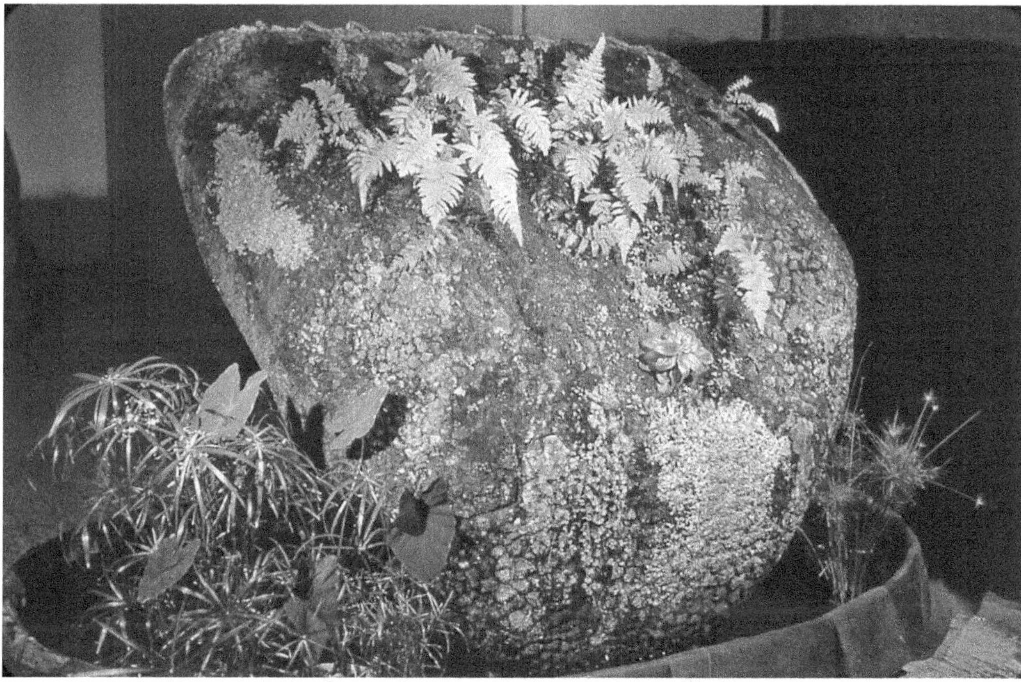

The mosses absorb toxins and even heavy metals, while the porous concrete substructure removes larger particulates and debris. *Prima Lingua,* made of concrete and volcanic rock in the shape of a giant tongue, stands in what began as a pool of polluted water. Constructing the work in 1996, Brookner pumped the water over the surface of the tongue. Over time vegetation has grown and thickened on the sculpture, gradually purifying the pool.

Significantly, Brookner chose a tongue as the sculptural motif. The artist describes the tongue as literally licking the water in which it stands. Indeed, the pouring water calls to mind dripping saliva. There are several particularities to the tongue that convey the relation between the sculpture, the water, and the subsequent growth of vegetation. In foregrounding the role of the tongue to lick the water clean, Brookner invokes a specific mode of sensorial experience that cannot be expressed by any other body part. The act of licking involves two kinds of sensation: touching and tasting. Tongues feel contour and texture, sensing through tactile exploration. However, they need only apply their surface against something in order to taste. Tasting, unlike touching, is a matter of receiving flavor; it is produced through chemical reaction. As in Derges's photograms, then, the contact between the artwork and elemental movement appears through the transformation of the work's surface. Though the tongue of *Prima Lingua* is large and thick, it is the receptivity of its surface that is the focus of the artwork (Figure 49). Not coincidentally, the tongue pushes out, flattened and wide, rather than lying supine. The tongue offers the lively growth of mosses and plants as though they were a burst of flavor. The aesthetic richness of the work is hinged not simply on the tongue as a sculptural object or on the vegetation in and of itself but also on the particular way the tongue cues the experience of the vegetation—allowing it to blossom uninterrupted by a penetrating touch.

Additionally, the tongue marks a passage between the interior and the exterior of the body. Unlike any other appendage, the tongue is located in a liminal zone, able to both reach outside and retract inside. Brookner seizes this aspect of the tongue as that which externalizes expression and invites sensation inward, to make a point about the interconnectedness of the earth and the body. The tongue is (usually) the primary instrument by which one consolidates language as speech. Yet whereas the discursive realm is often considered to be separate from and superior to the terrestrial sphere, Brookner secures their inextricability. Natural processes become a primary language, a *prima lingua,* to which we are privy before human language. Whereas Mendieta and Derges deploy their artworks as vehicles to face the earth from within the elemental in the contact between two surfaces, as, in Irigaray's image, two lips gathered "on the edge of speech," Brookner attempts a facing of the earth *as* this moment of poise that leads to enunciation. Language, here, is shown to arise from an elemental basis, carried up through the body in the same way the plants grow as a result of the continual flow of water pumped over the tongue. The tongue in itself does not form a word; it exposes the unintelligible transaction of sensations that precede and inspire speech. Moreover, it is housed not in a mouth but in a system of elementals—in water, air, and light. Brookner's tongue thus exteriorizes the body; it is exposed flesh that reacts with external nature, thereby revealing that language is spurred forth by the internal sensations of the friction between the body and the earth.

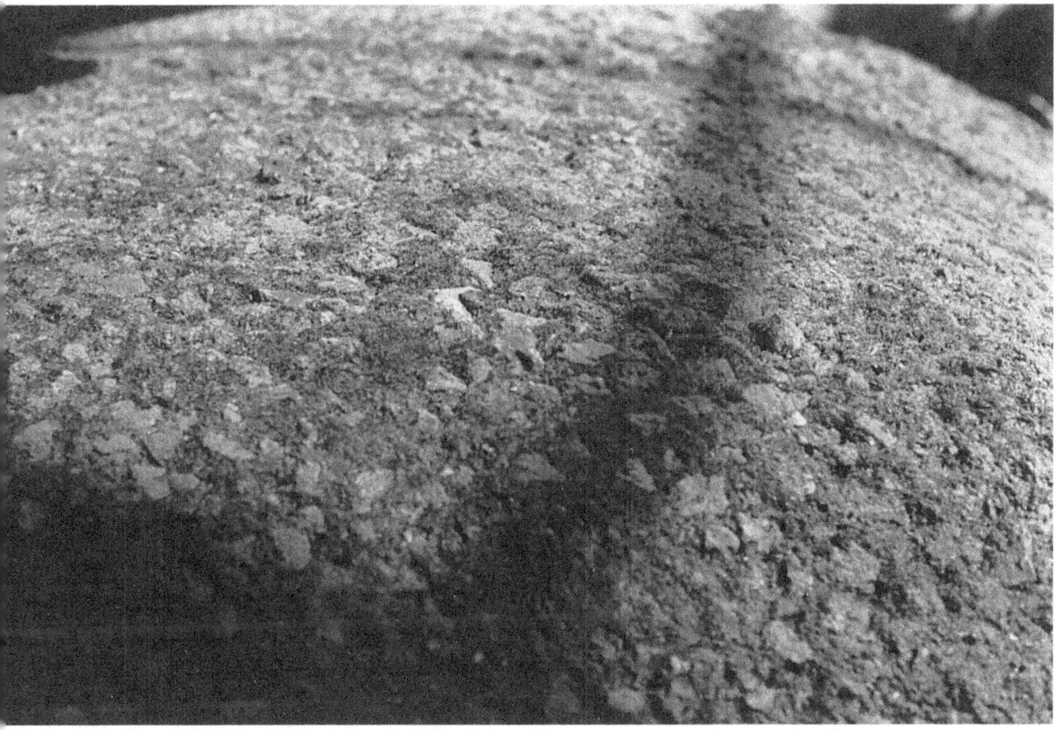

FIGURE 49. Jackie Brookner, *Prima Lingua* (detail), shown here in 1996. Copyright Jackie Brookner.

The face of the earth, encompassed by the growth on the tongue, parallels the articulation of a word. The artwork underscores, however, that the emergence of the face, like speech, is contingent on a subtle connectivity and division between two: between the speaker and the listener, or in this particular case, between the internal body and the external realm of elementals. The perception of the earth, like the communication of language, is predicated on its subtle expressiveness. In turning internal processes of speech into external processes of taste and touch, Brookner shows the influx of sensations that precede and inform discursive meaning. She then figures the face as an expression of language founded on that influx; vegetation and organisms take root and flourish because of the tongue's passive offering of itself as surface.

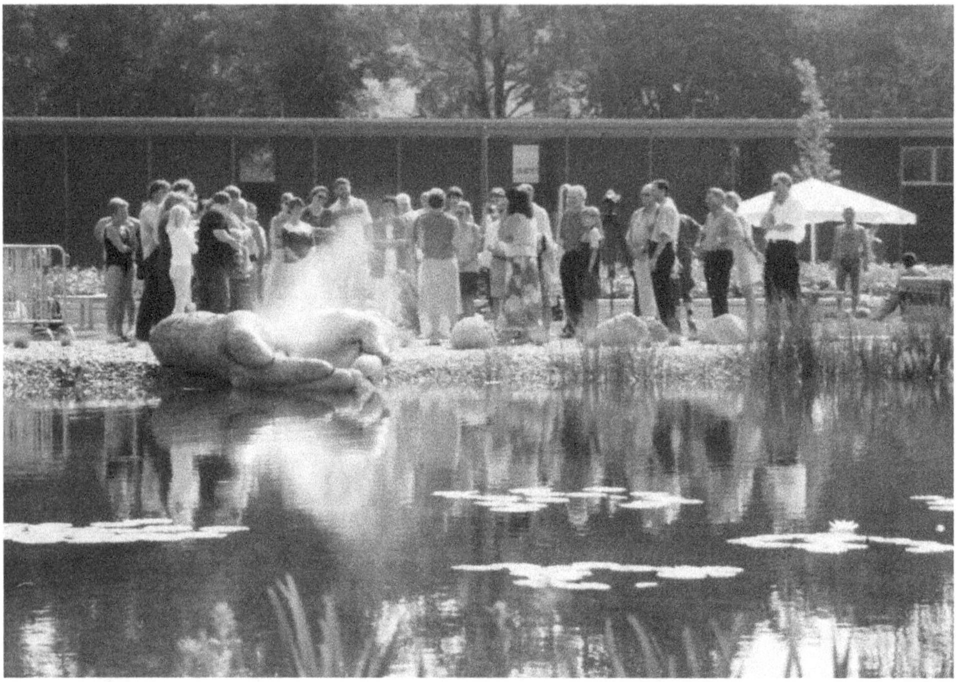

FIGURE 50. Jackie Brookner, *The Gift of Water,* 2001. Textile reinforced concrete, mosses, wetland plants, misting fountain. Grossenheim, Germany. Copyright Jackie Brookner.

In much the way Smithson recovers the elemental within the dense sediment of material language, Brookner's work intertwines language with the fluid dynamics of the elemental. However, instead of positioning words as material sediment, the continuous pouring of water over the tongue stimulates the emergence of what we might call vegetal utterances that rise up and fall away. The artist states that the piece is a visible image of transformation, revealing decay as part of creation.[26] But even more subtly, in offering the tongue as a receptive surface, the work makes the earth visible in the midst of its transformation. In this respect, Brookner's work reiterates John Sallis's point that the face of the earth exposes its physiognomy while also withholding itself. In its involution within the elemental, its simultaneous thrust forward and push back against the water that pours over it, the tongue

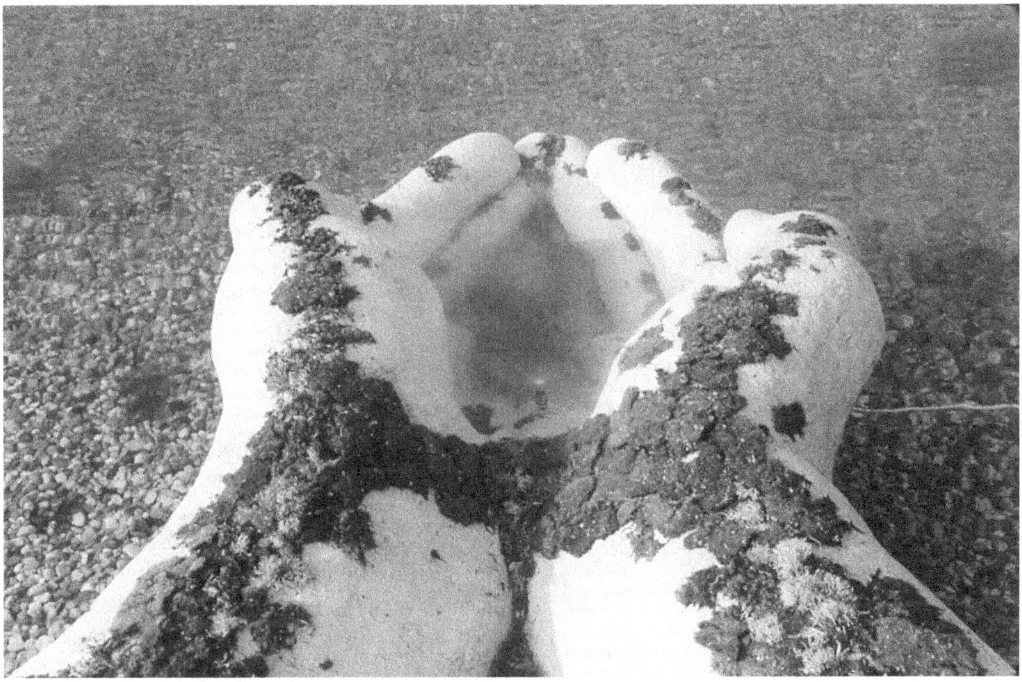

FIGURE 51. Jackie Brookner, *The Gift of Water,* 2001. Mosses growing on hands. Copyright Jackie Brookner.

gives rise to Brookner's micro-ecosystem. Natural activity is open-ended; it blooms but is never secured as a closed object to be held or seen in a perceptual grip. The continual transformation of the tongue forecloses the possibility that sensation is strictly a means to intelligibility. The tongue's location within the system of growth and decay opens a different approach to sensation, through its tactile support.

Like *Prima Lingua,* Brookner's other biosculptures substantiate a passage through which the elemental flows and mediates a sensual experience of nature and similarly posit the receiving of sensation as an ethical mode of perception. Her public work *The Gift of Water* (Figures 50 and 51), executed in Grossenheim, Germany, in 2001, features a literal wellspring that consolidates an ecological and phenomenological circuitry between the artwork and the site. The sculptural component of the work, a pair of giant hands, open with one resting on the other, is part of a natural water filtration system. The hands are made of a lightweight, textile-reinforced concrete, on which the purifying mosses and bacteria grow. A misting fountain spraying from between the hands aerates the water and moistens the mosses, which in turn purify the water. *The Gift of Water* was made as part of a new public swimming complex in which the water is filtered entirely by wetland plants without the use of chlorine or other chemicals.

The gesture of the giant hands, which reach from the bank into the pond, expresses the reciprocity of the artwork's relationship to the site—its simultaneous receiving and giving. Though the hands are not pressed against one another like those in Irigaray's image of reciprocal touch, the artwork expresses a similar relation of feeling–felt if we read it in terms of the contact between the hands and the pond. The hands are gathered together, open to receive the water. The suggestion that the hands are taking the water as though cupping it in order to drink, however, is inverted into a gesture of donation. The misting fountain projects a stream of water from the hands back into the pond. The title of the work, *The Gift of Water,* therefore has two directions. Clean water is given as a gift to the human public from the wetland ecosystem, but at the same time the artwork returns that gift of water to the ecosystem, since it acts as a catalyst for the growth of vegetation that cleans the water.

The artwork mediates the encounter between the public and the natural regeneration of the site. But it is the reversal of this exchange—the overturn of receiving into gift—that fosters the emergence of the face of that site. Water is an essential aesthetic component of the work: the pond reflects the light, it is touched by the giant hands, and it projects out from them in a misty cloud. But further, the work mobilizes the water to express its function to visitors and to the ecosystem. Water weaves the sculpture and the site together into a system of mutual support, in a succinct image of how the elemental binds us to the earth. Further, the pond is the medium by which mosses and plants can appear and grow on the surface of the sculpture. The hands assert the ecological growth, interestingly, through the immediacy of touch. The relation is not carried out as a grasp that would suffocate nature in the moment of its vulnerable exposure. Instead, the hands are positioned to receive touch through the giving of surface. Brookner thereby inspires the aesthetic and sensuous pleasure of water, transforming it into an ethical encounter—a facing of the earth through sensibility.

Because it is a public work connected to an existing wetland, the question of site returns in *The Gift of Water* in a more pressing way than in the self-regulating ecosystem of *Prima Lingua.* That is to say, more than being a sculptural object, *The Gift of Water* functions within a larger arena of experience: it is a filtration system installed within a natural place and a public space. The giant hands are not discrete objects; they are propositions to the visitor of how to approach the site at large. Insofar as it internalizes the perceptual experience of reciprocity that it creates with the ecosystem, *The Gift of Water* is better categorized as an installation than as a discrete sculpture. Alex Potts explains that installation work can be understood within a certain dialectical oscillation between a positivistic insistence on firmly defined entities on the one hand, and a radical undoing and unfixing of the definable object on the other.[27] The space of an installation into which a spectator enters has its own materiality and definition conjured up by a fabric of enclosure. Potts argues that the shape of the installation resides in the framing that focuses the viewer's looking, as though the "thingness" of the sculptural object has been turned inside out. He stresses that the shift from sculpture to installation is a symptom of sculpture's absorption of its conditions of staging and display, as well as a troubling of the modes of viewing and perception that those conditions give rise to.

My goal in positing that *The Gift of Water* is an installation instead of either a site-specific work (the more general characterization) or a public sculpture is to emphasize Brookner's appeal to the public about how to approach the swimming complex: to receive it as one would a gift, rather than to take it and occupy it as one's own. The giant hands punctuate the complex and embody the system of interrelatedness between humans and ecosystem. Otherwise put: they suggest a mode of confrontation with the wetland environment. Mick Smith makes the point that tangibility is the touchstone of a modern reality oriented toward the instrumentalization of matter—toward "things that exhibit a paradigmatic materiality, that are solid, fixed, bounded, isolable."[28] Instrumental logic operates in accordance with a mechanics of solids, denying that which is permeable, fluid, and less tangible. Brookner's hands signal that the swimming pond cannot be understood as a bounded space that is fixed and available to a colonizing touch. The openness of the hands, which allows for the uprising of water from between them and the growth of mosses on their surface, is a recommendation of how to conceptualize the site as sensuous but not tangible, as material but alive and changing. In Potts's description, an installation isolates an architectonic shaping and disperses focus to the staged environment.[29] However, *The Gift of Water* problematizes the logic of enclosure that defines installation. In its insistence on an ethical mode of contact, it invites entry into the pond but shifts its orientation to the ecological workings of the earth that sustains it. It thereby insists on a different kind of sensibility, one oriented not toward the preservation of nature within a closed framework but rather toward a subtle awareness of the co-implication of the swimming pond and the wetland. In this way, like Olafur Eliasson's works, Brookner's installation is an ecotechnology that interrogates the limits of its own closed system and posits a means of contact with the earth that lies beyond it.

## Surfaces of Sensation

The interplay of three-dimensional space and two-dimensional surface in earth art is a strategy by which artists redefine sensation through receptivity. Receptivity takes place through a conscientious recession that inaugurates an opening of sensorial possibilities.

For these artists, one cannot convey the body–earth relation simply by evoking immersion in an elemental plenum; there is always the risk that natural processes will be subsumed into a purely anthropocentric or solipsistic perceptual experience. Ethical contact requires an involution, a retraction from the immersive experience, a turn to face the other, as well as the earth itself, across and through the limits of the body. The recurrent assertion of a receptive surface—be it the bodily imprint, the photogram, or the reconfiguration of installation as ecotechnology—is a cue to the intertwinement and insurmountable division between the body and the earth. Mendieta, Derges, and Brookner demonstrate that an ethical relation is negotiated not only through sensation but through sensation in a particular mode of withdrawal that discloses this threshold or partition. Their works do not simply extol the earth's otherness; they are preoccupied with the limit of our perception and the conscious assertion of the body *as* that limit. The artists foster an ethical stance by predicating the artwork on techniques of receptivity. More strongly, by receding from the earth, they forego a position of privilege within it and locate the body as a receptive surface that turns against it.

CONCLUSION

# Facing the Earth Ethically

In a 2006 press release, Greenpeace reported on the danger of accumulating plastics, also known as "marine debris," in the world's oceans.[1] Estimating that over 267 species of animals were being contaminated through the ingestion of plastic waste floating in the water or aggregating on seabeds and shores, not to mention the multitudes of ocean creatures becoming entangled in this human litter, the report presented a sobering account of the impact of environmental negligence. Perhaps the most disturbing information in the report was on the "world's largest floating dump," the North Pacific Gyre. A giant vortex of trash, roughly estimated to be the size of Texas, has amassed between Hawaii and North America at the epicenter of a system of wind and water currents. It holds in suspension plastic waste from Asia, the Pacific, and North America. Not only does the gyre choke and ensnare marine life in the area and contaminate every level of the food chain, but it also stands as a tragic image of the consequences of the environmental predicament humans have created. In addition to putting other species and their worlds in peril, our solipsism has become self-destructive. Blanketing one of our elemental sources with waste that is, not coincidentally, solid, suffocating, and impenetrable, the trash vortex is a clear symptom of a paradigmatic contact that denies an ethical communicability with the planet. A reconsideration not merely of resource management but of our mode of encounter with the earth has never been more vital.

## Ichi Ikeda's Future Compass

Since the 1980s the Japanese artist Ichi Ikeda has incorporated water into his performances and installations, pursuing a mandate to show how environmental conditions inform human relations via elementals and to open possibilities for an ethical approach to the planet. Ikeda organizes public exhibitions designed to raise awareness about the planet's diminishing supply of water. His works, however, situate water not only as a topic of ecological concern but also as the medium that connects the earth and its inhabitants and that is the fluid basis of what we might think of as an emerging global consciousness—a commitment to others beyond anthropocentric boundaries such as national borders and local community. Water, in Ikeda's artworks, is the medium for ethical feeling, yielding sensibility and ceding a response to the other's imperative.

An active member of the art scene in Tokyo in the sixties and seventies, Ikeda participated in avant-garde theater, staging plays by Samuel Beckett and Eugène Ionesco, as well as founding his own theater company for which he was a playwright, art director, and actor. His roots in existentialist and absurdist performance translated into a long-standing interest in water as an artistic medium, for it does not conform to the will of the artist, and at the same time its abundant sensorial qualities lend it an aesthetic power. In an interview in 2007 he explains, "The process of art is a way of improvising at unraveling my entangled self, not some ritual thing. Instead of forming a concept into a shape, my performance sculpture is more like the unraveling of a cord. Nothing surpasses water as a medium of expression: it holds no bodily form and can metamorphose as a living entity."[2] Like Smithson's *Spiral Jetty,* Mendieta's *siluetas,* Turrell's *Skyspaces,* and Eliasson's installations,

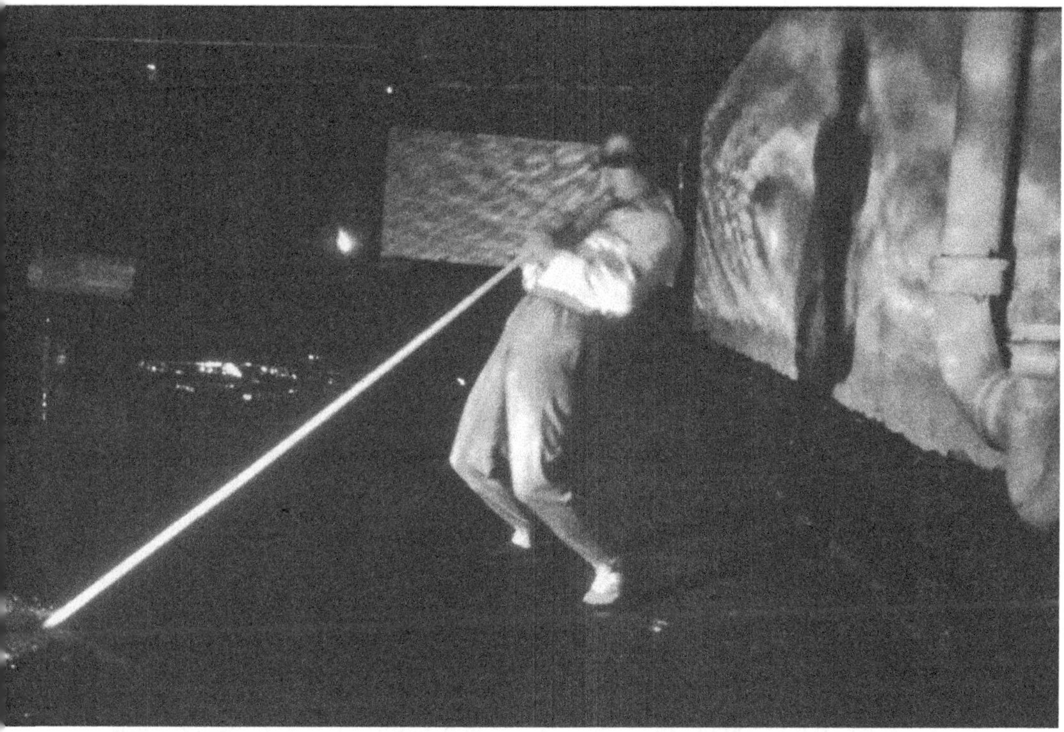

FIGURE 52. Ichi Ikeda, *Water Mirror*, Franklin Furnace Gallery, 1988. Copyright Ichi Ikeda Art Project.

Ikeda's works with water show his interest in the power of elementals to disassemble the boundaries of the art object and correspondingly reconfigure the limits of the viewing subject.

Interestingly, Ikeda raises the issue of the communicability of water in his description of it as a "medium of expression." The importance of water lies not only in its position as a precious natural resource but also in its irreducible qualities—how it defies concept and form yet also moves as a living thing. In the same way that Turrell attempts to give *thingness* to light and color, Ikeda considers water in terms both of the way it encompasses space and of the play of visual effects on its surface in a performance work called *Water Mirror* installed at the Franklin Furnace Gallery in New York in 1988 (Figure 52). Aiming to create a work that would reveal the relationship between the city of New York and the Hudson River on which it depends, Ikeda began by drawing water from the Hudson, putting it into containers, and pushing them in a cart through the Lower East Side and onto the subway. Then he redesigned the gallery space in order to display it. Sectioning off an area of the gallery, the artist painted the walls white. The floor was painted aquamarine and fitted with a shallow pool for the water. Finally, lights from the ceiling shone on the surface of the water, creating shadowy forms and ripples on the white walls. To galvanize the constructed space, Ikeda set the water in motion by stepping into the pool and blowing into it through a long hose.

There are two aspects of this performance that speak to the paradigm of earth art. First, the laborious process of collecting and transporting the water across the city works against the otherwise dormant presence of the Hudson. In some respects, this part of the performance acts as a kind of ecotechnology. By linking the river to urban pathways, containing the water in large plastic receptacles, and routing them to the gallery, Ikeda emulates the seizure and management of the river as a standing reserve. Second, however, he opens the aesthetic and ethical dimensions of the performance by bringing water into visibility and illuminating its surface effects. The presence of the river water in the building was disconcerting, not only because it was displaced but also because the river is widely known to be polluted. But the gesture of blowing against the water, which animates it with inviting movement, is symbolically regenerative. Like the image of Drury's camera obscura, the reflections in the mirror and play of shadows on the ceiling escape perceptual fixity, and for precisely this reason the water brought the entire gallery to life. Ikeda describes his performance as a way of introducing "fertile breaths" into the environment: "A building starts to breathe like a living creature when it's surrounded by wave reflections created by breathing."[3] The artist thereby forges a contact between the city and the river by activating the elemental surface, bringing it forward through contact with his breath.

Ikeda has developed these two aspects of the performance—the enactment of storing water and the mobilization of an aesthetic experience of the elemental—in his works since the nineties. However, his more recent works are geared more directly to an awareness of the global water supply. As one of twelve artists chosen to appear in the UN's fiftieth-anniversary calendar and since exhibiting at the Third

World Water Forum in Japan in 2003, Ikeda is now recognized by global political organizations. From this platform he has oriented his works toward public action while nevertheless insisting on maintaining the rich aesthetic dimension of his earlier performances. For example, Ikeda held what he called a *Big Hands Conference* in Bangkok, Thailand, in 2000 (Figure 53). For this installation he staged a conference of hands, actually large photostats of pairs of hands, twelve sets in all, gathered together around a large table and hung above twelve chairs. On the table in the middle, the artist projected an image of his own hands immersed in water, open and holding it. The gesture of cupped hands suggested the receiving of water; however, this inviting image was interrupted by the printed text in the center of each pair of hands. The hands were imprinted with captions about environmental disasters related to water, such as "Because of water pollution, 20% of fresh water fish species are nearly to the point of extinction"; "The diseases related to water are supposed to cause one child to die every 8 seconds"; and "After 50 years from now, it is supposed [the] number of people suffering seriously from shortage of water will reach to 66 countries, two-thirds of the population of the world" (Figure 54).

The photographs, like Ikeda's earlier performance in New York, emphasize the rippling surface of the water and the reflection of light. The warnings of depleted supply, disease, and toxicity undercut the implied plenitude of the image of the hands immersed in water. The installation was a direct call to action, much like Irland's *A Gathering of Waters,* in which the artwork reconfigures social relations on the basis of an ecological imperative. In fact, Ikeda's goal for *Big Hands Conference* was to solicit spectators' signatures to a "Water Sender's Agreement," whose signatories committed to take action to relay water to people in the future. The agreement, a paper contract that participants actually signed, reads, "Let us all be Water Senders, sending water, one of the Earth's most precious resources, to all people living in the future, regardless of cultural, national or religious differences and disagreements." As in Brookner's *The Gift of Water,* the artist positioned the image of two open hands as an image of simultaneous giving and receiving.

The "Water Sender's Agreement" is linked to Ikeda's broader ambition—what he calls his *World Water Ekiden* projects—to assemble communities in order to construct large holding containers of water, with the goal of storing it for future generations. The organizing tenet of the *World Water Ekiden* projects is the idea

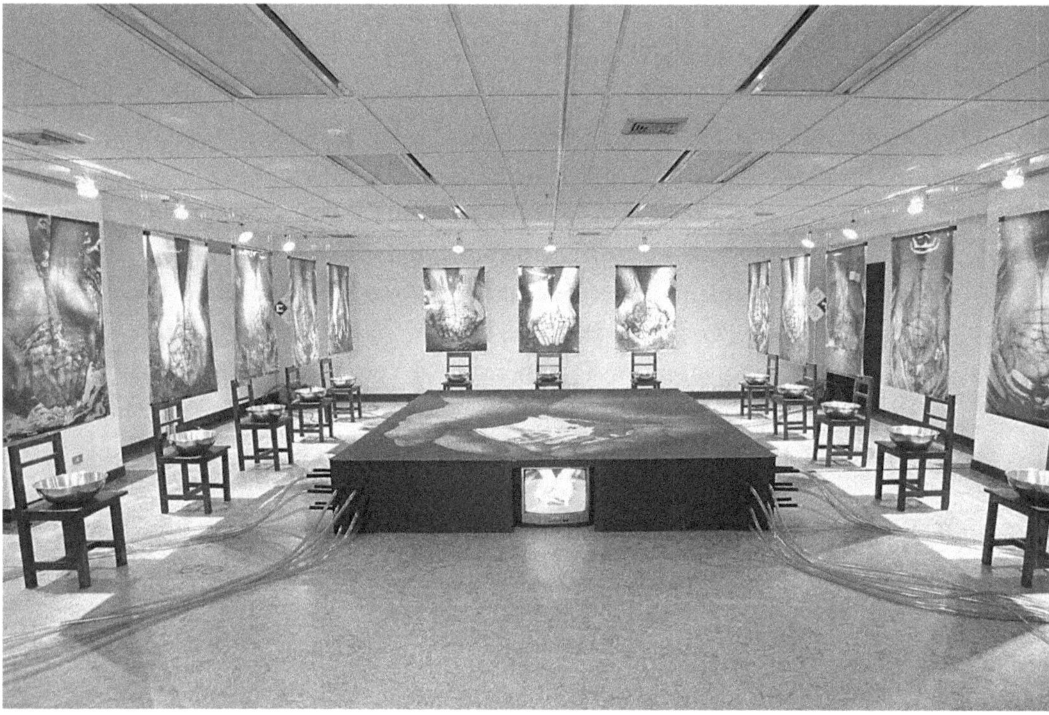

FIGURE 53. Ichi Ikeda, *Big Hands Conference,* Bangkok, Thailand, 2000. Copyright Ichi Ikeda Art Project.

that, according to the World Health Organization, each person needs eighty liters of water daily to maintain a basic standard of health, though some live with as little as five liters a day. Ikeda thus conceived of a clear plastic, cubical receptacle that would hold eighty liters of water and made this the building block of his installations around the world. Touring major cities in Japan, Southeast Asia, and the United States, Ikeda presents eighty-liter water boxes with information about global water shortages. However, his installations also aim to show that water is the elemental basis of our lived experience of the earth and of others in the world. For every person who signs a "Water Sender's Agreement," Ikeda fills an eighty-liter unit affixed with photographic transparencies of the donor's hands cupping the water. In Kawaguchi City, for a work entitled *Future Compass,* he acquired enough cubes to fill a large reservoir that holds eighty thousand liters of water, or a daily

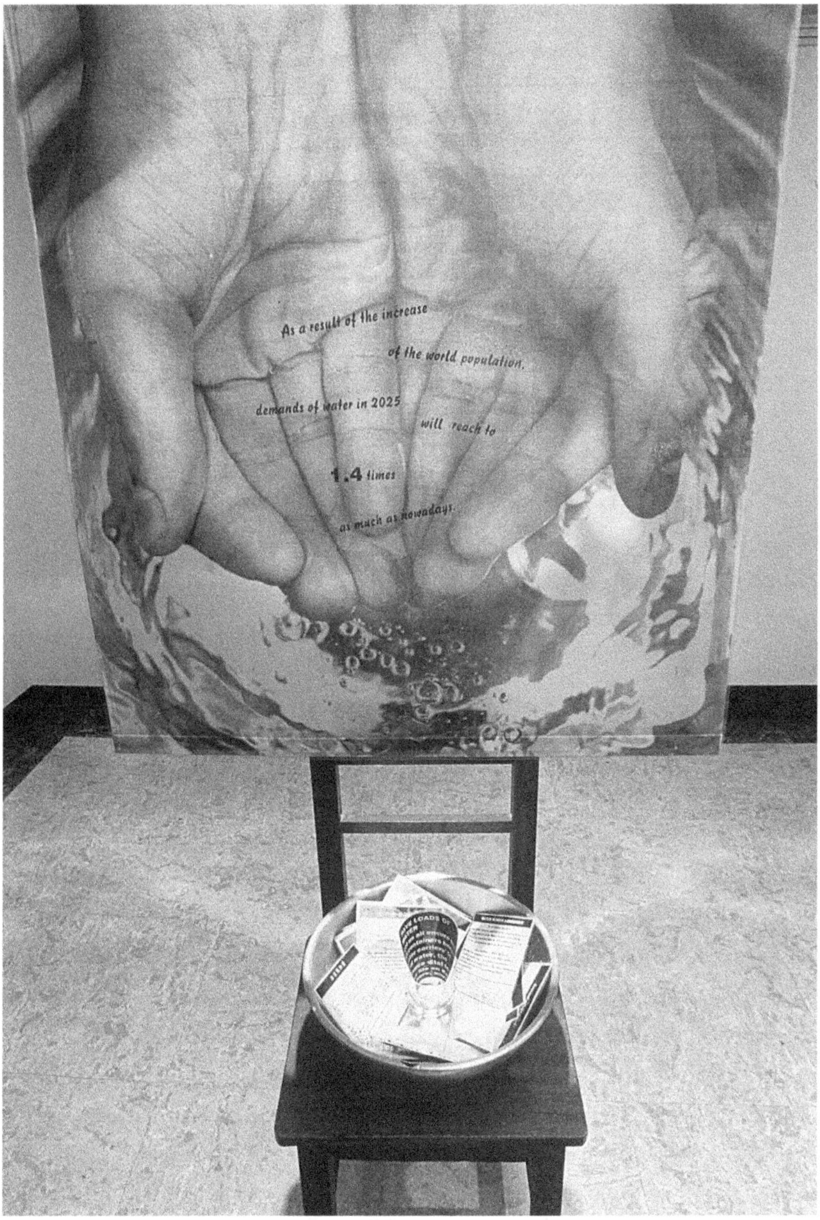


FIGURE 54. Ichi Ikeda, *Big Hands Conference* (detail), Bangkok, Thailand, 2000. Copyright Ichi Ikeda Art Project.

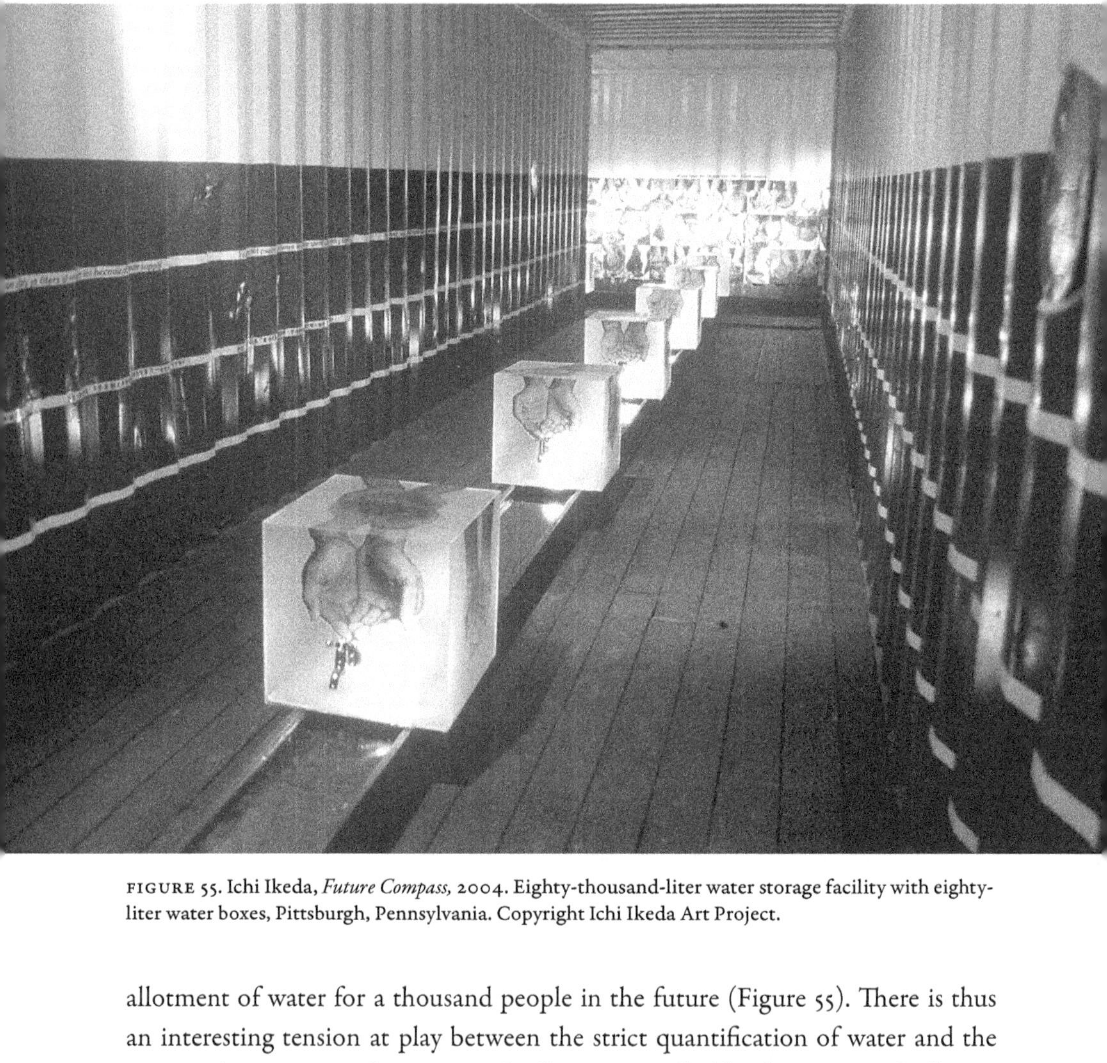

FIGURE 55. Ichi Ikeda, *Future Compass,* 2004. Eighty-thousand-liter water storage facility with eighty-liter water boxes, Pittsburgh, Pennsylvania. Copyright Ichi Ikeda Art Project.

allotment of water for a thousand people in the future (Figure 55). There is thus an interesting tension at play between the strict quantification of water and the imagined movement of water into the future, propelled by the gesture of offering. Though the water has been harnessed for exclusively human use, the implication is that the performance of donation, which requires a distinct denial of the participant's use of the water for her or his own purposes, returns to it its elemental qualities.

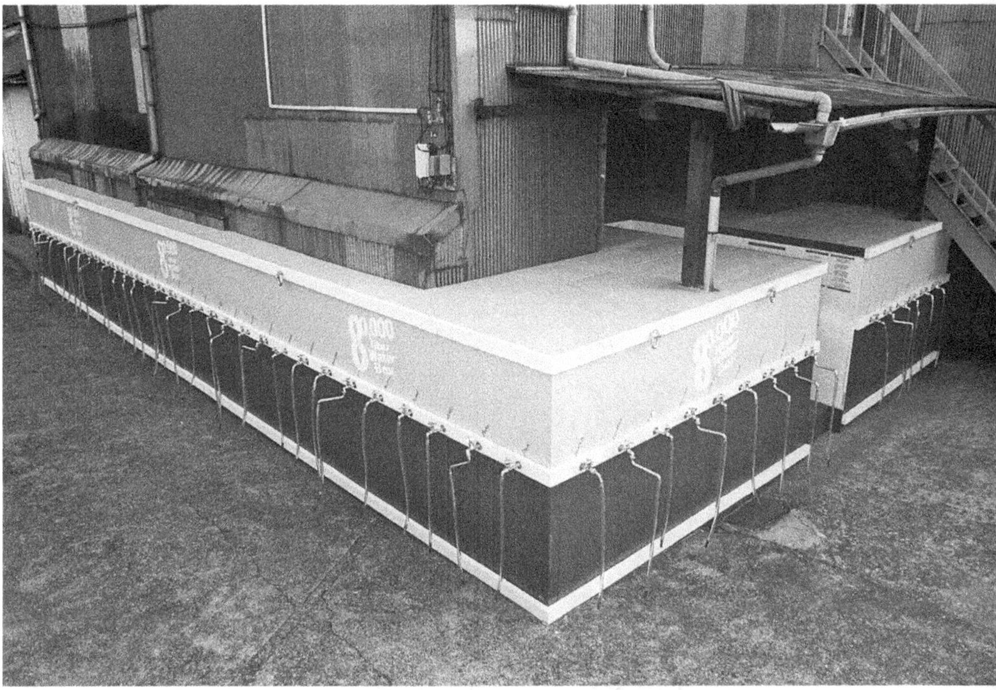

FIGURE 56. Ichi Ikeda, *Kawaguchi Water Factory,* 2005. Eighty-thousand-liter water storage unit with forty-eight taps, Kawaguchi City, Japan. Copyright Ichi Ikeda Art Project.

Ikeda's prognosticated future is not entirely abstract, nor is it even so distant. For his *Kawaguchi Water Factory,* organized in Kawaguchi City, Japan, in 2005, Ikeda built a water purification and storage facility aiming to collect the 80,000 liters of water for the forty-eight countries that are predicted to suffer from water shortage by the year 2025 (Figure 56). The artist converted an old iron foundry into a warehouse and fitted it with equipment to collect and clean rainwater. The large storage container was built against the exterior wall of the factory, and Ikeda installed forty-eight taps into it, one water line for each country anticipated to be struck with drought. Certainly, the *Kawaguchi Water Factory* is not intended to replace the necessary political legislation that would prevent water pollution and shortage. Rather, it is underpinned by the idea of an *ekiden,* or relay race. Just as a team passes

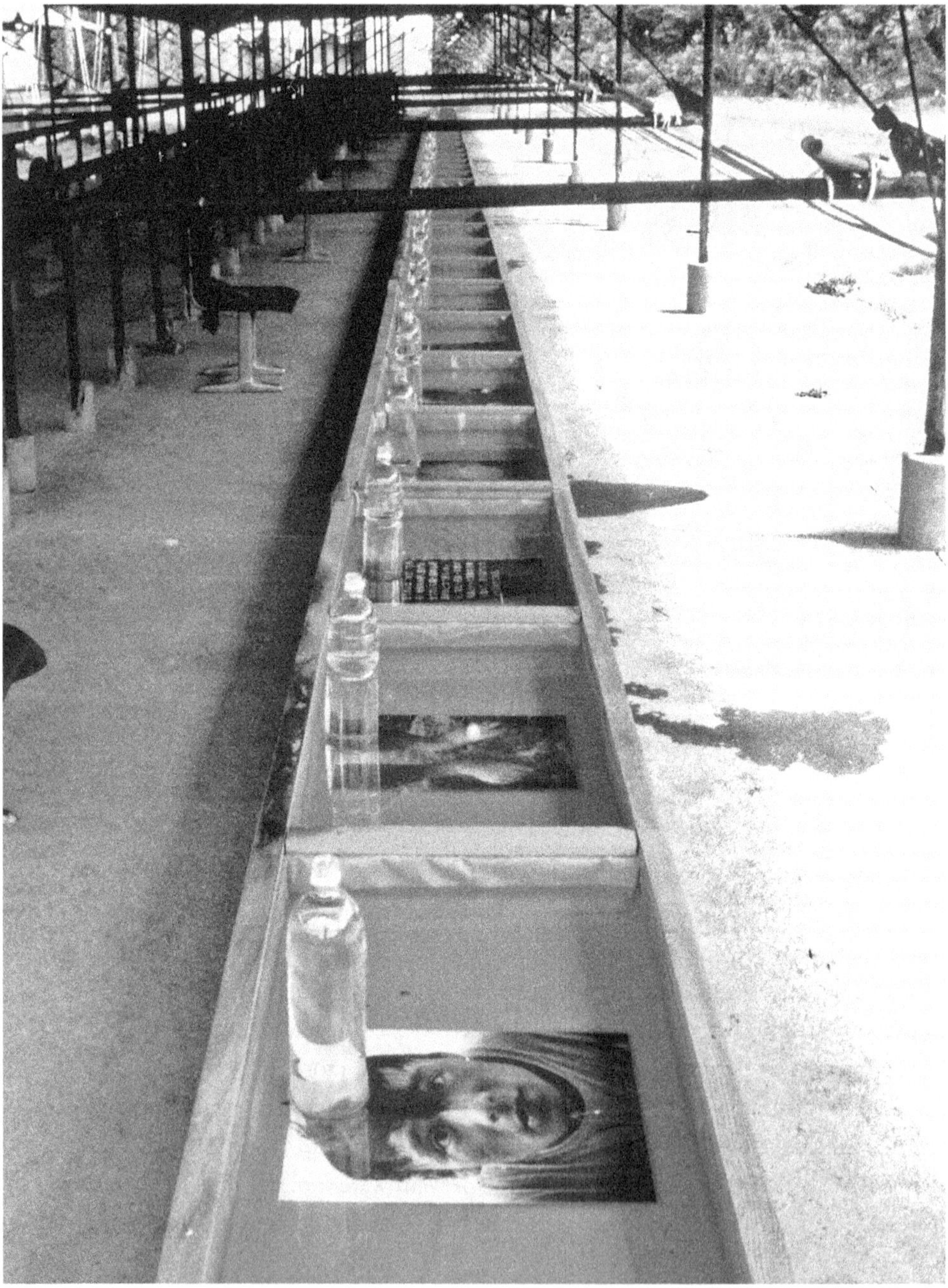

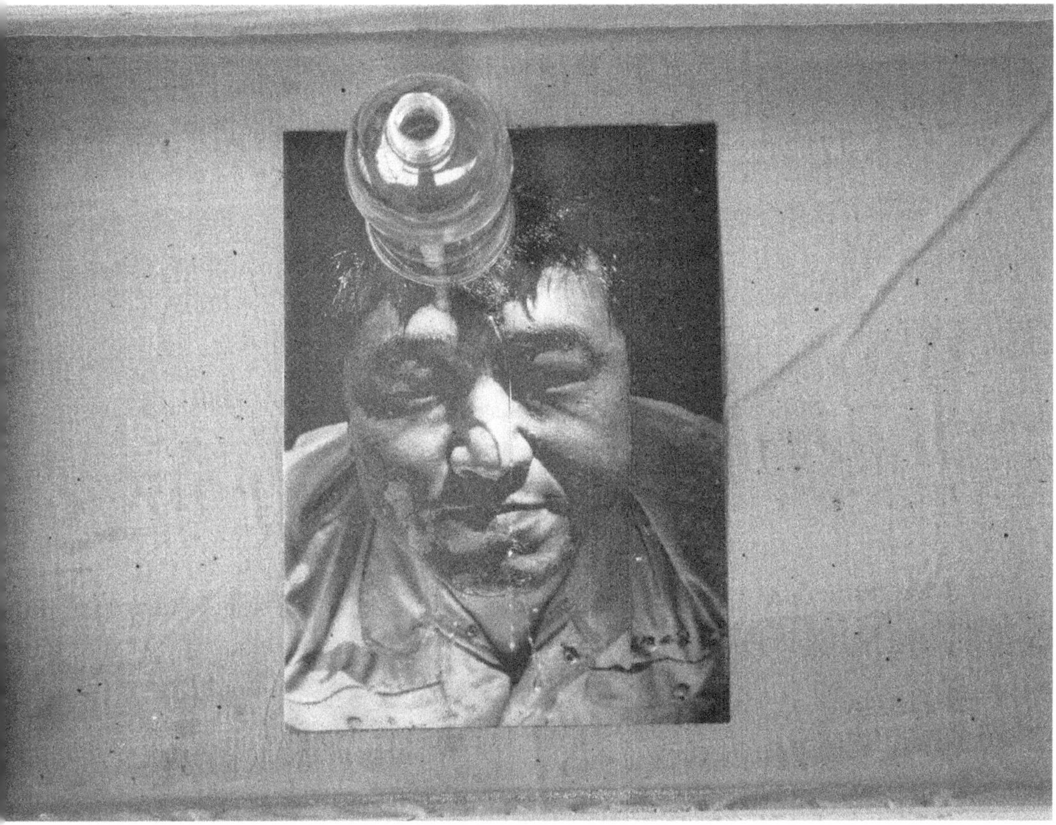

*opposite* FIGURE 57. Ichi Ikeda, *Kaseda Water Market,* 1998. Water boxes, photographs, air pumps. Copyright Ichi Ikeda Art Project.

*above* FIGURE 58. Ichi Ikeda, *Kaseda Water Market,* detail of Kaseda water station, 1998. Copyright Ichi Ikeda Art Project.

a baton from one member to the next, moving it forward in a race, Ikeda stages a flow of water across geographic distance, past the divisions of national borders, and over the time between the present and the future.

But the *World Water Ekiden* is not necessarily a statement of generalized humanism. To the contrary: what is at stake is the uncertainty of the water's destination, which calls into question the future condition of the planet and its inhabitants, who will face the consequences of our decisions in the present. This uncertainty is directly related to the alterity of the elemental. As Stephen Ross explains, what is dangerous about the earth is the way in which its abundance exceeds human order. By "abundance," Ross refers to the earth's unpredictable unfolding into the future: "Abundance is the material expression of a future and of other species and kinds that we may never hope to make stable." He concludes that what is required of an ecological ethic is a celebration of biodiversity as "salutation and exaltation—toward a *parousia,* a future [to] come, toward others we do not know and cannot imagine."[4]

Ikeda's *World Water Ekiden* projects confront communities with their most basic human need—the need for water—and transfigure it into a performance of offering. Water is the subject and also the dominant aesthetic component of the installations; it is poured into containers, touched by hands, and often illuminated by spotlights. At the same time, the undercurrent of the artwork is always a response to an other. Ikeda answers the imperative for water through its sensuousness, deploying it not only as a basic necessity but also as a medium of aesthetic and ethical exchange and political action. The ethical imperative toward other people is to be heeded not just in the abstract but also through sensibility. As Lingis explains, the face-to-face encounter takes place as answering the destitution of the other with one's own bread (or in this case, water). Facing is the other's claim on one's own sustenance, "made wholly of the substance of the sensuous element."[5] Ikeda consolidates an ethical statement by inviting participants to partake in the sensation of water and to offer up this sensual experience to an unknown other.

*Kaseda Water Market* from 1998 realized this alternative economy of elementals (Figure 57, 58). The market involved two stages. First, it assembled a group of water senders at the conjunction of the Kaseda and Takeda rivers. Converging at this meeting point, which was marked with a bamboo "water hut" and a pathway to the riverfront, participants gathered water to be transported to the second stage, the water market. Converting a livestock market into an exhibition space, Ikeda arranged for forty water senders to display their own water boxes. The blue water boxes had photographic transparencies of the senders' hands, faces, and feet immersed in the water and pasted to the bottom. Additionally, the boxes were outfitted with air pumps to agitate the water inside, once again calling attention to its sensuous properties. The exchange itself—the basic premise of the water market—was to transfer water from present-day Kaseda to the seven oceans in the future.

The future orientation of Ikeda's work and the centrality of acts of donation complicate the potentially possessive activity of collecting and storing water. While the cubes and storage units could be interpreted as an act of misanthropic stockpiling, by covering the cubes with the images of the open hands and using air pumps and reflecting lights, Ikeda insists that water cannot be possessed, grasped, or delimited as an object; water's fundamental nature is to flow and to exceed limits. Indeed, this is why Irigaray codes the ethical feeling itself as fluid. Ethics stems from the excess and dynamism of the elemental, contradicting the solidity and self-enclosure of instrumental principles. In this way, it is possible to read Ikeda's deployment of water as implicated in an uprising of ethical sensation; the gesture of the big hands initiates a face-to-face encounter with an unknown other. Moreover, the fact that the water of the *Kaseda Water Market* is destined for the oceans, and not for future humans, underscores the openness of the artwork's gesture.

The hands that punctuate Ikeda's works encompass both an appeal from the earth and a reply. Because they reroute the participant's need into a gift, they position the hands in a symbolic torsion within the elemental: they take in the water and they push it outward, calling out in need and answering that need simultaneously. This involution is facilitated by the water, which surfaces against the hands, rippling and reflecting. It thereby mediates the human–earth encounter, substantiating a constitutive relation through the gesture of offering. In this way, Ikeda summarizes what emerged in early earth art as a simultaneously recessive and exteriorized subject, linking it to a global politics that is oriented toward its elemental basis.

## Basia Irland Dissolving Text

The withdrawal from representation appears most strongly in the way earth art reconfigures text into receptive surfaces. Though Owens rightly points to the textualization of art as one of the most significant shifts from modernism to postmodernism, at the same time, earth art enacted a deconstructive interplay between natural forces and the material text. It is therefore important to clarify that earth

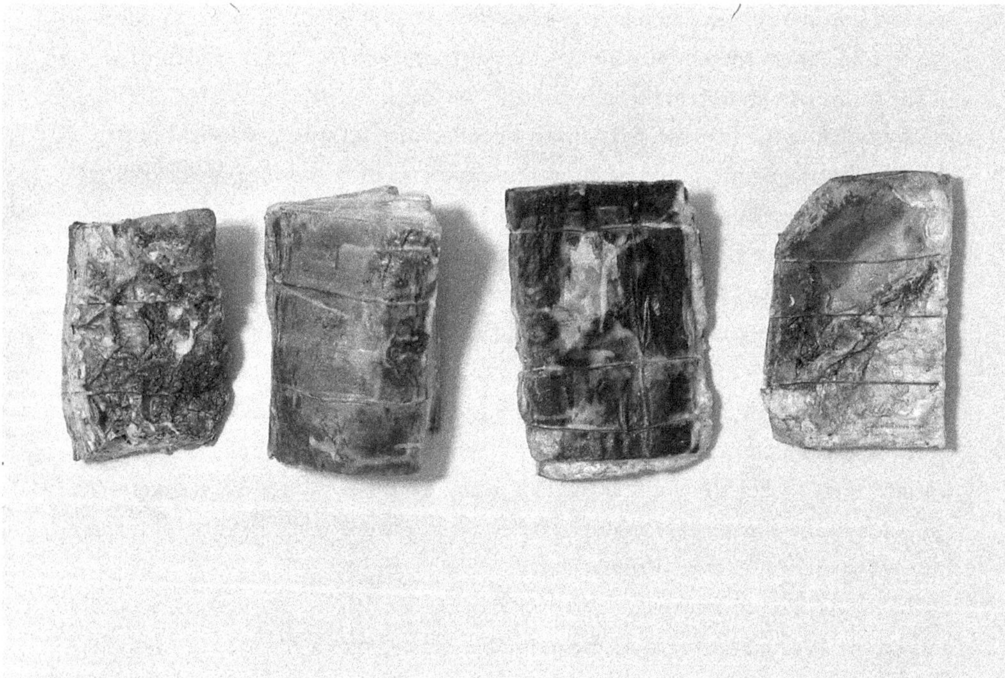

FIGURE 59. Basia Irland, *River Books* (*Hydrolibros* series), 1989. Beeswax, wire, cord, books. Copyright Basia Irland.

art redirected the textual drive of conceptual art and its legacies, bringing language and representation to its limits through the expansive force of elementals. The textualization of art must therefore be understood not as a merely discursive turn, by which art can be read and its meaning affixed by the shifting contexts in which it is read, but rather as a strategy to cultivate receptivity, so that the artwork precludes any such "reading" and instead unlimits the senses.

Basia Irland's *Hydrolibros* series speaks directly to this alternate trajectory. Irland began a series of ruined texts after discovering a heap of discarded library books that had been lying in the open air on the banks of the Rio Grande in a gorge near Taos, New Mexico. In *River Books,* Irland recovered some of the books, preserving them by binding them in cord and wire, then covering them in beeswax (Figure 59). Tightly bound and coated in this way, the books cannot be opened and

FIGURE 60. Basia Irland, *Ice Book. Boulder Creek: Continental Divide to Confluence,* 2007. Ice and mountain maple, columbine flower, and blue spruce seeds. Copyright Basia Irland.

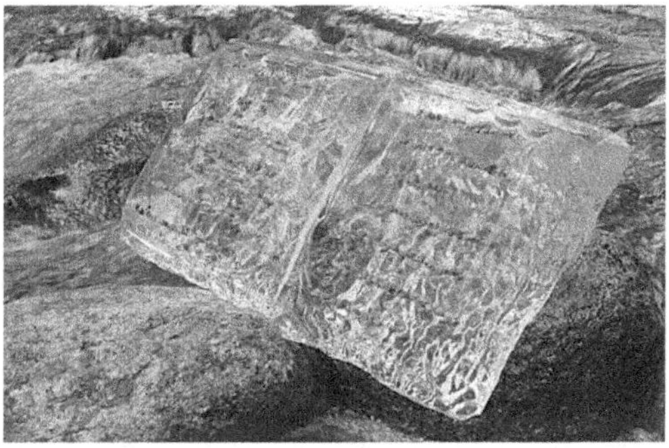

read, yet their colored and textured surfaces yield the traces of water that have deteriorated their pages. Like Smithson's film of *Spiral Jetty,* which is encrypted with blinding sunlight and rippling water, Irland's *River Books* stand as relics of the Rio Grande but also disclose its currents and incessant flow. Indeed, Irland observes that the books stand as a testament to a natural cycle of growth and decay since the very pages of the books came from trees that were harvested and processed. The textual artwork is therefore not a signal of the transcendence of the earthly sphere by discursive knowledge. Instead, it is an integral part of the earth, constituted and disassembled by an elemental basis.

Irland poignantly demonstrates the co-implication of text and the elemental in her ice books, the first of which was a 250-pound ice sculpture installed in Boulder Creek, Colorado, in 2008, marking the beginning of a larger project entitled *Receding/Reseeding* (Figure 60). A variation of her gathering projects (see chapter 1), Irland constructs her ice books by inviting local participants to collect water in a canteen, which is then decanted and handed to another group of people downstream, and so forth. For the ice book in Colorado, the artist froze the gathered water and sculpted the ice into a book, embedded with rows of mountain maple, columbine flower, and blue spruce seeds suggesting lines of text. The artist conceived of this work as the release of an "ecological language" as the ice sculpture melted back into the creek, carrying with it the seeds, which would collect along the banks and then grow, helping to sequester carbon to purify the water and fortify the ground. Subsequently, the artist has continued the series of ice books in Antwerp, Paris, Washington State, New Mexico, and North Carolina.

Significantly, Irland presents the ecologically charged act of reseeding the banks of rivers as an ethical gesture of recession, hence the title of the series, *Receding/Reseeding.* Not only can recession be understood in terms of the literal melting of the ice book as it dissolves into the river, but more strongly, the performance posits the ephemeral text as a recessive position in relation to the river. Irland locates the book at the liminal zone between the limits of human knowledge and the limitlessness of the elemental. The mingling of water to make the ice book corresponds to a disassembly of the anthropocentrism of local boundaries and interweaves the participants in the elemental medium of water. The newfound ecological orientation bypasses human solipsism and is the catalyst for the restorative offering to the river, an act encapsulated by the slow undoing of the book as the water washes over it. That is, the offering works because it anticipates the river's excess of the human frameworks that the book signifies (the realm of language, history, and social and subjective formations). The recession of the book thereby corresponds to the heightened receptivity of the participants.

## After the Flood: Helen Mayer Harrison and Newton Harrison

Whereas Irland opens the way for an ecological orientation through public activism, the artists Helen Mayer Harrison and Newton Harrison imagine new forms of human habitation in response to the problems of environmental crisis. Since the early 1970s, the Harrisons have been pioneers of ecologically oriented art, their work straddling the domains of site-reclamation, installation, poetry, landscape design, and architecture. Through their collaboration with scientists, engineers, architects, and other specialists in sustainable development, the artists have attempted to narrow the gap between the labor of restoration and aesthetic appreciation of the living environment. However, their optimism that governments will implement the necessary measures to avoid the serious effects of environmental negligence has waned over the decades. In their 2008 project *Greenhouse Britain,* the artists address the consequences of global warming, insisting that the current plans for controlling greenhouse-gas emissions are insufficient to keep the global temperature rise to less than two degrees. This means that the rising ocean levels,

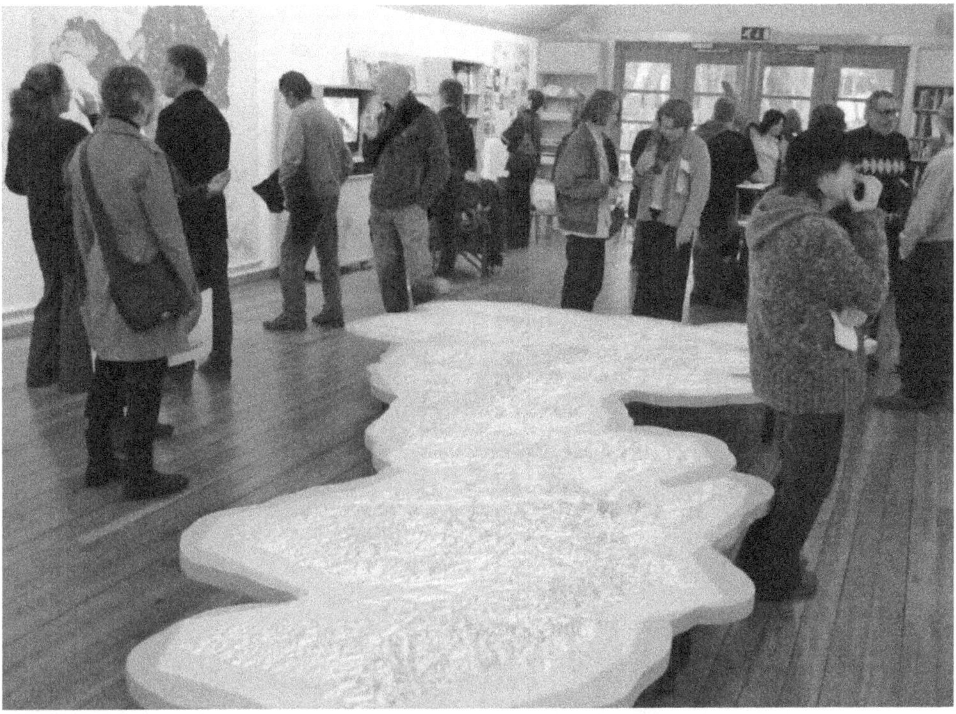

FIGURE 61. Helen Mayer Harrison and Newton Harrison, in consultation with the Tyndall Centre for Climate Change Research, *Greenhouse Britain,* 2008. Model of topographic map of United Kingdom, 7½ × 14 feet, with six projectors above. Copyright The Harrison Studio, Britain.

and the consequent displacement of millions of people, will demand massive restructuration.

*Greenhouse Britain* is both an online virtual exhibition and a touring installation in which the artists imagine the consequences of a rise of one to five meters in water levels on the island of Great Britain and propose a plan for the withdrawal and relocation of up to 2,200,000 people who occupy the ten thousand square kilometers of land that would be washed out. The project consists in mapping the areas that will be affected by the rising shorelines and suggesting ways of rebuilding sustainable living conditions. For the installation, the artists constructed a topographical model of Britain on which were projected images of the encroaching water and

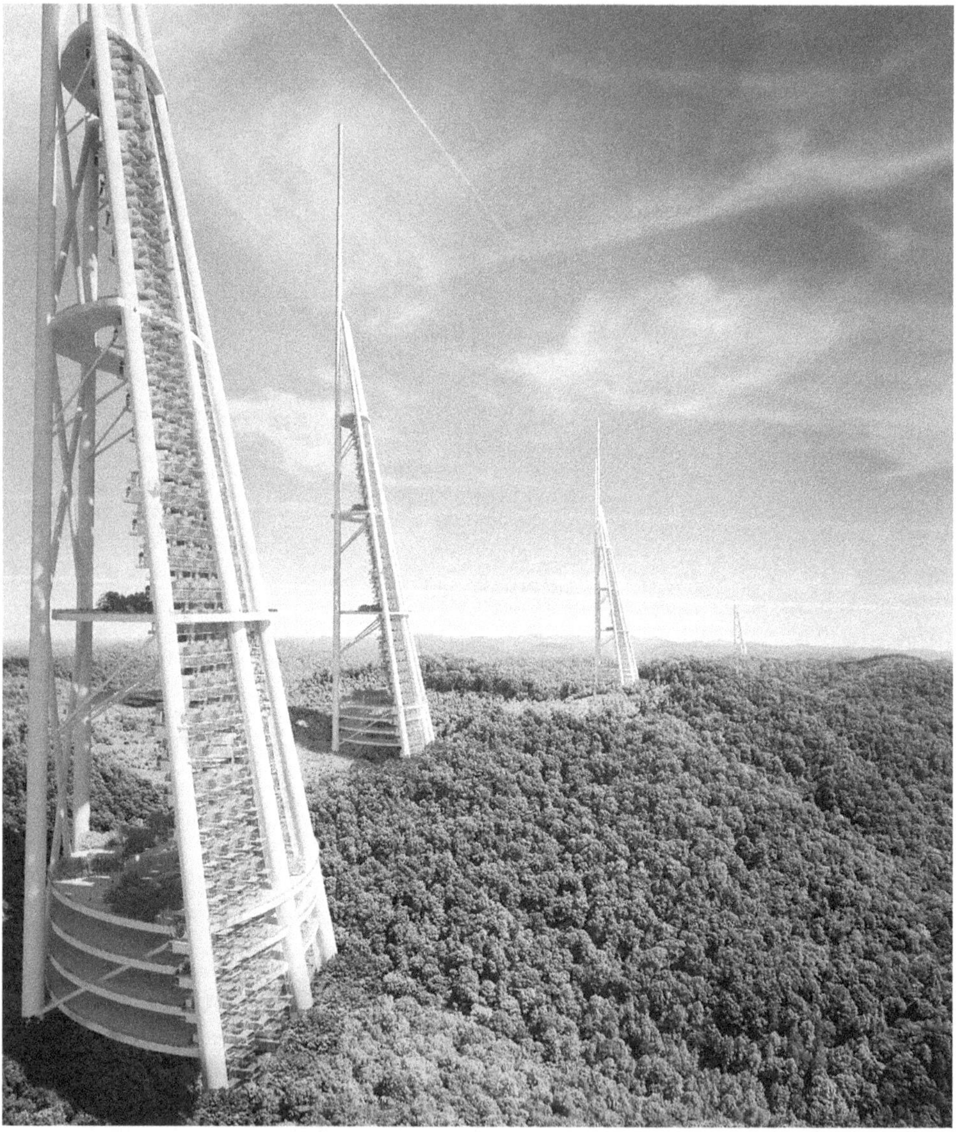

FIGURE 62. Helen Mayer Harrison, Newton Harrison, and APG (Architectural Planning Group, Bristol, United Kingdom), *Greenhouse Britain,* Eco Tower, 2008. Copyright APG, Bristol, UK. Courtesy of The Harrison Studio, Britain.

FIGURE 63. Helen Mayer Harrison and Newton Harrison, *Greenhouse Britain,* drawing of Eco Tower, 2008. Copyright APG, Bristol, UK. Courtesy of The Harrison Studio, Britain.

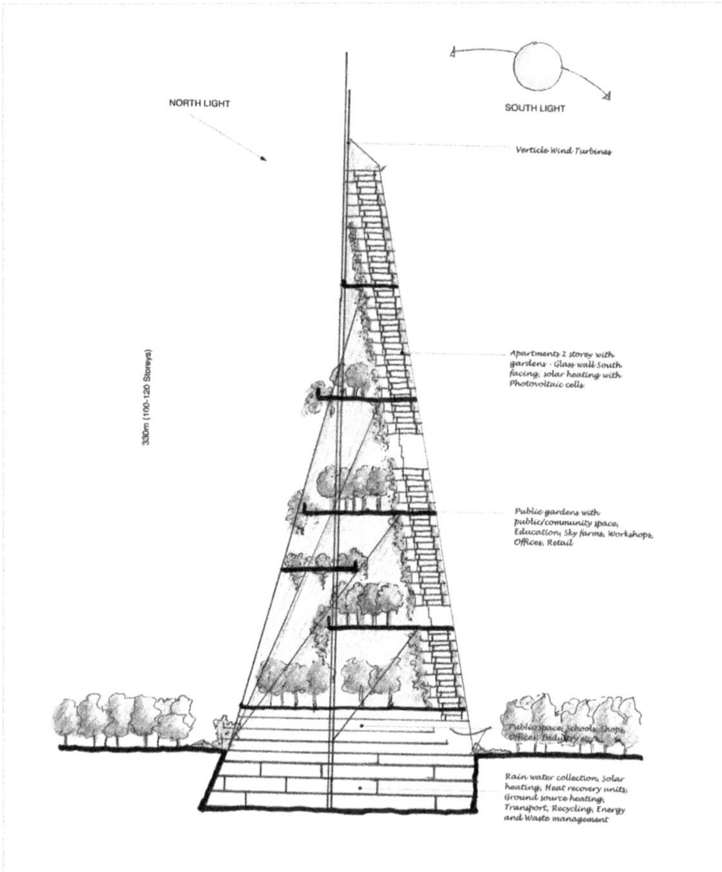


storm surges (Figure 61). In addition to this, the artists devised a new plan for the withdrawal of the affected populations into high-rise cities. For example, the artists propose a set of towers along the Thames and Lea Valley river basins, each of which would house fifteen thousand people (Figures 62 and 63). The towers would face south, would be designed with a glass-pane facade that would allow for the gathering of solar power, and would have an underground system of heat recovery, rain collection, and waste management. Each of the towers would hold schools, offices, shops, and public spaces at its base and gardens and two-story apartments in the upper floors, and each would be topped with a wind turbine, another means of powering the system. Not only would the high-rise village house the displaced populations, but it would also allow for the growth of meadows and forest, which would allow for the sequestering of carbon. In this way, the Harrisons reinstate subsoil ecosystems and increase the absorption of carbon emissions.

What is significant about the *Greenhouse Britain* project, in addition to its incorporation of innovative sustainable technologies, is the way in which it outlines a vertical movement, consisting in both a withdrawal from the earth and the advancement of systems that are receptive to elementals in order to reduce destructive human impact. In their solar orientation, the diagonal glass-pane towers redirect whole cities in the way Turrell's *Skyspaces* tilt the spectator's perspective in order to open perception to the senses. While it might be argued that the proposed ecotechnologies merely put elementals on standing reserve, it would be more accurate to say that it is only through a complete alteration of human settlement that we can cohabit with elementals. That is to say, the project is based not on an anthropocentric system of resource management but rather on a fundamental shift of consciousness, both ethical and aesthetic. This shift entails a retraction, not simply a literal withdrawal from the land but a fundamental recession that stems from the acknowledgment that human necessity is preceded by and inextricable from the earth's imperative. It is with this in mind that *Greenhouse Britain* recapitulates the convergence of the aesthetic and the ethical, best described by Heidegger when he writes, "The first step to vigilance is the step back from the thinking that merely represents . . . to the thinking that responds and recalls."[6]

# Notes

## Introduction

1. Mark Dion, "Mark Dion," in *Art in the Twenty-first Century* (New York: Abrams, 2007), 88.

2. Ibid.

3. See David Wood, *The Step Back: Ethics and Politics after Deconstruction* (Albany: State University of New York Press, 2005), for its clear assessment of the idea of recessive ethics, or as he terms it following John Keats, a "negative capability."

4. David Nash, "Real Living Art: A Conversation with David Nash," interview by John Grande, *Sculpture* 20, no. 10 (December 2001): 30.

5. Douglas Crimp, "Serra's Public Sculpture: Redefining Site Specificity," in *Richard Serra,* ed. Ernst Gerhard Güse (New York: Rizzoli, 1988).

6. Rosalyn Deutsche, *Evictions: Art and Spatial Politics* (Cambridge: MIT Press, 1996). See also Deutsche, "Uneven Development: Public Art in New York City," *October* 47 (Winter 1988): 3–52.

7. Lucy Lippard, *Six Years: The Dematerialization of the Art Object from 1966–1972* (New York: Praeger, 1973).

8. Miwon Kwon, *One Place after Another: Site-Specific Art and Locational Identity* (Cambridge: MIT Press, 2002), 29.

9. Kwon notes that though these categories did emerge corresponding to a roughly linear progression of concerns over the last thirty to forty years, they often overlap in artistic practice and are not necessarily chronological.

10. Val Plumwood, *Environmental Culture: The Ecological Crisis of Reason* (New York: Routledge, 2002), 4.

11. Val Plumwood, *Feminism and the Mastery of Nature* (New York: Routledge, 1993). Plumwood explains that "hyperseparation" is one tactic by which the paradigmatic "master" denies his or her dependency on the "other" by segregating that other and thus securing his or her own identity as self-determined.

12. Jacques Derrida, *Writing and Difference,* trans. Alan Bass (London: Routledge, 1978), 279.

13. Stephen David Ross, "Biodiversity, Exuberance, and Abundance," in *Rethinking Nature: Essays in Environmental Philosophy,* ed. Bruce V. Foltz and Robert Frodeman (Bloomington: Indiana University Press, 2004), 246.

14. J. E. Lovelock, *Gaia: A New Look at Life on Earth* (Oxford: Oxford University Press, 1979), 145.

15. Edward Casey, "Mapping the Earth in Works of Art," in Foltz and Frodeman, *Rethinking Nature,* 262.

16. Edmund Husserl, "Origin of the Spatiality of Nature," trans. Fred Kersten, in *Husserl: Shorter Works,* ed. Peter McCormick and Frederick A. Elliston (Notre Dame, Ind.: University of Notre Dame Press, 1981), 227.

17. John Sallis, "The Elemental Earth," in Foltz and Frodeman, *Rethinking Nature,* 142–143.

18. Martin Heidegger, "The Origin of the Work of Art," in *Poetry, Language, Thought,* ed. Albert Hofstadter (New York: Harper and Row, 1971), 46.

19. Fred Kersten, introduction to *Husserl: Shorter Works,* 217.

20. Husserl, "Origin of the Spatiality of Nature," 228.

21. Casey, "Mapping the Earth in Works of Art," 263.

22. Robin Kelsey, "Landscape as Not Belonging," in *Landscape Theory,* ed. Rachael Ziady DeLue and James Elkins (New York: Routledge, 2008), 204.

23. See Maurice Merleau-Ponty, *The Phenomenology of Perception,* trans. Colin Smith (New York: Routledge, 2002); and Merleau-Ponty, *The Visible and the Invisible,* ed. Claude Lefort, trans. Alphonso Lingis (Evanston, Ill.: Northwestern University Press, 1968).

24. See Luce Irigaray, *An Ethics of Sexual Difference,* trans. Carolyn Burke and Gillian C. Gill (Ithaca, N.Y.: Cornell University Press, 1984).

## 1. Contemporary Art and the Nature of Site

1. Robert Smithson, *The Writings of Robert Smithson,* ed. Nancy Holt (New York: New York University Press, 1979), 22.

2. Robert Smithson, "A Tour of the Monuments of Passaic, New Jersey," in *Robert Smithson: The Collected Writings,* ed. Jack Flam (Berkeley and Los Angeles: University of California Press, 1996), 68–74.

3. Rosalind Krauss, *Passages in Modern Sculpture* (New York: Viking Press, 1977), 262.

4. Rosalind Krauss, "Richard Serra: Sculpture," in *Richard Serra,* ed. Hal Foster and Gordon Hughes (Cambridge: MIT Press, 2000), 130.

5. Krauss, *Passages in Modern Sculpture,* 270.

6. Merleau-Ponty, *Phenomenology of Perception,* 394.

7. Richard Serra, *Richard Serra: Interviews, etc., 1970–1980* (Yonkers, N.Y.: Hudson River Museum, 1980), 26.

8. Ibid., 28.

9. Yve-Alain Bois, "A Picturesque Stroll around *Clara-Clara,*" in Güse, *Richard Serra,* 46.

10. Merleau-Ponty, *Phenomenology of Perception,* 352–353.

11. Sue Spaid, *Ecovention: Current Art to Transform Ecologies* (Cincinnati, Ohio: Cincinnati Museum of Contemporary Art, 2002), 73.

12. Betty Beaumont, quoted in Barbara Matilsky, *Fragile Ecologies* (New York: Rizzoli, 1992), 101.

13. Aviva Rahmani, "Project Statement," www.ghostnets.com/ghostnets/state.html.

14. See Miwon Kwon, "From Site to Community," in *One Place after Another.*

15. Rahmani, "Project Statement."

16. Joseph Beuys, "Coyote, I Like America and America Likes Me," in *Energy Plan for the Western Man: Joseph Beuys in America,* ed. Carin Kuoni (New York: Four Walls Eight Windows, 1990), 141.

17. Ibid., 142.

18. See Benjamin Buchloh, "The Twilight of the Idol," and "Reconsidering Joseph Beuys Once Again," in *Joseph Beuys: Mapping the Legacy,* ed. Gene Ray (New York: Distributed Art Publishers, 2001).

19. Joseph Beuys, "Manifesto on the Foundation of a 'Free International School for Creativity and Interdisciplinary Research,'" in Beuys, *Energy Plan for the Western Man,* 153.

20. Joseph Beuys, "Interview with Richard Demarco," in Beuys, *Energy Plan for the Western Man,* 110.

21. Kwon, *One Place after Another,* 157.

22. Lucy Lippard, *The Lure of the Local: Senses of Place in a Multicentered Society* (New York: New Press, 1997), 18.

23. Ibid., 292.

24. Spaid, *Ecovention,* 49.

25. Ibid.

26. Charlotte Townsend Gault, "First Nations Culture: Who Knows What?" *Canadian Journal of Communication* 23, no. 1 (1998): 31–43.

27. Hans Haacke, quoted in Jack Burnham, *Hans Haacke, Wind and Water Sculpture* (Evanston, Ill.: Northwestern University Press, 1967), 8.

28. Andy Goldsworthy, "Black Stone/Rain Shadow," in *Rivers and Tides: Andy Goldsworthy Working with Time,* DVD, directed by Thomas Riedelsheimer (New York: New Video Group, 2004).

29. Nick Kaye, *Site-Specific Art: Performance, Place, and Documentation* (New York: Routledge, 2000), 156.

30. Dennis Oppenheim, interview by Willoughby Sharp, in *Dennis Oppenheim: Explorations* (Milan: Edizioni Charta, 2001), 119.

31. Ibid.

32. Amelia Jones, *Body Art: Performing the Subject* (Minneapolis: University of Minnesota Press, 1998), 27.

33. Merleau-Ponty, *The Visible and the Invisible,* 130.

34. Mick Smith, *An Ethics of Place: Radical Ecology, Postmodernity, and Social Theory* (Albany: State University of New York Press, 2001), 209.

35. Ibid., 173.

36. Ibid., 181.

37. Tina Chanter, *Ethics of Eros: Irigaray's Rewriting of the Philosophers* (New York: Routledge, 1995), 221.

38. Smith, *An Ethics of Place,* 184.

39. Rosalind Krauss, "Sculpture in the Expanded Field," in *Theories of Contemporary Art,* ed. Richard Hertz (Englewood Cliffs, N.J.: Prentice Hall, 1985).

40. Craig Owens, "Earthwords," *October* 10 (Autumn 1979): 122.

41. Irigaray, *An Ethics of Sexual Difference* (1984 ed.), 191.

42. Ibid., 197.

1. Owens, "Earthwords," 120–130; and Owens, "The Allegorical Impulse: Toward a Theory of Postmodernism," part 1, *October* 12 (Spring 1980): 67–86, and part 2, *October* 13 (Summer 1980): 59–80. Owens's discussion of allegory was bolstered by Joel Fineman's essay "The Structure of Allegorical Desire," *October* 12 (Spring 1980): 46–66, and is further considered in Stephen Melville's 1981 essay "Notes on the Re-emergence of Allegory, the Forgetting of Modernism, the Necessity of Rhetoric, and the Conditions of Publicity in Art and Criticism," *October* 19 (Winter 1981): 55–92.

2. There are of course photographs, maps, and other paraphernalia that accompany the work, but the sculpture, film, and essay are generally considered the essential corpus of the work.

3. Roland Barthes, "The Death of the Author," in *Image/Music/Text,* trans. Stephen Heath (London: Fontana Press, 1977), 142.

4. Ibid., 148.

5. Ibid.

6. Lawrence Alloway, "Sites/Nonsites," in *Robert Smithson: Sculpture,* ed. Robert Hobbs (Ithaca, N.Y.: Cornell University Press, 1981), 42.

7. Owens, "Earthwords," 122.

8. "Nature is simply another 18th- and 19th-century fiction." Robert Smithson, "A Museum of Language in the Vicinity of Art," in *The Collected Writings,* ed. Flam, 85.

9. Robert Smithson, "A Sedimentation of the Mind: Earth Projects," in *The Collected Writings,* ed. Flam, 106.

10. Ibid., 107.

11. Ibid.

12. Robert Smithson, "Incidents of Mirror-Travel in the Yucatan," in *The Collected Writings,* ed. Flam, 122.

13. Ibid., 125.

14. Robert Smithson, "Fragments of a Conversation," ed. William C. Lipke, in *The Collected Writings,* ed. Flam, 190.

15. Owens, "Earthwords," 124.

16. Owens, "The Allegorical Impulse," part 1, 75.

17. Owens, "Earthwords," 129.

18. Fineman, "The Structure of Allegorical Desire," 50.

19. Ibid., 51.

20. Owens, "Earthwords," 126.

21. Quoted in Owens, "The Allegorical Impulse," part 1, 77.

22. Krauss, *Passages in Modern Sculpture,* 280–282.

23. Robert Smithson, "The Spiral Jetty," in *The Collected Writings,* ed. Flam, 149.

24. Ric Collier and Jim Edwards, "The Spiral Jetty Re-emergence," *Sculpture* 23, no. 6 (July–August 2004): 29.

25. Owens, "The Allegorical Impulse," part 1, 74.

26. Owens, "Earthwords," 128.

27. Owens, "The Allegorical Impulse," part 1, 69.

28. Owens "Earthwords," 128.

29. Walter Benjamin, *The Origin of German Tragic Drama* (London: New Left Books, 1977), 45.

30. Smithson, "The Spiral Jetty," 146.

31. Ibid., 153.

32. Ibid., 149.

33. Ibid., 146.

34. Ibid., 148.

35. Ibid., 147.

36. Ibid., 148.

37. Ibid., 147.

38. Ibid., 147–149.

39. Ibid., 150.

40. Ibid., 147.

41. Ibid., 151.

42. Ibid., 148.

43. Ibid., 150.

44. Ibid., 131.

45. Ibid., 148.

46. Ibid.

47. Ibid., 152.

48. Elizabeth Grosz, *Volatile Bodies: Toward a Corporeal Feminism* (Bloomington: Indiana University Press, 1994), 104.

49. Ibid.

50. Merleau-Ponty, *The Visible and the Invisible,* 152.

51. Smithson, "The Spiral Jetty," 148.

52. Luce Irigaray, *An Ethics of Sexual Difference,* trans. Carolyn Burke and Gillian C. Gill (Ithaca, N.Y.: Cornell University Press, 1993), 156.

53. Smithson, "A Tour of the Monuments of Passaic, New Jersey," 69.

54. Owens, "The Allegorical Impulse," part 1, 70.

55. Walter Benjamin, quoted in Owens, "The Allegorical Impulse," part 1, 71.

56. Owens, "The Allegorical Impulse," part 1, 71.

57. Owens, "Earthwords," 129.

58. Ann Reynolds, "Reproducing Nature: The Museum of Natural History as Nonsite," *October* 45 (Summer 1988), 109.

59. Ann Reynolds, *Robert Smithson: Learning from New Jersey and Elsewhere* (Cambridge: MIT Press, 2003), 225. It is interesting to note, however, that when Reynolds went to *Spiral Jetty* in 2004, she revised her analysis somewhat. In an essay published in 2005, she argues for the primacy of the textual descriptions and suggests that these become folded into the phenomenological experience of the sculpture. In this way, she acknowledges that the texts and the actual site remain knotted together, and indeed, that the site is never entirely replaced by the texts. She writes, "Descriptions can even take the place of what they describe and appear to render their referents unnecessary unless, or at least until, that referent returns." Reynolds, "At the Jetty," in *Robert Smithson "Spiral Jetty": True Fictions, False Realities,* ed. Lynne Cooke and Karen Kelly (New York: Dia Art Foundation, 2005), 74.

60. Robert Smithson, "Conversation in Salt Lake City: Interview with Gianni Pettena," in *The Collected Writings,* ed. Flam, 298.

61. Robert Smithson, "Entropy Made Visible: Interview with Alison Sky," in *The Collected Writings,* ed. Flam, 302.

62. Smithson, "A Sedimentation of the Mind," 107.

63. Walter Benjamin, "The Work of Art in the Age of Mechanical Reproduction," in *Illuminations,* ed. Hannah Arendt, trans. Harry Zorn (London: Pimlico, 1999), 214–215.

64. Smithson, "A Sedimentation of the Mind," 113.

65. Smithson, "Entropy Made Visible," 301.

66. Suzaan Boettger, *Earthworks: Art and the Landscape of the Sixties* (Berkeley and Los Angeles: University of California Press, 2002), 204.

67. Gary Shapiro, *Earthwards: Robert Smithson and Art after Babel* (Berkeley and Los Angeles: University of California Press, 1995), 196.

68. Boettger, *Earthworks,* 205.

69. Jennifer L. Roberts, *Mirror-Travels: Robert Smithson and History* (New Haven: Yale University Press, 2004).

70. Ibid., 18–19.

71. Ibid., 44.

72. Ibid., 45.

73. Smithson, quoted in ibid.

74. Ibid., 40.

75. Smithson, ". . . The Earth, Subject to Cataclysms, Is a Cruel Master," interview with Gregoire Müller," in *The Collected Writings,* ed. Flam, 259.

76. Ibid., 261.

77. Benjamin, *The Origin of German Tragic Drama,* 183–184.

78. Mick Smith, "Environmental Anamnesis: Walter Benjamin and the Ethics of Extinction," *Environmental Ethics* 23 (Winter 2001): 369.

79. Ibid., 370.

## 3. Ecotechnology and the Receptive Surface

1. John Sallis, "The Elemental Earth," in Foltz and Frodeman, *Rethinking Nature,* 137.

2. Ibid., 135.

3. Martin Heidegger, "The Question Concerning Technology," in *The Question Concerning Technology, and Other Essays,* trans. William Lovitt (New York: Garland Publishing, 1977), 17.

4. Jean-Luc Nancy, *The Creation of the World or Globalization,* trans. François Raffoul and David Pettigrew (Albany: State University of New York Press, 2007), 94.

5. Heidegger, "The Question Concerning Technology," 33.

6. John Sallis, *Force of the Imagination: The Sense of the Elemental* (Bloomington: University of Indiana Press, 2000), 24.

7. Heidegger, "The Question Concerning Technology," 34.

8. Ibid., 35.

9. Ibid., 34.

10. Ibid., 33.

11. James Turrell, *Air Mass* (London: South Bank Centre, 1993), 26.

12. Sallis, "The Elemental Earth," 145.

13. Ibid.

14. Irigaray, *An Ethics of Sexual Difference* (1984 ed.), 183.

15. *Luce Irigaray Key Writings,* ed. Luce Irigaray (New York: Continuum, 2004), 30.

16. Irigaray, *An Ethics of Sexual Difference* (1984 ed.), 161.

17. Ibid., 81.

18. Jean-Luc Nancy, "The Sublime Offering," in *Of the Sublime: Presence in Question,* trans. Jeffrey S. Librett (Albany: State University of New York Press, 1993), 45–46.

19. Turrell, *Air Mass,* 58.

20. Craig Adcock, "Light, Space, Time: The Visual Parameters of Roden Crater," in *Occluded Front: James Turrell,* ed. Julia Brown (Los Angeles: Lapis Press, 1986), 108.

21. Ibid., 113–114.

22. Ibid., 126–127.

23. Nancy, "The Sublime Offering," 45–46.

24. James Turrell, interview by Julia Brown, in Brown, *Occluded Front,* 22.

25. Leo Steinberg, "Other Criteria," in *Other Criteria: Confrontations with Twentieth-Century Art* (New York: Oxford University Press, 1972), 81.

26. Ibid., 84.

27. Ibid., 83.

28. Ibid., 84.

29. Turrell, quoted in Brown, *Occluded Front,* 34.

30. Turrell, *Air Mass,* 26.

31. Ibid., 21–25.

32. Ibid., 40.

33. Ibid., 25. ". . . without solid form, [the] penetration of vision can be halted."

34. Giorgio Agamben, *The Open,* trans. Kevin Attell (Stanford: Stanford University Press, 2002).

35. Martin Heidegger, *The Fundamental Concepts of Metaphysics: World, Finitude, Solitude,* trans. William McNeill and Nicholas Walker (Bloomington: Indiana University Press, 1995), 247.

36. Agamben, *The Open,* 65.

37. Heidegger, *Fundamental Concepts of Metaphysics,* 255.

38. Agamben, *The Open,* 70.

39. Ibid., 90.

40. Ibid., 65.

41. Ibid., 91.

42. Chris Drury, *Found Moments in Time and Space* (New York: Abrams, 1998), 20.

43. Ibid.

44. Luce Irigaray, *The Way of Love,* trans. Heidi Bostic and Stephen Pluhacek (New York: Continuum, 2002), 163–164.

45. Ibid., 164.

46. Drury, *Found Moments in Time and Space,* 117.

47. Jonathan Crary, *Techniques of the Observer: On Vision and Modernity in the Nineteenth Century* (Cambridge: MIT Press, 1991).

48. Merleau-Ponty, *The Visible and the Invisible,* 133.

49. Rudolf Sagmeister, "The Mediated Motion," in *The Mediated Motion: Olafur Eliasson* (Bregenz: Kunsthaus Bregenz, 2001), 44.

50. Jonathan Crary, "Illuminations of the Unforeseen," in *Olafur Eliasson: Your Color Memory,* ed. Richard Torchia (Glenside, Pa.: Arcadia University Art Gallery, 2006), 24.

51. Nancy, "The Sublime Offering," 49.

52. "Daniel Birnbaum in Conversation with Olafur Eliasson," in *Olafur Eliasson,* ed. Madeleine Grynsztejn (New York: Phaidon Press, 2002), 22.

53. Nancy, "The Sublime Offering," 34.

54. Jonathan Crary, "Visionary Events," in *Olafur Eliasson,* ed. Kunsthalle Basel (Basel: Kunsthalle Basel, 1997).

55. Olafur Eliasson, "Dear Everybody," in *Olafur Eliasson* (New York: Phaidon Press, 2002), 134.

## 4. The Body as Limit

1. Sallis, "The Elemental Earth," 142.

2. Emmanuel Levinas, *Totality and Infinity: An Essay on Exteriority,* trans. Alphonso Lingis (Pittsburgh, Pa.: Duquesne University Press, 1969), 50–51.

3. Peggy Phelan, *Unmarked: The Politics of Performance* (New York: Routledge, 1993), 148.

4. Ibid., 150.

5. Georges Didi-Huberman, *L'Empreinte* (Paris: Éditions du centre Georges Pompidou, 1997), 77.

6. Jones, *Body Art,* 35.

7. Anne Raine, "Embodied Geographies: Subjectivity and Materiality in the Work of Ana Mendieta," in *Generations and Geographies in the Visual Arts—Feminist Readings,* ed. Griselda Pollock (New York: Routledge, 1996), 245.

8. Ibid., 245.

9. Mieke Bal, *Quoting Caravaggio: Contemporary Art, Preposterous History* (Chicago: University of Chicago Press, 1999), 51.

10. Raine, "Embodied Geographies," 246.

11. Sergei Eisenstein, quoted in Bois, "A Picturesque Stroll around *Clara-Clara,*" 48.

12. Merleau-Ponty, *The Visible and the Invisible,* 130–131.

13. Irigaray, *An Ethics of Sexual Difference* (1993 ed.), 156.

14. Ibid., 182–183.

15. Ibid., 161.

16. Alphonso Lingis, *The Community of Those Who Have Nothing in Common* (Bloomington: Indiana University Press, 1994), 122.

17. Alphonso Lingis, *Sensation: Intelligibility in Sensibility* (New Brunswick, N.J.: Humanities Press, 1996), 101.

18. Lingis, *The Community of Those Who Have Nothing in Common,* 125.

19. Susan Derges, "A Technical Note," in *Woman Thinking River,* ed. Frish Brandt and James Danziger (New York: Danziger Gallery and Fraenkel Gallery, 1999), 79.

20. Charlotte Cotton, "Water Forms," in Brandt and Danziger, *Woman Thinking River,* 9.

21. Steinberg, "Other Criteria," 84.

22. Casey, "Mapping the Earth in Works of Art," 261.

23. Sallis, "The Elemental Earth," 142.

24. Irigaray, *The Way of Love,* 163–164.

25. Jackie Brookner, Biosculptures, www.jackiebrookner.net/biosculpture.htm.

26. Ibid.

27. Alex Potts, "Installation and Sculpture," *Oxford Art Journal* 24, no. 2 (2001): 17.

28. Smith, *An Ethics of Place,* 171.

29. Potts, "Installation and Sculpture," 17.

## Conclusion

1. Michelle Allsopp, Adam Walters, Dan Santillo, and Paul Johnson, *Plastic Debris in the World's Oceans* (Amsterdam: Greenpeace International, 2006).

2. Ichi Ikeda, "Water Mirror: A Conversation with Ichi Ikeda," interview by John K. Grande, *Sculpture* 26, no. 7 (September 2007): 22.

3. Ibid., 24.

4. Ross, "Biodiversity, Exuberance, and Abundance," 256.

5. Lingis, *Sensation,* 86.

6. Martin Heidegger, *Poetry, Language, Thought,* trans. A. Hofstadter (New York: Harper and Row, 1975), 181.

# Index

**AMANDA BOETZKES** is assistant professor of contemporary art and theory at the University of Alberta.

Printed in the USA
CPSIA information can be obtained
at www.ICGtesting.com
LVHW011739210824
788805LV00012B/91

9 780816 665891